BYLINES IN DESPAIR

Bylines in Despair

HERBERT HOOVER, THE GREAT DEPRESSION, AND THE U.S. NEWS MEDIA

LOUIS W. LIEBOVICH

Westport, Connecticut
London

Library of Congress Cataloging-in-Publication Data

Liebovich, Louis.
    Bylines in despair : Herbert Hoover, the Great Depression, and the
U.S. news media / Louis W. Liebovich.
      p.   cm.
    Includes bibliographical references (p.) and index.
    ISBN 0–275–94843–9 (alk. paper)
    1. Hoover, Herbert, 1874–1964. 2. Depressions—1929—United
States. 3. United States—Politics and government—1929–1933.
4. Presidents in the press—United States—History—20th century.
5. Mass media—Political aspects—United States—History—20th
century. I. Title.
E802.L52   1994
973.91'6'092—dc20   93–50679

British Library Cataloguing in Publication Data is available.

Library of Congress Catalog Card Number: 93–50679
ISBN: 0–275–94843–9

First published in 1994

Praeger Publishers, 88 Post Road West, Westport, CT 06881
An imprint of Greenwood Publishing Group, Inc.

Printed in the United States of America

The paper used in this book complies with the
Permanent Paper Standard issued by the National
Information Standards Organization (Z39.48–1984).

10 9 8 7 6 5 4 3 2 1

For my parents, Albert and Dorothy,
who know firsthand of the Great Depression

Contents

Acknowledgments

The author wishes to extend a note of sincere appreciation to the entire staff of the Herbert Hoover Presidential Library in West Branch, Iowa, and to director Richard Norton Smith. A special recognition is also proffered to archivists Dwight M. Miller and Dale C. Mayer, whose suggestions concerning appropriate manuscripts were invaluable. A thank you is extended to the Herbert Hoover Presidential Library Association for grants awarded in support of research for this book. Without the association's financial commitment, this book would not have been possible. A word of thanks is offered to my wife, Shirley, who worked tirelessly to help gather articles and documents that bolstered my search for evidence.

A thank you also is extended to Robert Reid, associate professor of journalism at the University of Illinois at Urbana-Champaign, and Thomas B. Littlewood, professor of journalism at the University of Illinois, for their suggestions and help. A note of appreciation is offered to the University of Illinois vice chancellor's office, which funded a mini-grant for travel. Donald Lisio, professor of history at Coe College in Cedar Rapids, Iowa, also played an instrumental part in the compilation of information for the chapter on the Bonus March.

Finally, a note of gratitude is extended to my family, including especially my wife, but also by children, Cynthia, Andrew, and Rebecca, for their patience while this work was completed.

Prologue

Each week during the 1970s, in the television series, "All in the Family," Archie and Edith Bunker sang an opening song harkening to their ficti- tious, stereotyped childhoods. In the song they mentioned that the na- tion could use Herbert Hoover again, thus suggesting that Hoover would have agreed with Archie's narrowminded attitudes and that Hoover was the embodiment of traditional prejudice and government indifference in the 1920s and 1930s. On the one hand, during the opening credits of one of the most popular programs in the history of modern television, the song, "Those Were the Days," conjured the incarnation of Hoover and a bygone era of tradition and simple, honest relationships. Herbert Hoover was seen as the last vestige of a hard-working, unrestrained, cap- italistic society. On the other hand, the silly rhyme also reflected the overall message of the TV series: bigotry of the Hoover era was carried into 1970s society by an older generation, who harbored too many mis- creants with values such as Archie's.

Mirroring a long-held caricature of Hoover, the song suggested that the president represented not only intolerance but also lack of charity and indifference to misery. Certainly, social values of the "All in the Family" generation were different from those in 1932, and Hoover would not have been elected in 1972; but Hoover lived 40 years earlier when, for most of his life, he was considered a visionary, a man ahead of his times. The 1970s TV image of Hoover as a harbinger of establishment values left a distorted impression in order to appeal to a new, young audience or simply to engender the misguided attitudes of the writers and producers of the weekly series.

This is not an isolated misrepresentation. Unflattering portrayals of Herbert Hoover are common, even those created during the years since his death. Repeatedly he is seen as the progenitor of depression and sorrow, but, in truth, his timing was more his bane than was his attitude. The *London Times* observed, in his 1964 obituary; "(Hoover) will be remembered as one of the unluckiest men ever to be elected President of the United States. Had he held office at a time of normal strain his rule would probably have been noted for quiet success and smooth progress."[1]

In fact, Hoover was one of few presidents who gained early popularity through public service outside politics and who repeatedly dedicated himself to helping the needy. He was first the beneficiary of and then the victim of public imagery. A complex, worldly man filled with compassion, human understanding, and business savvy, he rose to power through the willing creation of a misplaced perception and sank to the depths through an equally unfair portrayal. Circumstances, his poor judgment, and caricatures created by some reporters, editors, and political enemies destroyed his public career and made him a pariah for years to come, just as successful promotion helped to build his early success. How he was perceived turned out to be much more important than who he was and what he stood for. This book is about how media affected the life of Herbert Hoover and his presidency and about press relations in a crucial earlier era in this century. It is about both the real Hoover and the false images, both positive and negative, that burnished and tarnished his presidency and his reputation.

Hoover amassed a fortune in mining engineering before he reached age 40. This, even though he lost both his parents before he was ten. Reporters in the 1920s found Hoover's storybook financial achievements great copy. Hoover was, in fact, the embodiment of the nineteenth-century hero: the boy who rose from humble beginnings to become a successful businessman through independence, hard work, and determination. Later in the twentieth century, after the Hoover presidency, Americans adopted other kinds of heroes such as movie stars, athletes, and rock singers. Hard work became not so important as public appeal and style, but in his time Hoover represented everything most Americans hoped for—power, success, and wealth mixed with decency and compassion, not flash and conspicuous consumption.

That such a man could become president was a testimony to the success of American democracy. That he could become one of the most despised and misunderstood American presidents of all time is a testimony to bad luck, to the fickleness of public life, to the power of public opinion and opinion makers, and to Hoover's own inability to adapt to changing times.

Hoover's successes and failures, then, were not just of his own doing but also, in part, the results of what he was perceived as doing. The disgraced president of 1933 was no more or less a humanitarian and extraordinary genius than the mining engineer of 1910, but public judgment had certainly changed. Hoover learned that the modern presidency had as much to do with imagery as policy.

In March 1929 Hoover ascended to the presidency of the United States after handily defeating New York Governor Al Smith four months earlier. The Republicans had dominated national politics and the presidency for more than 30 years. Only Woodrow Wilson's eight-year tenure, a direct result of a rift between Theodore Roosevelt and William Howard Taft in 1912, had interrupted a line of six Republican presidencies dating back to William McKinley's election over William Jennings Bryan in 1896. Republicans dominated both houses of Congress, and the country had just completed a most prosperous year.

Hoover had served nobly in public office overseas under Wilson. He worked tirelessly to aid stranded Americans and starving Europeans during and after World War I. He also directed the purchase, storage, and supply of food in the United States during all but the first month of U.S. participation in the war. Hoover's efficiency and compassion earned the respect of Europeans and Americans alike. Later, as an aggressive and active secretary of commerce under Warren Harding and Calvin Coolidge in the 1920s, he solidified his position as a leader of the Republican Party, despite his early allegiance to a Democratic administration.

When Coolidge, in the summer of 1927, announced suddenly that he would not be a candidate for president, party leaders quickly turned to Hoover. He was a self-made millionaire, a compassionate public servant, and a shrewd politician. He was untainted. He had never held an elected public office before his successful bid for the presidency, and he kept his distance from grimy political infighting as he sided with the progressive, reform-minded wing of the party. This despite the stale, do-nothing, laissez-faire attitudes of his two predecessors, Harding and Coolidge. Americans wanted a business hero who would protect them from unscrupulous capitalists while funneling continued prosperity to their doorsteps. Hoover promised to do just that.

Reporters in Washington and their editors back home also looked forward to a Hoover presidency. Many powerful newspapers were Republican. Hoover's ideals and philosophies suited most magazine and newspaper publishers and editors. Even William Randolph Hearst, an ar-

dent Democrat and the most influential publisher in the country, supported Hoover in 1928. Reporters, after years of second-class treatment
from Woodrow Wilson, Warren Harding, and Calvin Coolidge, looked
forward to working with Hoover. He seemed to understand the value of
good relations with reporters and promised them free and open discussions, laying the foundations for the same type of amicable press relations
he had established during his eight years as secretary of commerce.

Few would have predicted in early 1929 that this hard-working, well-
respected president would four years later become one of the most despised and criticized persons ever to occupy the Oval Office. The tragic
events of the 1930s Great Depression so thoroughly eradicated the earlier
Hoover image of hero and humanitarian that the ramshackle shanty
towns where the poor and destitute were forced to live came to be known
derisively as "Hoovervilles."

In late 1929 and early 1930 the country descended into the worst economic disaster in history. But how Hoover dropped so drastically in the
public's esteem and how the world came to regard Hoover's name as the
equivalent of failure requires a more complex analysis. In truth, despite
spending billions of federal dollars, Franklin D. Roosevelt was only mar-
ginally more successful in combatting the depression. Americans remained out of work in record numbers as late as 1940. However, voters
perceived that Roosevelt fought the depression on their behalf. Hoover
was a victim of circumstance, but also a casualty of his own shortcomings.
He was neither an orator nor a showman, which is what the country
needed in the 1930s.

This book is a result of an academic search for information. I lecture
on the press and the presidency in the twentieth century. In searching
for course material on the Hoover Administration, I found, to my disappointment, only Craig Lloyd's book about Hoover's promotional activities, mostly prior to his presidency, and a few scattered articles. Press
historians skip quickly through the Harding, Coolidge, and Hoover years
to concentrate on the expanding role of the press during the Roosevelt
presidency. Roosevelt manipulated and influenced reporters and the public masterfully. Hoover did not, and he was driven out of office. Americans
do not like failures.

Yet, there are as many historical lessons and fascinating stories in the
Hoover presidency as in Roosevelt's. The years 1929 to 1933 were crucial
ones. Skipping over press-presidential relations during this time, merely
because of Hoover's shortcomings or because the country was mired in
a ruinous economic catastrophe, is a distortion of history. Failure is just
as relevant to our past as is success. The great promoter of 1927 turned
into a quintessential public relations disaster after the Wall Street crash.
Years of unchecked success led to disaster, and Hoover emerged a beaten

and bitter man, a victim of circumstances and self-destruction. All that is usually remembered now are the years of decline. His life was a success, and his presidency a failure, but Herbert Hoover never changed his attitudes or his visions whether they were coated with a veneer of victory or one of defeat. The story of Herbert Hoover and the U.S. media is a complex one that has waited 60 years to be told.

NOTE

1. Herbert Hoover obituary, *London Times*, Oct. 21, 1964.

BYLINES IN DESPAIR

1

The Unlikely Road to Success

Born in the tiny village of West Branch, Iowa, in 1874 to Quaker parents, the young Hoover worked hard at an early age. His brother Theodore was three years older and his sister, May, two years younger than he. His paternal ancestors had migrated to the United States in 1738 from Switzerland and westward to Iowa in the nineteenth century, and his maternal ancestors had emigrated to the United States as early as 1630. His father, Jesse, who was a blacksmith, died from "rheumatism of the heart," as a local obituary described it in 1880 when Jesse was 34 and Herbert was six, and his mother, Hulda, died of pneumonia three years later when she was 35.[1]

The orphaned Hoover children were placed with various relatives in Iowa and Arkansas for a year. In 1884, Herbert, at age 10, was sent to Oregon to live with his uncle and aunt, Henry John and Laura Minthorn, in Newberg, Oregon. Young Herbert lived his formative years with neither his parents nor even his brother and sister, who stayed with other relatives.[2]

All his youth, Herbert adhered to a strict morality dictated by his Quaker faith, accepting the precepts of hard work and honest faith, while elevating truthfulness and duty much above materialistic success.[3] A shy but determined boy, Hoover was hardly an aspirant for public adulation.

Neither a mesmerizing speaker nor a publicity seeker, he seemed an unlikely candidate for jousting with hard-bitten reporters in his later years and delivering speeches to millions of listeners over network radio. Hoover was a nineteenth-century man raised with Victorian values. He did not live the patrician luxury of his presidential successor Franklin D. Roosevelt, whose wealthy and doting parents mapped their only child's road to adult accomplishment. Hoover learned at an early age to expect no luck and to labor against whatever odds he might encounter; he also learned to keep his problems to himself and to see the world in clear blacks and whites. He overcame impediments without help and expected others to do the same. His religion and his understanding aunt and uncle were all he had. He always found it hard to warm to people. Twenty-five years after Hoover's death, long-time companion and former *Chicago Tribune* reporter Walter Trohan said of him:

He was an engineer. His mind was sort of a slide-rule. You put figures in one side and they came out the other in a certain way. He didn't have enough hokum or con man in him to be a politician. Most politicians are great for wit and humor. By telling jokes and patting you on the back, they imply a certain camaraderie and don't have to answer your questions. FDR was magnificent at it. Hoover wasn't like that. He liked people but would not embrace people easily.[4]

In his memoirs Hoover commented little about his adolescence, except to say that in West Branch he enjoyed the usual pleasures: sliding down a long, snowy hill during the winter and fishing during the summer. Hoover did not write his memoirs until the late 1940s and early 1950s, nearly 20 years after the nation had resoundingly rejected him at the polls and later shunned him as a public disgrace. Hoover could have used the recollections of his early youth as a bitter forum for denouncing his detractors and pointing out how he understood the terrible struggles of life, but he did not. He emphasized only those few pleasant experiences of his formative years and did not dwell on the rest.[5] Only in discussing politics did his bitterness emerge. This was typical of Hoover. In 1931 while the United Press carried a series of articles about Hoover's boyhood, Hoover's press secretary Theodore Joslin asked the president what his ambition was as a boy. Hoover answered: "To be able to earn my own living without the help of anybody, anywhere."[6]

The Minthorns moved to Salem, Oregon, in 1888 and established a Quaker land-settlement business there. At age 15, Hoover helped in the office during the day and attended school at night. On occasion, the boy, a Republican, would take the opportunity to debate politics with a retiree in town who voted Democratic. Hoover met many influential people in Salem, some who later launched his Oregon presidential campaign in 1928. One of those acquaintances was a reporter for the *Oregon States-*

man in Salem named Bill Hindricks. Hindricks was the young Hoover's only early contact with the press, but Hoover remarked on their friendship only in passing in his later recollections.[7] Hoover was interested in journalism and reporters, but as a way of informing himself about the world, not as a career goal, though he often wrote newspaper and magazine articles when he became a public figure.

In 1891, at age 17, young Hoover enrolled in a newly created university, Stanford, in Palo Alto, California, to begin his studies in geology. Though his father had left him a modest life insurance annuity through a trust, Hoover had to work at odd jobs to pay his college costs. Those jobs ranged from typing for the geology department to delivering newspapers to operating a laundry agency. During the summer months, he was a surveyor in Arkansas and Nevada, earning as much as $60 a month plus expenses. Back at school, he managed the baseball team's finances and scheduling and later did the same for the newly created football team. He was treasurer of the junior class. In all these responsibilities, he learned how to juggle finances and handle planning details. These specialties, not public speaking or popular leadership, marked Hoover's later life, too. Hoover got things done. Students knew to turn to him for management of their money and for organization, and so did politicians and voters later in his life. In his senior year, he met freshman Lou Henry, originally from Waterloo, Iowa. After he graduated with a B.A. in geology, they corresponded while he traveled the world as a mining engineer and she remained at Stanford. They were married in 1899 in Monterey, California, her home town at that time.[8]

For the remainder of his life, nothing about Hoover was unremarkable, neither his accomplishments nor his failures. For the next 30 years, success after success spilled into his life. Not until his presidency did Herbert Clark Hoover experience anything but career advancement. Probably not even the young couple, Herbert and Lou, who moved to China soon after the wedding, would have predicted the golden years that lay ahead.

After graduation, Hoover worked in the western United States at a variety of jobs, mostly as a common laborer in mines. His first job as an engineer in Colorado in 1895 brought him $150 a month plus expenses. But he recalled 55 years later: "From that day to this I have never again asked for or looked for an engineering job of any kind. They have come of their own accord."[9] He then lived in Australia managing gold-mining interests for the British firm of Bewick, Moreing and Company before returning to marry Lou Henry and depart for another mining position based in Peking, China.

His Quaker faith and his orphaned youth made Hoover a fearless adventurer. Lou Hoover was no less daring. Both learned to adapt to foreign cultures and to speak Chinese. During the Boxer rebellion in 1900, the Hoovers managed to escape the antiforeign wrath of xenophobic Chinese mobs by seeking refuge in the Port at Taku, where foreign warships were docked 60 miles from Peking. A fighting force comprised in part of American Marines eventually rescued the foreigners held up there.[10]

Hoover's loyal service to the British mining firm and his success in obtaining concessions from the Chinese government won him a partnership in Bewick, Moreing in 1900, accompanied by a hefty salary boost and $250,000 in company stock.[11] Money was never a problem again for the Hoovers. Between 1902 and 1907 they traveled extensively, as he supervised mining operations around the globe. Frequently, the Hoovers spent weeks aboard ocean liners before docking in a strange land and setting up housekeeping in another temporary residence. Their two sons, Herbert Jr. and Allan, were born in 1903 and 1907. During this time, Bewick, Moreing expanded greatly, particularly in Western Australia, where a gold rush took place.[12]

In 1898 Hoover delivered two papers on mining engineering to conventions in Buffalo and New York City. Both were published in the trade journal, *Transactions*. T. A. Rickard, editor of the New York–based *Engineering and Mining Journal*, who met Hoover in Australia, encouraged the young mining engineer to continue his technical writing. By 1905 Hoover had written several papers, which were incorporated into a book edited by Rickard.[13] A second book, *Principles of Mining*, was published in 1909.[14] Hoover was not a great writer, but his initial foray into publishing showed his sound grasp of engineering concepts and allowed him an understanding of the problems that writers face. Often, during his years as Belgian relief director, as food administrator, and as Secretary of Commerce, Hoover wrote articles for magazines explaining his position on this or that issue or discussing the nature of his work. Rickard's cousin, Edgar, was publisher of *The Mining Magazine* from 1909 to 1914 and later became an assistant to Hoover, when Hoover was relief director and food administrator. Edgar Rickard continued as a close confidant and financial advisor to Hoover for many years after.[15]

By 1910 the Hoovers had amassed a fortune estimated at between $3 million and $5 million. Not needing money any longer, Hoover sought to escape the pressures of a large firm. He established his own consulting company in 1908.[16] In the next six years, the Hoovers still traveled, not as frequently or as far (around the United States and to Great Britain, Germany, and Russia usually),[17] but enough to interrupt home life continually. This contributed to his international experience, but the long absences from the United States also kept Herbert Hoover isolated from an active role in politics and public life. Were he politically ambitious (he was not at that time), he could not have followed up on those ambitions. He traveled worldwide and established his principal living quarters in London far away from the political pulse of the United States. Later, political opponents would charge that he had wanted to or even had switched his citizenship to Great Britain.

Contacts with journalists were perfunctory and infrequent. Hoover spent time with newspaper people, but usually only for social reasons or by happenstance. In 1900, for instance, the Hoovers hosted a group of reporters, who found themselves trapped with other foreigners at Taku during the Boxer Rebellion in China.[18] Hoover also maintained a personal relationship with Will Irwin, a correspondent with the *Saturday Evening Post* and a former classmate at Stanford.[19]

However, editors and reporters knew that Hoover was a powerful businessman who could provide stories and introductions to important news sources and wished to remain in the Hoovers' good graces. In 1909 an Associated Press correspondent was to have delivered some money to a woman in Paris on behalf of Mrs. Hoover and another man. Somehow, a mixup occurred, and the recipient was led to believe the money came from Robert M. Collins, the London Bureau chief of the Associated Press. Collins quickly dispatched a humble apology to Mrs. Hoover for the mixup, obviously not wanting to make an enemy of such an influential woman.[20]

In 1914, Hoover unsuccessfully sought to purchase the *Sacramento Union*, which obviously would have greatly enhanced his influence in both political and journalistic circles. He did briefly acquire partial ownership six years later.[21] Historian George Nash observes that Hoover was fascinated by the press and by its power.[22] But otherwise, except within the mining engineering profession, Hoover remained away from public scrutiny, ignored by party politicians and out of newspaper columns.

This early absence of public notoriety was not entirely unique to presidents of this time period. Woodrow Wilson, a Princeton history professor, lived a private life until he became president of the university and then governor of New Jersey late in life. Warren Harding, a small-town Ohio newspaper publisher, had only served one term in the United States Senate before his election as president. Still, most politicians of the day worked their way up through the ranks identifying closely with their party goals, while earning friends and enemies through backroom deals that either elevated or downgraded their political careers. Hoover, in contrast, disliked politics and what happened in those smoke-filled rooms seemed to have little direct impact on his life. The year 1914 brought his fortieth birthday and the knowledge that he had accomplished more than he had dreamed possible as a boy. Hoover biographer Dorothy Horton McGee describes Hoover as the most successful mining engineer in the world at this time.[23] Hoover's destiny seemed obvious and simple. He would fill out his years as an engineering consultant, raise his family, and retire in comfort, but then a Serbian nationalist intervened.

WORLD WAR I

On June 28, 1914, in the Bosnian capital of Sarajevo, a Serbian assassin named Gavrilo Princip shot and killed the Archduke Franz Ferdinand, the heir to the Austro-Hungarian throne, and his wife. Austria-Hungary, with Germany's backing, demanded on apology and several concessions from Serbia. Wishing to avoid war, the Serbs accepted all the Austrians' demands except the placing of Austrian troops in Serbia, but to no avail. Hoover noted in his memoirs that Americans hardly paid attention to the unfolding events in Europe "So well informed a newspaper as *The New York Times* from July 1st to July 22nd carried no alarming European news on the front page—Austria got only a minor mention from time to time on the fourth page inside."[24] In response to the Serb refusal to allow occupational troops in their country, Austria on July 28 declared war and invaded Serbia. In 1882 Germany and Austria-Hungry had formed an alliance. A similar pact, the Entente, had been signed by Great Britain, France, and Russia in 1907. Serbia was tied to the latter alliance, and so when Austria invaded Serbia the Triple Entente came to Serbia's defense, spreading the war worldwide. Though Germany quickly conquered and overran Belgium by October, the war then stalemated along a 450-mile series of trenches cutting across Europe from the Atlantic near Dunkerque in France to Alsace-Lorraine at the Swiss frontier in the east.[25]

For Americans in Europe the immediate problem was not warring armies, but jittery bankers who would not accept U.S. currency. In London, the American consulate was besieged by U.S. citizens who had nowhere to turn. No London merchant would accept their money, leaving them with no sustenance or hope of purchasing passage home. American Consul General Robert P. Skinner, an old friend, asked Hoover's help. Hoover loaned his company's own British currency to thousands of stranded travelers, organized a volunteer staff of 500 to see to the needs of more than 100,000 Americans in Great Britain and the continent, secured temporary lodging for the refugees, and organized passage to allow them to return to the United States. Hoover's service brought him regular press attention for the first time in his life, but naturally the focus of most foreign news coverage was upon military and political events, not upon Hoover's work. Though concern for thousands of stranded travelers troubled Americans, news items about the relief committee were small and inconsequential, based usually upon statements released by Hoover's office about the committee's progress.[26]

Under Hoover's direction, the American Citizens' Relief Committee worked for several months to bring stranded Americans home. Woodrow Wilson had turned to Hoover in a difficult, confused hour and the Great Organizer had responded. By accident, his life of public service had begun. "I did not realize it at that moment, but on Monday, August 3rd, my engineering career was over forever," Hoover recalled.[27]

The German-Austrian occupation left many Belgians homeless, hungry, and destitute. The Belgium Army had resisted mightily, buying precious time for Allied forces bracing against the German advance, but the fierce warfare took a heavy toll, leaving the country in a shambles. In September 1914 even before Hoover had completed his work with the relief committee, a friend asked Hoover to volunteer to help provide food and other staples for the suffering Belgians. The United States remained neutral, and so Americans were allowed to cross battle lines. Hoover sought the help of Melville E. Stone, general manager of the Associated Press, in inquiring about procedures for providing relief, and later turned to, among others, Ben S. Allen, London correspondent for the Associated Press, to aid the relief effort.[28] Allen later became a member of Hoover's Food Administration staff in May 1917.[29] In 1914, coincidentally, Hoover and Allen were thinking of pooling their resources to purchase the *Sacramento Union*. Eventually Allen did purchase the *Union* with Hoover's help and became managing editor after the war.[30]

Without hesitation Hoover jumped into the task of avoiding massive starvation in Belgium, accepting no salary for his work and giving up his lucrative consulting work. Hoover encouraged public support in the United States by cultivating American reporters in Europe and by churning out public-relations-type promotional material for the relief effort. Stanford classmate Will Irwin wrote articles publicizing the agency's work.[31] For the next 30 months, Hoover solicited aid for the Belgians from people around the world and worked tirelessly to negotiate movement of the supplies from his base in London through German lines to Brussels. He often had to argue with both the British and the Germans. The effort was extended in 1915 to Northern France, where two million French lived under German occupation.

Not only had Hoover fed millions of starving Europeans, but he had learned the value of public relations in gaining popular support for his relief effort, but as biographer David Burner points out, Hoover refused to accept any accolades or credit. He was shy, and his Quaker faith dictated that he help others, while shunning personal aggrandizement.[32] The Belgian food relief effort not only launched Hoover's public career, but probably also exemplified his best qualities: charity, compassion, organization, and selfless devotion. This time was, in many ways, the height of his career. Yet, it happened in far-away Europe, away from American readers. Hoover's insistence upon no personal publicity also kept his name from the headlines. Newspapers at this time carried hundreds of articles about the relief committee, usually on inside pages under modest headlines, but certainly in large quantity. Yet, Hoover's name was always men-

tioned only in passing. Irwin in June of 1917 felt it necessary to explain
to readers of the *Saturday Evening Post* just who this Hoover man was.[33]

The stalemated war dragged on hopelessly as millions of Europeans
died in trenches. Woodrow Wilson tried to maintain American neutrality,
but the sinking of the British liner *Lusitania* on May 7, 1915, by a German
U-boat cost more than a thousand lives, including 128 Americans and so
angered Americans that they called for war. The frenzy abated only after
a German apology bought a precarious neutrality. Eventually, in early
1917, the Germans resumed unrestricted U-boat warfare against American ships, and in April 1917 Wilson sought and received a declaration of
war.

On May 19, 1917, Wilson named Hoover head of the United States
Food Administration, handing him the responsibility of redirecting the
distribution of all U.S. food. Hoover was to see that soldiers ate well and
that the country's remaining staples were fairly and equitably divided
among civilians. Historian Robert D. Cuff points out that it was highly
unusual that Hoover should be given such a responsibility independent
of all cabinet posts in the government. Wilson hoped that the food administration would operate not like a bureaucratic government agency
but like a private business. Hoover relied upon the voluntary assistance
of the nation's food producers and distributors and sought to instill his
staff with a patriotic spirit.[34] Cuff observed, "Hoover was the very model
of modern disaster manager and a fitting symbol of how the structure of
a system of thought—voluntarism—fundamentally reflected the structure
of a particular system of war organization—the American mobilization
effort."[35] In a written statement issued to reporters on the day of his
appointment, Hoover said he would not accept any pay for directing the
nation's food distribution and would ask most assistants to work as volunteers.[36]

The food administration adapted the slogan, 'Food Will Win the War,"
and staffers sent letters to thousands of newspaper editors urging them
to publish articles about food conservation. Ben Allen, Hoover's old
friend from the AP London Bureau, took over publicity for Hoover's bureau, and 21,000 newspaper editors and reporters were asked in writing
to convince Americans to conserve food.[37] Profit ceilings were set for
retail food sales, and 1918 crop prices were fixed. Wilson wrote to Hoover on June 12 that the voluntary work toward national mobilization of
food resources should begin immediately. He suggested that housewives
and food producers probably were anxious to follow Hoover's direction.
"I give you full authority to undertake any steps necessary for the proper
organization and stimulation of their efforts," Wilson wrote.[38] Congress
took until August 1917 to give Hoover authorization to control food distribution, but he moved quickly after his appointment to set the frame-

work for his agency and to work toward streamlining the nation's food distribution system in anticipation of congressional action.

More importantly to Hoover's future, the food administration brought him to Washington, the center of government and the focus of the nation's newspapers. Obviously, as people had to eat, whatever Hoover did from May 1917 to the end of the war in November 1918 was news. Newspapers across the nation carried front-page coverage of Hoover's appointment, but reporters not surprisingly emphasized probable guidelines to be implemented under the new food program and hardly discussed Hoover personally. The *San Francisco Chronicle*, for instance, a newspaper whose editors were close to Hoover in later years, never picked up on his local Stanford connection and only described the new food administrator as the "Belgian relief worker."[39] The *Atlanta Constitution* said that if food policies developed in the manner that Hoover predicted, the nation would be wise to follow his leadership and urged Congress to act quickly to give Hoover the power to begin redirecting the nation's food supply. The *Constitution* did not comment on Hoover personally, however.[40]

But as news of his appointment circulated, curious reporters began to chronicle Hoover's background and his work in Belgium. *The Boston Globe* commented editorially:

Mr. Hoover is one of the men whom war raises to greatness. His efficiency in Belgium was such as to impress all Europe. . . . But to it he brings ideals and a spirit that are of incalculable value. . . . He wants no salary for himself or his staff. He seeks no rewards. He plays no politics.[41]

Hoover would become "better known than 'Three-Fingered' Hoover whom Eugene Field made famous," the *Globe* predicted.[42] *The New York Times* gushed:

There is neither politics nor favoritism in the selection of Mr. Hoover to take charge of the food interests of this country. The president has approached this appointment in precisely the spirit suited to a war emergency. . . . If there is another man in all the country as good as Mr. Hoover for this indispensable work, he would still lack Mr. Hoover's nearly three years of experience. And if a special school of experience had been established solely to train such a man, it couldn't have been better than that from which he had graduated with the highest honors. Mr. Hoover was a very successful mining engineer when the war broke out. He dropped everything to take up the Belgian relief work.[43]

The *Times* editorial and many other magazine and newspaper articles and editorials supported Hoover. The commentary came from small and large newspapers and from magazines as diverse as *New Republic*, *Saturday Evening Post*, and *National Geographic*. This revealed how much

Hoover's image had improved since the early days of the war and how much trust some of the nation's editors had placed in him. It also reflected the tendencies of emerging prominent newspapers and magazines in the United States. Hoover seemed to be the perfect subject for editors interested in reporting with fewer political overtones. This rise of objectivity affected the presentation of the news during the World War I era.[44] Hoover, the inscrutable relief worker, and his approach to the public service were pure news. His politics were more or less unknown, and his purposes, as *The Times* noted, seemed to be free of political taint. His accumulated wealth and selfless work ethic not only made him a hero in a traditional nineteenth-century sense, but his apolitical nature also made him news in a new twentieth-century journalistic sense. Newspapers remained politically partisan, but their news pages reflected this bias much less than papers of earlier generations. Hoover, the humanitarian, captured the fancy of American editors at just the right time.

Still, it is interesting to note that the man who had been imbued with the power to control all food in the country was relatively unknown to Americans. Despite the scattered biographical pieces, he hardly held the same public identification as most prominent political figures in the nation.

Hoover, then, remained a popular public figure, but an enigma, while his reputation grew. He had discouraged personal identification, and newspapers and readers were much more concerned about how the food administration would affect their eating habits and their wallets anyway. He was famous largely because of his work and his successes. At the same time, no person coming under public scrutiny had a better basis for support. Hoover had succeeded in Belgium, had asked for no salary, and had undertaken a new task that all Americans wanted him to complete satisfactorily. Their basic comfort depended upon his success. After the American Grocer's Association, forced to abide by whatever Hoover dictated during the war, surprisingly hailed Hoover's work in June 1917, *The New York Times* observed: "Hoover is attracting the praise of those whom he must control. . . . It is difficult to say what his methods may be in the strenuous days ahead. But he begins with praise and cooperation."[45] Hoover's reputation as an organizer and humanitarian finally attracted great nationwide publicity, but newspapers hardly bothered to go much beyond reporting his public statements and the day-to-day complexities of food administration. Hoover became popular without most Americans having the slightest clue as to who he was and what he actually stood for. In the months that followed, the nation watched. "Hoover Ready to Buy Whole Wheat Crop," read the headline on the lead story of the Aug. 18, 1917, *The New York Times*.[46] "Sugar Industry Put under Hoover," this newspaper declared a month later.[47] "Mr. Hoover to Fight the Food-Pirates," proclaimed *Literary Digest*.[48]

Despite the kind words that greeted his appointment, Hoover's entire public career hung in he balance for the 18 months that he oversaw the food administration. During the previous American incursion, the Spanish-American War in 1898, Army food distribution had been badly mismanaged and plagued by widespread corruption. Wilson wished to avoid a repetition of that experience, but leaders in Washington still feared the worst.[49] With the food administration free of any particular cabinet office, Hoover had the freedom to operate quickly and without interference, but he also shouldered the entire responsibility for success or failure. He convinced Wilson not to appoint a food board but, because of the absolute need for efficiency, to leave all of the logistics to one man. Success or failure would be entirely credited to Hoover.[50]

Poor crops in both 1916 and 1917 complicated the task. The United States had plenty of food to feed Americans, but could the nation's farmers also feed Europe? Because Australia and India were too far away to guarantee steady supplies to Europe past German U-boats, American food distribution was crucial to the Allied effort after May 1917.[51] Hoover himself understood the task of explaining to American housewives the importance of their helping with food conservation. This personal appeal in magazines such as the *Ladies Home Journal*, *Good Housekeeping*, and the *National Geographic* placed the food administrator one-on-one with American homemakers and helped to make him famous. He reached Americans at every level. One article in *Literary Digest* in November of 1917 was "especially designed for high school use."[52]

Despite the pressure, Hoover succeeded magnificently. Food shipments to Europe doubled in one year, though the Germans intensified their U-boat campaign. The U.S. government spent less than $8 million for food administration, and Americans experienced little rationing or shortage.[53] By Armistice Day, Nov. 11, 1918, in the heady atmosphere of a total Allied victory, it was clear to Americans and U.S. opinion makers that Hoover's plans and leadership were instrumental to success. Americans equated Herbert Hoover with governmental competence, though they had watched his every move carefully and skeptically.

At the same time, the unyielding vengeance and avarice of the French, British, and Italian governments after World War I left many Americans discouraged and bitter. The Great War afforded few political heroes and left U.S. voters fed up and dissatisfied. Hoover stood out as one of the few causes for optimism that emerged from the terrible conflict. Yet, he was an engineer and had never sought political office. Could such a man take an even greater leadership role in this country? Americans wondered about this shy business tycoon and, as months passed, the name Hoover came up ever more frequently in discussions about presidential candidates. He would never be able to escape public attention again, and so reluctantly he was now neither an engineer nor a humanitarian, but a politician.

POST-WAR POLITICS

Just three months after the Armistice, Wilson appointed Hoover head of the American delegation to the Supreme Economic Council, the body charged with re-creating a viable world economic system. Concurrently, Hoover accepted the directorship of the American Relief Administration, charged with coordinating food supplies to Europe's 370 million people and preventing starvation, especially among children.[54] The economic council proved to be a traumatic experience in the realities of world politics. Thirty years later, Hoover remembered his first meeting: "This morning session was at once an enlightenment in national intrigue, self-ishness, nationalism, heartlessness, rivalry and suspicion, which seemed to ooze from every pore—but with polished politeness."[55] As relief administrator, Hoover faced a host of frustrating problems. How could he provide aid to defeated Germany? Which countries should get priority? Should food be shipped to the Bolshevik-led and newly created Soviet Union? How could he relieve an oversupply of American pork without American farmers losing money?[56]

While his efforts to protect the starving captured less attention than had his earlier duties as wartime food administrator, Hoover's work continued. Millions escaped starvation after World War I because of Herbert Hoover. He stood by the hungry and displaced of Europe, even if fewer and fewer headlines contained his name. Hoover stories after the war usually dealt with some sort of petty complaint. These stories about angry governments, which charged that Hoover had shortchanged them on food distribution generated little interest.[57]

Without the slightest political effort, Hoover had positioned himself for consideration as a candidate in the 1920 presidential election. A strange turn of events after the conclusion of World War I pushed Hoover deeper into public life at a time when he would have preferred to rest and spend time with his family in California.

At first it seemed that Hoover would quietly retire. After returning home in September 1919, he kept busy writing articles for magazines about what needed to be done to rebuild Europe[58] and helped prepare a documentary film, entitled "Starvation," for distribution in New York in early 1920. The film depicted hunger in Europe through what were considered then to be graphic scenes.[59] Still, he was far away from and unspoiled by divisive politics, and he became a sought-after political commodity. In his excellent recreation of the 1920 election, historian Wesley Bagby describes Hoover as "second only to Wilson, the best known American in 1920."[60]

The divisiveness stemmed, in part, from Wilson's insistence upon American leadership in the League of Nations, which defied the mood of the country. Americans were fed up with European squabbling. Hoover, much to the dismay of many Republican regulars, advocated a U.S. role in the League, though a less active one than Wilson.[61]

Inside the Wilson administration, there was also an even more troublesome and uglier side in the years 1917 to 1919. To encourage enthusiastic American support for the war, Wilson had created a governmental information agency, a public relations arm of the White House, called the Committee for Public Information. Headed by a former Colorado newspaper editor George Creel, the committee flooded the nation's newspapers with press releases and used all manner of public relations gambits to generate popular support for the war. For instance, uniformed soldiers made pitches in movie houses for Americans to buy War Bonds. The Creel Committee exceeded its original charge by often exaggerating American victories or by using heavy-handed tactics against newspapers or groups who were opposed to American participation in the war.[62] This trampling of individual rights carried over after the war. Attorney General A. Mitchell Palmer, harboring his own presidential ambitions and capitalizing on anti-Bolshevik hysteria that swept the country after the Russian revolution, jailed many leftists and closed down socialist newspapers in 1919, creating a climate of fear in the country.

Spending most of his time in Europe and away from the mainstream of the Wilson Administration, Hoover remained untouched by these excesses. "Mr. Hoover is one war leader who isn't nursing a presidential 'bee' as a desired reward for his services," observed the *Kansas City Times* in March 1919. "Hoover wasn't a politician when he took the job as food administrator and didn't mix in politics while he had it," the newspaper concluded.[63]

Hoover was greeted as a hero upon his return from Europe in September 1919. "Vastness of Hoover's Work Realized As He Returns," read a September 14, 1919, banner headline in the special articles section of *The New York Times*. Praising his work in bringing relief and recovery to war-torn Europe, *The Times* observed: "Hoover has been the nearest approach to a dictator in Europe since Napoleon."[64] By January, newspapers and magazines openly speculated that Hoover would be a front-runner for the Democratic nomination. Readers flooded newspapers with letters of support for the former food administrator. "For the present, at least, we propose to print in the Mail Bag no more individual opinions favorable to the presidential nomination of Herbert Hoover," *Boston Herald* editorial writers advised readers on January 13, 1920. "There are too many of them and space conditions require a cessation." The editorial writers noted that readers did not seem to care whether Hoover was a Republican or Democrat and advised Hoover to remain independent of both parties until June 1920, just before the conventions.[65]

Newspapers and magazines stumbled over each other praising him and speculating on his political chances. In a speech in New York on January 14, 1920, to the National Wholesale Dry Goods Association Julius Barnes, director of the U.S. Wheat corporation and a close Hoover confidant, told the gathered businessmen and eager reporters that Hoover was not a candidate, but that he might be, if drafted. The statement only confused the news gatherers and whetted their interest. Contradictory headlines predicting a Democratic candidacy or a Republican candidacy or no candidacy appeared on front pages and on editorial pages the next morning.[66]

In the next few weeks Hoover speculation filled hundreds of thousands of column inches of newsprint. "Boom for Hoover Grows in Volume," declared the *Philadelphia Public Ledger*.[67] "Launch Hoover Boom in Washington State," read a headline in the *Washington (D.C.) Star*.[68] "A demand for Hoover keeps appearing here and there, especially in Washington," the *Nebraska State Journal* noted.[69] Hoover supporter David Lawrence wrote a special article for the *Chicago Daily News* identifying Hoover as the dark horse that Democrats probably would turn to.[70] "Hoover Watched by Leaders of Both Parties," proclaimed a *Washington News* headline.[71] Articles and editorials dotted newspapers and magazines from San Francisco to New York.[72] Former President William Howard Taft wrote articles for the *Philadelphia Public Ledger* and the *Washington Post* suggesting that Hoover should declare himself a Republican, because he could not win as a Democrat. He counseled Republicans to rethink their attitudes against the League of Nations to accommodate Hoover's pro-League stance.[73]

Both Republican and Democratic newspapers and politicians eagerly sought a Hoover candidacy. Hoover boosters for the Democratic nomination were Ralph Pulitzer and Frank I. Cobb, publisher and editor respectively of the *New York World*; Cyrus Curtis, publisher of the *Saturday Evening Post*; and John S. Cohen, editor of the *Atlanta Journal*.

The Democratic *World* endorsed Hoover on January 20, 1920. "We should be glad to support Mr. Hoover as a Democratic candidate for President on a platform that represents the historical principles of the Democratic Party," the *World* told its readers. "We should be glad to support him as an independent candidate on a platform of progressive liberalism. We should not hesitate to support him as the Republican candidate. . . . "[74] This, from a newspaper that, under Joseph Pulitzer, had almost singlehandedly defeated Republican candidate James G. Blaine in 1884 and had bitterly opposed Republican candidates for 40 years. *Collier's* magazine was stunned by the *World*'s choice.[75] The Pulitzer flagship newspaper, along with William Randolph Hearst's *New York Journal*, were the leading Democratic newspapers in the country, and the *World* had chosen to support a man who had not even revealed his party affiliation. The uncharacteristic endorsement made news. Other newspapers carried articles about the *World*'s decision.[76] For weeks after their editorial endorsement, the *World*'s editors tried to pump up a Hoover candidacy by publishing stories focusing on praise from other newspaper editors, other public figures, and ad hoc groups. Headlines such as "Hoover As a Candidate Well Spoken of by Voters in All Walks of Life," "More College Men Declare for Him," "World's Appeal for Hoover Attracts Press of Country," "Mass of Citizens Praise the World for Urging Hoover," "New Hampshire Women Favor Hoover's Candidacy," "Admiration for Hoover's Ability Is Expressed by Congressmen," "William Taft Indorses [*sic*] Hoover As Candidate," "Hoover Winner if Named, Editors Wire the World," and "Big Business Men Feel Hoover Would Help Settle Conditions" appeared in the *World* in the days after the newspaper's endorsement.[77]

Pulitzer and Cobb sought to portray Hoover as a man of the people and build a groundswell of support that would swamp party politicians. At the same time the newspapermen hoped voters would see Hoover opponents as self-interested politicians concerned only with maintaining backroom politics. "Politicians are Shaken by The World's Hoover Boom; Popular Response Is Quick," read a *World* headline two days after the endorsement.[78] Another declared, "Hoover's Name Rousing a Nationwide Demand: Old Guard to Fight Him."[79]

Cohen offered to help organize the South for Hoover. In California, the *San Francisco Bulletin*, the *San Francisco News*, the *Los Angeles Times*, the *Los Angeles Express*, and, not surprisingly, the *Sacramento Union* all supported Hoover.[80] Freelance writers, politicians, and businessmen such as William Hard, Will Irwin, Mark Sullivan, Vernon Kellogg, Lewis Strauss, William Brown Meloney, and even Barnes, persons who had known Hoover for years or who had worked with him in Europe, wrote articles for all manner of newspapers and magazines, seeking to boost Hoover's chances.[81] Charlotte Kellogg, Vernon Kellogg's wife, wrote a flattering article about Lou Henry Hoover for the June 1920 edition of *Woman's Home Companion*.[82] Rose Wilder Lane published the first book about Hoover, entitled *The Making of Herbert Hoover*, in early 1920. A sympathetic treatment of Hoover, the book revealed for the first time to many Americans Hoover the person, instead of Hoover the administrator.[83] She and Charles Field collaborated on a series of articles in *Sunset* magazine that not coincidentally appeared from April through September 1920 while the 1920 campaign heated up. Field, editor of *Sunset*, was a former classmate of Hoover's at Stanford.[84] Opposition newspapers claimed Hoover was too much an Anglophile and that he had cheated his way to success as a mining engineer.

THE 1920 PRIMARIES

Hoover, a lifelong Republican, did not commit himself to a candidacy or to either party. On Feb. 7 he declared he was not a candidate, saying, "I have not sought and am not seeking the presidency."[85] The *Baltimore Sun*, a Democratic newspaper, editorialized on February 10 that the 1920 election was unique because diverse groups sought candidates who did not mesh well with either party. Referring to Hoover, the *Sun* noted: "Politicians there, great and small, begin to realize that what may be called the Hoover group of Americans—that is Americans who are for America first and party second—are going to decide the election."[86]

On March 9, Hoover told supporters in California that he was an independent Progressive, but that he was not seeking the nomination.[87] Two days later, supporters started an independent presidential campaign for Hoover anyway. Because official Washington sensed that an outsider might emerge from nowhere to capture the Republican Party's nomination, opposition to a Hoover candidacy grew in Congress.[88] *Collier's* came to Hoover's defense. Staff reporter Webb Waldron wrote in early April: "When you read the name Hoover, you think of great storehouses of food, American ships unloading needed provisions, distribution of food to a starving Europe. . . . [He is] the supreme illustration of American character."[89] On the other hand, the liberal *Nation* labeled a Hoover candidacy "absurd" because he was "detached from the influences that would make him a popular choice."[90] The attorney general of Michigan ruled that Hoover's name could appear on both primary ballots in the Michigan primary.[91]

Only 20 states held primaries in 1920 and, though there was a plentiful supply of candidates, no person emerged as a front-runner for either party. The Republican Party's most forceful personality, Theodore Roosevelt, had died in 1919, confounding the expectations of party regulars who looked to him to win the 1920 nomination. Wilson, partially paralyzed by a stroke he suffered while touring the West in September 1919 as he sought voter support for the League of Nations, insisted until the spring of 1920 that he might wish to seek a third term.[92] This not only kept the Democratic race in doubt, but also prevented William Gibbs McAdoo, Wilson's son-in-law and the former Secretary of the Treasury, from actively campaigning.[93] This did not keep McAdoo from opposing Hoover's nomination on the Democratic side, however. He loathed the thought of a nonparty man like Hoover getting the nomination. He labeled Hoover a "cast-off Republican" and said his nomination would wreck the party.[94]

Party bosses kept delegates under their control by fielding slates of uncommitted delegates in primaries or by merely dictating who would attend the conventions in those states that had no primaries. The primaries had no impact on the final nominations. The eventual Democratic nominee, Governor James Cox of Ohio entered few primaries. Hoover's position remained ambiguous until he committed to the Republicans on March 30 amid much discussion among political observers.[95] In the Michigan primary four days later, he finished fourth on the Republican side but first on the Democratic ballot.[96] The day after the Michigan primary, Hoover campaign manager F. W. Dowling denied Hoover would split the party with a third-party candidacy. Hoover repeated that pledge five days later, adding that he would not accept the Democratic nomination under any circumstances, either.[97] Other Republican candidates included Warren Harding, senator from Ohio; Hiram Johnson, the Progressive senator from California who had alienated party regulars by serving as Theodore Roosevelt's running mate in 1912 on the breakaway Progressive ticket; Generals Leonard Wood and John J. Pershing, heroes of the war; Calvin Coolidge and Henry Cabot Lodge, governor and senator of Massachusetts respectively; and Frank Lowden, reform governor of Illinois. Democratic contenders included McAdoo, Palmer, and William Jennings Bryan. Bryan had been the party standard-bearer in 1896, 1900, and 1908.

On May 4, Hoover lost badly in California to Johnson, polling only 210,000 votes to Johnson's 370,000. This was actually a respectable showing for a campaign that Hoover had tried to discourage and that had no formal organization, but the resounding defeat effectively ended the Hoover boom.[98] In something of a Hoover postmortem, the *Nation* observed weeks later:

The practical choice before the Republicans is limited. Mr. Herbert Hoover has the barest chance of obtaining the nomination. Were Mr. Hoover nominated by the Republicans, he would, beyond the shadow of a doubt, be the next president of the United States. But his selection would be a miracle.[99]

World editorial writers were bitter, saying Hoover "practically threw away the presidency" by declaring himself a Republican instead of remaining independent. "Up to that time his position was impregnable. . . . The managing politicians were panic stricken. If the Republicans rejected him at Chicago, the Democrats were certain to nominate him, and his nomination spelled his election," the *World* editorialized.[100] Many other newspapers and magazines mourned Hoover's loss or praised both Hoover and Johnson for their egalitarian campaigns.[101]

Cox won on the 44th ballot in San Francisco and Harding on the 10th ballot in Chicago, setting the stage for a battle between two newspaper publishers. Relying largely on his personal appeal and on his opposition to the League, Harding hardly even campaigned and yet trounced Cox. He polled more than 16 million votes to Cox's eight million and 404 electoral votes to Cox's 127.[102] Interestingly, the first commercial radio broadcast in the history of the nation carried the election results over Pittsburgh station KDKA.

Hoover did not discuss the 1920 election much in his memoirs, except to say that he had been a registered Republican since age 21, but had respect for some ideals and people in both parties. He noted, too, that he had no interest in the presidency then and had tried to block all support for his candidacy, only reluctantly entering his name in the California primary. "I did not make a single political speech or statement in the primary," he recalled. He described the California primary votes for him as "extremely good, considering all the circumstances.[103] His only mention of newspapers was a complaint about "isolationist newspapers" that directed "slander and abuse" at him.[104]

The role that newspapers and magazines played in the spontaneous Hoover boom in 1920 has largely been forgotten. The almost evangelical zeal for Hoover, first reflected in the *World* and later in many other Republican and Democratic newspapers and magazines, represented a truly bipartisan movement for a nonpolitician for president. Despite Hoover's attitude toward the boom and Johnson's victory in the California primary, newspapers and magazines moved away from strict party partisanship in 1920, if only for a short while, and backed a candidate they felt represented the will of the people. This was a marked change in media politics, and Herbert Hoover was the catalyst for the change. This Progressive spirit in magazines and newspapers remained strong during the primary campaign of 1920, though it was stifled by the selection of Warren Harding and by his dismal performance as president from 1921 to 1923. Still, the enthusiasm for Hoover boded well for the man who claimed in 1920 he had no interest in the White House. The *Baltimore Sun*'s declaration in February 1920 that independent voters, who put the nation first and party second, would decide the election did not come true. Wanting a return to "normalcy" in 1920, Americans were not ready for a technician president who favored the League of Nations. They let party politicians decide who would be president. The *Sun*'s prediction was premature by eight years.

Meanwhile, just before Harding's election, Hoover had helped his old friend from the London bureau of the Associated Press, Ben Allen, purchase the *Sacramento Union*. Allen took over as managing editor and promptly brought the newspaper nearly to bankruptcy. Allen asked the Hoovers for more money. "Lou and myself [*sic*] simply cannot go further. You will have to skin down to running expenses and make the best terms possible for your friends who so loyally support you," a peeved Hoover responded. In the end, Allen, on the verge of a nervous breakdown, was forced to sell to an attorney whom he hated. He wrote a letter of apology to Hoover for losing his money and savagely attacked the attorney, a man named Meredith, as having arranged financing through "the worst elements in Sacramento." He added, "The paper has already accepted advertising from the lowest jackass brandy joints in the town."[105] Allen took the unprecedented step of issuing a lengthy press release explaining why he sold the *Union*. The statement was published in area newspapers. In it, Allen explained at length the financial problems the newspaper had faced and asserted that Meredith promised to run "a clean and fearless paper devoted to the interests of its readers."[106] He also wrote that his financial backers—obviously, many knew that Hoover had a strong financial interest—had had no interest in controlling the news in Sacramento and had left editorial decisions to him.[107] He added:

I conducted this paper with as much independence as if I possessed a million dollars in working capital. If I failed it was not because I failed to give my readers a newspaper fairly reflecting those ideals which in my opinion must be followed if one is to continue to own his own soul. For my editorial policies I have no apologies to make. If they hurt individuals and interests the fault must be assumed by the community; certainly I do not feel it. As a matter of fact which may or may not be interesting to anyone except myself I am inordinately proud of the enemies I made by the policies of this paper while I was responsible for its editorial content.[108]

Allen later in 1923 bounced back to become president of the Rural World Publishing Company in Los Angeles and editor of the "California Farmer" magazine.[109] According to an interview Hoover gave in 1930, Hoover later invested in the *Washington Herald* and became a silent partner briefly, about the same time as he acquired part ownership of the *Sacramento Union*.[110]

The experience with the *Sacramento Union* serves to underscore several points. Allen probably turned his private financial affairs into a public debacle to embarrass Meredith—despite his protestations in the article to the contrary—to protect Hoover from any embarrassment should ownership by Meredith turn out as badly as Allen expected, to salve his own ego and publicly cleanse himself, and finally to convince readers that his intentions were to create an independent, unbiased newspaper. Hoover learned from the experience and never involved himself in personal ownership of a newspaper again, though offers would come later.

Just as with the Hoover boom in the 1920 primary campaign, the Allen newspaper ownership points out how some newspaper people in the 1920s had begun to regard objectivity as crucial to reader allegiance and trust. Newspapers had largely been unabashedly biased, closely identifying with one political party or the other. Most would continue this way for another three decades at least. But Allen's discomfiture over financial failure and his anger at Meredith showed that he had been looking toward a different kind of newspaper. The statement he issued to the public seemed overblown and self-serving, but it is significant that he felt he owed the public any explanations. Owners rarely explained their motivations to the public, assuming that ownership gave them the right to pursue any editorial policies of their choosing. His close relationship with Hoover would have colored the *Union*'s editorial perspective had Allen continued his tutelage, but the fact that he was self-conscious over any possible bias is a clear indication of how newspapers were changing. Significantly, as has been mentioned, Hoover seemed to be the kind of man who would appeal to this type of emerging professional journalist. He had come to politics at a time when his kind was viewed favorably by journalists and the public. He was a man free from party machinery and even disdainful of it.

NOTES

1. J. C. Hoover obituary, *West Branch Local Record*, Dec. 16, 1880, p. 1; and Hulda Hoover obituary, *West Branch Times*, Feb. 28, 1884. For a genealogy of the Hoover family and a biography of his early years, see Herbert Hoover, *The Memoirs of Herbert Hoover: Years of Adventure 1874–1920* (New York: Macmillan, 1951) [hereafter referred to as Hoover memoirs, vol. 1], p. 1; also see Charles W. Corkran, "Hoover," *Iowa Illustrated Magazine*, special edition, 1965, p. 12.

2. Hoover memoirs, vol. 1, pp. 4–12.

3. For a more complete rendition of the Hoover youth in Iowa, see David Burner, *Herbert Hoover: A Public Life* (New York: Knopf, 1979), pp. 1–12.

4. Walter Trohan interview with author, Sept. 19, 1989.

5. Hoover memoirs, vol. 1, pp. 1–15.

6. Theodore Joslin diary, May 13, 1931, entry, Joslin Personal Papers, Box 10, Herbert Hoover Presidential Library, West Branch, Iowa.

7. Ibid., p. 14.

8. Ibid., pp. 16–24. Also see Corkran, "Hoover," pp. 12–13; Burner, *Herbert Hoover*, pp. 17–21; and Dorothy Horton McGee, *Herbert Hoover: Engineer, Humanitarian, Statesman* (New York: Dodd, Mead, 1959), pp. 18–28.

9. Hoover memoirs, vol.1, p. 27.

10. Ibid., pp. 47–53.

11. Burner, *Herbert Hoover*, p. 38.

12. Ibid., pp. 44–52; Hoover memoirs, vol. 1, pp. 73–98; Corkran, "Hoover," p. 15; McGee, *Herbert Hoover*, pp. 78–87.

13. See T. A. Rickard, W. R. Ingalls, H. C. Hoover, and R. Gilman Brown, *The Economics of Mining* (New York, 1905) as quoted in Joseph S. Davis, "Herbert Hoover, 1874–1964: Another Appraisal," *South Atlantic Quarterly*, 68, no. 3 (Summer 1969): 296–97.

14. See Hoover memoirs, vol. 1, p. 87.

15. Ibid. Also see Edgar Rickard diary and personal papers, HHPL; and *Who's Who in America* (Chicago: A. N. Marquis Co.), pp. 2302–3.

16. Burner, *Herbert Hoover*, p. 54.

17. In his memoirs Hoover actually lists the countries he visited during the years 1909 to 1914. Hoover memoirs, vol. 1, pp. 99–100.

18. Ibid., pp. 53.

19. Ibid., p. 155.

20. Robert M. Collins letter to LHH, June 11, 1909, Lou Henry Hoover Papers, Personal Correspondence, 1874–1920, Box 1, HHPL.

21. George H. Nash, "The Social Philosophy of Herbert Hoover" in Lee Nash (ed.), *Understanding Herbert Hoover: Ten Perspectives* (Stanford, Calif.: Hoover Institution Press, 1987), p. 32. See also Burner, *Herbert Hoover*, p. 73.

22. George H. Nash, *The Life of Herbert Hoover: The Humanitarian 1914–1917* (New York: W. W. Norton, 1988), p. 177.

23. McGee, *Herbert Hoover*, p. 99.

24. Hoover memoirs, vol. 1, p. 137.

25. For an analysis of World War I, see Rene Albrecht-Carrie, *The Meaning of the First World War* (Englewood Cliffs, N.J.: Prentice-Hall, 1965); A.J.P. Taylor, *War by Timetable: How the First World War Began* (London: MacDonald and Co., 1969); and Luigi Albertini, *The Origins of the War of 1914*, vols. 1 and 2 (Westport, Conn.: Greenwood Press, 1980). See also H. C. Peterson and Gilbert C. Fite, *Opponents of War 1917–1918* (Madison: University of Wisconsin Press, 1956) for a discussion of American participation in the war.

26. See, for instance, "15,000 for Week's Relief/Fewer Americans, but Worse Off Financially in London," *The New York Times*, Aug. 28, 1914, p. 4; "Delay Is Dangerous," *The New York Times* editorial, Aug. 28, 1914, p. 8.

27. Hoover memoirs, vol. 1, p. 148.

28. Ibid., pp. 153, 157.

29. See official list of personnel of Food Administration as of December 1, 1917, Ben. S. Allen Papers, Box 6, HHPL.

30. Ibid., HH correspondence of April 11, 1921, and Sept. 12, 1921.

31. See, for instance, Will Irwin, " 'Bert' Hoover: American Chief Agent for Belgian Relief," Jan. 17, 1917, *New York World* society section, p. 1; "The American Ideal Again," *New York World* editorial, Jan. 17, 1915. Also see Burner, *Herbert Hoover*, pp. 73, 91.

32. Ibid., pp. 91–92.

33. Will Irwin, "The Autocrat of the Dinner Table," *Saturday Evening Post*, June 23, 1917, pp. 26–30, 61. For other articles on Hoover and the Belgian relief team, see Irwin, "A Chance for Us All to Help Belgium," *The Metropolitan* magazine, February 1916. For other articles about Hoover and the Belgian Relief effort, see, for instance, "Germans Exempt Belgian Grain Crop," *The New York Times*, Jan. 29, 1915, p. 4; "Americans to Feed 2,500,000 French," *The New York Times*, p. 5; "$50,000,000 Belgian Aid in Eight Months," *The New York Times*, Sept. 20, 1915, p. 7; "Hoover and His Way of Bringing Things to Pass," *Current Opinion*, 62 (January 1917): 21–22. "Belgian Relief Must Go On," *Brooklyn Daily Eagle* editorial. Feb. 14, 1917; "Food Control," *New Republic*, March 10, 1917, pp. 66–67; Alonzo Engelbert Taylor, "The Control of Food Supplies in Blockaded Germany," *Saturday Evening Post*, Feb. 24, 1917, pp. 18–19; Taylor, "Hoover Would Fit Well in American War Cabinet," *Philadelphia Public Ledger*, March 6, 1917; George Barr Baker, "The Pope and the 'Lone Crusader,' " *American Magazine*, March 1917, pp. 16–19, 117–19; "Hoover Hailed by Liberated French,"

New York Sun, March 31, 1917; "The Great Relief Work of the Belgian Relief Commission," *The New York Times Current History*, April 1917, pp. 131–36; John H. Gade (Relief Staffer), "Belgium's Plight," *National Geographic*, 31 (May 1917): 21–22; Charlotte Kellogg, "A Cinema of the C.R.B.," *American Mercury*, April 1917, pp. 535–45.

34. Robert D. Cuff, "Herbert Hoover, the Ideology of Voluntarism and War Organization during the Great War," *Journal of American History*, 64, no. 2 (September 1977), pp. 358–60.

35. Ibid., p. 361.

36. See especially "President Tells of Necessity for Food Control," *St. Louis Post-Dispatch*, May 20, 1917, p. 1; and "Absolute Power to Control Food Asked by Wilson," *Atlanta Constitution*, May 20, 1917, p. 1.

37. Burner, *Herbert Hoover*, p. 102; Richard Norton Smith, *An Uncommon Man: The Triumph of Herbert Hoover* (New York: Simon and Schuster, 1984), p. 89.

38. Woodrow Wilson to HH letter, June 12, 1917, pp. 1–3, Allen Papers, Box 6, HHPL.

39. *San Francisco Chronicle*, "Hoover to Direct Control of Food," p. 1, and "President Appoints Hoover Head of Food Control Board," p. 28, both May 29, 1917.

40. "The Food Control Plan," *Atlanta Constitution* editorial, June 12, 1917, p. 8. For other articles about Hoover's impending appointment or covering the appointment see "Hoover Heads Food Board, To Devote Services to U.S.," *San Francisco Examiner*, April 12, 1917; "Hoover Accepts Food Board Post," *The New York Times*, April 12, 1917; "Hoover Prepared to Take Control of Nation's Food," *New York World*, April 12, 1917; "Hoover Takes Post; Decries Food Waste; Wide Inquiry Abroad," *New York Sun*, April 12, 1917; 'First Duty of United States is to Supply Food—Hoover," *Palo Alto (Calif.) Times*, April 13, 1917.

41. *Boston Globe* editorial, May 21, 1917. For other coverage and editorials on Hoover's appointment see "President Urges Food Control Plan," *Boston Globe*, May 20, 1917, pp. 1, 9; "Regulating Food Prices," *Wall Street Journal* news-editorial, May 21, 1917, p. 1; "Hoover Given Wide Powers as Controller," *Chicago Tribune*, May 20, 1917, p. 1; "Hoover Outlines Cardinal Principles of Food Control," *Chicago Tribune*, p. 9, May 20, 1917.

42. "Editorial Points," *Boston Globe*, May 21, 1917, p. 6.

43. "The Right Man for the Place," *The New York Times* editorial, May 22, 1917, p. 22. For other biographical articles about or editorial praise of Hoover and his wife, see "Mr. Hoover as Food Controller," *The New York Times* editorial, April 13, 1917; "Personal Glimpses—Hoover in the Making," *Literary Digest*, June 30, 1917; Donald Wilhelm, "Hoover and His Food Organization," *American Review of Reviews*, September 1917, pp. 283–86; "Hoover's Boyhood Spent in Newberg and Salem, Oregon," *(Portland) Oregon Journal*, August 19, 1917, society section, p. 1; "Hoover Self-Made: Began at $2 a Day," *New York Tribune*, April 12, 1917; "Hoover's Silent Partner," *Literary Digest*, 55, no. 10 (Sept. 8, 1917); "Herbert C. Hoover's Unselfish Services to the World," *Munsey's Magazine*, June 1917, pp. 65–66; "Who's Hoover—Want Food at Fair Prices? Then You Want to Know the Man Who Fed Belgium and May Feed the World," *Boston Post*, May 27, 1917, section D, p. 1; "How Hoover Won His Wife at College," *Boston Post*,

June 10, 1917, section D, p. 1; Montrose J. Moses, "Who's Hoover," *The Independent* magazine, June 9, 1917, p. 460; and "Hoover—A Man for These Times," *American Review of Reviews*, June 1917, p. 572.

44. For a more complete explanation of the rise of objectivity see Michael Schudson, *Discovering the News: A Social History of American Newspapers* (New York: Basic, 1978), *pasim* but especially pp. 121–59. Also see Daniel Schiller, *Objectivity and the News: The Public and the Rise of Commercial Journalism* (Philadelphia: University of Pennsylvania Press, 1981), *passim* but especially pp. 179–97.

45. "Mr. Hoover's Engaging Ways," *The New York Times*, June 27, 1917, p. 8.

46. "Hoover Ready to Buy Whole Wheat Crop; Garfield Heads Board to Fix Price; Will Lower Cost of Flour and Bread," *The New York Times*, Aug. 18, 1917, p. 1.

47. "Sugar Industry Put under Hoover," *The New York Times*, Sept. 16, 1917, p. 1.

48. "Mr. Hoover to Fight the Food Pirates," *Literary Digest*, 54, no. 26 (June 30, 1917), p. 3. For other articles see Montague Glass, "Montague Glass and Morris Discuss 'Hooverizing' the Overhead," *Washington Star*, Nov. 11, 1917, part 4, p. 1; "Fighting over the Empty Sugar-Bowl," *Literary Digest*, 55, no. 26 (Dec. 29, 1917); William Almon Wolff, "Wheat—Meat—Sugar—Fat," *Collier's Weekly*, Dec. 26, 1917, pp. 6–7, 32–33; "Abusing Mr. Hoover," *Nation*, Sept. 27, 1917; "The Significance of Mr. Hoover," *North American Review*, September 1917, pp. 357–60; "Mr. Hoover Now in Authority," *American Review of Reviews*, September 1917; "Food Dictator for the United States," *New York Times Current History*, September 1917, p. 389; "The Food Control Bill," *Outlook*, August 22, 1917, p. 606; and "The Nation's Food As the Nation's Business," *Literary Digest*, 55, no. 7 (Aug. 18, 1917), pp. 9–11.

49. See comments by Assistant Secretary of Agriculture Vrooman on June 9 as quoted in "Pirates Control Prices of Food, Asserts Vrooman," *Atlanta Constitution*, June 10, 1917, p. 2.

50. Hoover memoirs, vol. 1, pp. 241–42.

51. Ibid., pp. 240–41; McGee, *Herbert Hoover*, p. 136.

52. United States Food Administration (actually written by Hoover), "The Causes of High Food Prices," *Literary Digest*, 55 no. 22 (Nov. 24, 1917). For other articles written by Hoover see "A Letter to You from Mr. Hoover," *Good Housekeeping*, 65 (October, 1917), p. 74; Dudley Harmon (ed.), "The Woman and the War," *Ladies' Home Journal*, August 1917, p. 25; "Why I Ask for Your Help," *Ladies' Home Journal*, October 1917, p. 18; and "The Food Armies of Liberty," *National Geographic* 32, no. 3 (September 1917), pp. 187–96.

53. Smith, *An Uncommon Man*, pp. 89–90.

54. Corkran, "Hoover," p. 15.

55. Hoover memoirs, vol. 1, p. 287.

56. See especially Burner, *Herbert Hoover*, pp. 114–37.

57. See, for instance, a *San Francisco Chronicle* editorial brief of Jan. 1, 1920, in which Armenians complained about critical remarks about their country that captured one paragraph on page 1 of the "Thoughts and Commentary" section; also see "Mr. Hoover, Matador," *New York Call* editorial, Oct. 5, 1919, in which

editors, disgusted with Hoover's food aid program to the Soviet Union, asked if Hoover's insistence upon such a program wasn't his just "throwing the bull "to work up a boom for the presidency.

58. See, for instance, United States Food Commission, "Food for All—A Fundamental War Problem," *Scientific American*, 118 (April 16, 1918), pp. 310–11; Herbert Hoover, "The Bankruptcy of Socialism," *Munsey's*, December 1919, pp. 438–42; Herbert Hoover, "Some Notes on Industrial Readjustment," *Saturday Evening Post*, 192, no. 26 (Dec. 27, 1919), pp. 4–5.

59. See " 'Starvation' Seen in Film," *The New York Times*, Jan. 10, 1920; "Film Shows Work of Hoover Abroad," *New York Sun*, Jan. 10, 1920; "Screen Scenes Show How American Food Has Saved Europe," *New York Tribune*, Jan. 10, 1920; "Starvation Scenes Are Shown in a Film," *New York World*, Jan. 10, 1920; "America Feeding Starving Europe Shown on Screen," *New York Herald*, Jan. 10, 1920.

60. Wesley Bagby, *Th Road to Normalcy: The Presidential Campaign and Election of 1920* (Baltimore: Johns Hopkins University Press, 1962), p. 42.

61. Ibid., p. 115.

62. See especially Stephen Vaughn, *Holding Fast the Inner Lines: Democracy, Nationalism, and the Committee on Public Information* (Chapel Hill: University of North Carolina Press, 1980), for a discussion of the Creel Committee.

63. " 'Food Shop' Broken Up," *Kansas City Times*, March 26, 1919, p. 1.

64. "Vastness of Hoover's Work Realized As He Returns," *The New York Times*, Sept. 14, 1919, section D, p. 1.

65. "No More Hoover Letters," *Boston Herald* editorial, Jan. 13, 1920.

66. See especially "Hoover Will Run for President If Nation Demands," *Philadelphia Public Ledger*, Jan. 15, 1920, p. 1; "Hoover Does Not Want Presidency, Says Friend," *Washington Times*, Jan. 15, 1920, p. 1; "Hoover Won't Enter Politics Unless Forced, Says Barnes," *Washington Post*, Jan. 15, 1920, p. 1; "Barnes Talks of Hoover for Presidency," *Washington Herald*, Jan. 15, 1920, p. 1; "Mr. Hoover Not Seeking Nomination," *Christian Science Monitor*, Jan. 16, 1920, p. 1; "Hoover's Politics," *Baltimore Sun* editorial, Jan. 16, 1920; "Perplexed Anew by the Hoover Riddle," *Baltimore Sun*, Jan. 16, 1920, p. 1; "Herbert Hoover," *The New York Times* editorial, Jan. 16, 1920.

67. "Boom Grows for Hoover in Volume," *Philadelphia Public Ledger*, Jan. 9, 1920, p. 1.

68. "Launch Hoover Boom in State," *Washington Star*, Dec. 11, 1919, p. 1.

69. Untitled editorial, *(Lincoln) Nebraska State Journal*, Jan. 7, 1920.

70. David Lawrence, "Hoover May Be Dark Horse of Democrats," *Chicago Daily News*, Jan. 8, 1920, p. 1.

71. "Hoover Watched by Leaders of Both Parties," *Washington News*, Jan. 3, 1920, p. 1.

72. See especially a roundup of editorial opinion from around the nation in "How the Papers Size Up the Hoover Boom," *Literary Digest* 65, no. 10 (March 6, 1920), pp. 14–16. Also see "Hoover the Man," *Los Angeles Times* editorial, Jan. 11, 1920; "Hoover Turns Oliver Twist Down," *New York Globe* editorial, Jan. 13, 1920; Edward H. Hamilton, "Non-Partisan Feeler out for Hoover," *San Francisco Examiner*, Jan. 23, 1920, p. 1; "Gen. Wood and Mr. Hoover," *Baltimore American*, Jan. 23, 1920, p. 1; "Hoover Presidential Boom Is Launched," *New York Tribune*, Jan. 21, 1920, p. 1; "New Push Given to Hoover's Boom," *The New York*

Times, Jan. 21, 1921, p. 1; "Hoover Boom Hits Washington, Giving Politicians Scare," *Philadelphia Inquirer*, Jan. 22, 1920, p. 1; "Democrats Divided over Hoover Boom," *New York Tribune*, Jan. 22, 1920, p. 1; "Hoover's Boom Stirs Capital," *New York Herald*, Jan. 22, 1920, p. 1; "Hoover's Big Boom Meets with Verbal Medley in Congress," *Philadelphia Press*, Jan. 22, 1920, p. 1; "Party Chiefs Keep Watch on Hoover Boom," *New York Sun*, Jan. 22, 1920, p. 1; "The Hoover Fascination," *New Haven Journal-Courier*, Jan. 22, 1920.

73. William H. Taft copyrighted article, "Hoover Can't Win As Democrat, Says Taft," *New York Herald*, Jan. 23, 1920, section 2, p. 1; and Taft, "Taft Warns Republicans to Compromise on League in View of Hoover Boom," *Washington Post*, Jan. 23, 1920, p. 1.

74. "Hoover for President," *New York World* editorial, Jan. 21, 1920; also see Burner, *Herbert Hoover*, p. 151; Eugene Lyons, *Our Unknown Ex-President: A Portrait of Herbert Hoover* (Garden City, N.Y.: Doubleday, 1948). p. 199.

75. See *Collier's* editorial, "Great Scott," Feb. 21, 1920, p. 14.

76. "Hoover, on Any Ticket, for U.S. President! Says New York World/Wilson Paper Throws Shell Into Democrat Ranks; Blow Falls Hard," *San Francisco Chronicle*, Jan. 22, 1920; "Hoover Candidacy Boomed by Pact Advocates," *San Francisco Call*, Jan. 22, 1920; Edward H. Hamilton, "Republicans of S.F. Start Hoover Move," *San Francisco Examiner*, Jan. 22, 1920; "New York World Backs Hoover for President," *Washington Times*, Jan. 22, 1920.

77. *World*, Jan. 22, 23, 25, Jan. 29, Feb. 2, and Feb.12.

78. *World*, Jan. 21, 1920, p. 1.

79. *World*, Feb. 23, 1920. See also "Gronna Opens War on Hoover's Boom for the Old Guard," *New York World*, Feb. 3, 1920, p. 1.

80. Bagby, *The Road to Normalcy*, p. 44.

81. See Hoover references in Mark Sullivan, "Palmer and McAdoo Lead in Democratic Contest," *New York Post*, April 11, 1920, p. 1; William Brown Meloney, "You're Gong to be Handed Something," *Everybody's Magazine*, April 1920, pp. 15–20, 88; Julius Barnes, "Herbert Hoover: Some Reasons for His Reputation," *Outlook*, April 14, 1920, pp. 642–44; Mark Sullivan, "Mark Sullivan Gives Resume of Hoover's Nomination Chances," *Philadelphia North American*, Jan. 25, 1920 (article also appeared in *New York Post*); Mark Sullivan, "For Rent: A White House," *Collier's*, Jan. 24, 1920, pp. 6, 7, 18, 28; and Lewis Strauss, Jr., "Herbert C. Hoover and the Jews," *The American Hebrew*, April 23, 1920, pp. 747, 759; Vernon Kellogg, "The Story of Hoover," *Everybody's Magazine*, February, March, and April 1920 editions.

82. Charlotte Kellogg, "What Is Mrs. Hoover Like?" *Woman's Home Companion*, June 1920, pp. 13, 66.

83. Rose Wilder Lane, *The Making of Herbert Hoover* (New York: Century, 1920); see also John M. Oskison book review in *The New York Times* book reviews (undated).

84. Rose Wilde Lane and Charles Field, "The Making of Herbert Hoover," *Sunset, The Pacific Monthly* magazine, 44, no. 4–45, no. 3 (April-September 1920).

85. "Hoover Announces He Is Not Candidate for Presidency," *Philadelphia Inquirer*, Feb. 8, 1920, p. 1; and "Hoover Not in Politics," *Washington Post*, Feb. 8, 1920, p. 1; "Mr. Hoover Denies He Is a Candidate," *Washington Star*; Herbert

Hoover, *The Memoirs of Herbert Hoover: The Cabinet and the Presidency, 1920–1933* (New York: Macmillan, 1952), p. 34. (Note that Hoover lists Feb. 9 as the day he announced he would not be a candidate, but newspaper clippings clearly indicate it was Feb. 7.)

86. "The Most Extraordinary Campaign in Our History," *Baltimore Sun* editorial, Feb. 10, 1920.

87. "Hoover Now Cuts All Party Ties," *The New York Times*, March 10, 1920, p. 1.

88. "Hoover Candidacy Fails to Obtain Congress Support," *The New York Times*, April 1, 1920, p. 1; "Reed Assails Hoover," *Washington Post*, Jan. 25, 1920; "Bryan Won't Consider Hoover's Candidacy," *The New York Times*, Jan. 24, 1920; "Penrose and Reed Join Hearst in Vilifying Hoover," *Philadelphia Public Ledger*, Jan. 24, 1920.

89. Webb Waldron, "About This Man Hoover," *Collier's*, April 3, 1920, p. 14.

90. "The American Presidency," *Nation* editorial, March 27, 1920, pp. 882–83.

91. "Rules Hoover's Name Can Go on 2 Ballots," *New York Post*, Feb. 6, 1920, p. 1.

92. See "Candidates for the Presidency/Party Confusion/Mr. Wilson and a Third Term," *The New York Times*, March 27, 1920; Bagby, *Road to Normalcy*, pp. 55–57.

93. Ibid., pp. 64–65.

94. Ibid., p. 67.

95. See "Hoover Announces He Would Run As a Republican," *New York World*, March 31, 1920, p. 1; "Hoover out for Republican Nomination; Wires California Friends He'll Accept, While Republicans Here Attack Him," *New York Times*, March 31, p. 1; *Providence (R.I.) Journal* editorial; *Washington Star* editorial; *Cleveland Plain Dealer* editorial; and *Boston Transcript* editorial, April 1, 1920; *New York Journal* editorial, March 31, 1920.

96. "Hoover sticks to Republicans," *The New York Times*, April 4, 1920, pp. 3, 12.

97. "Hoover Man Denies Third Party Talk," *The New York Times*, April 5, 1920, p. 17; "Hoover Says 'No' To the Democrats," *The New York Times*, April 10, 1920, p. 1.

98. "Johnson Has 155,338 Cal. Lead; Wood 8,116 in Ind.," *New York Tribune*, May 5, 1920, p. 1; "Senator's Lead in Home State May be 50,000," *Washington Herald*, May 5, 1920, p. 1; "Wood Has 5,393 Lead in Indiana; Hiram Johnson Wins in California; Hoover's Vote More Than 158,000," *New York Post*, May 5, 1920, p. 1.

99. "A Campaign of Confusion," *Nation*, June 5, 1920, p. 306.

100. "Hoover's Defeat," *New York World* editorial, May 6, 1920.

101. "Johnson's Day," *Richmond (Va.) News-Leader* editorial, May 5, 1920; "Herbert Hoover, Sportsman," *Boston Transcript* editorial, May 5, 1920; "The Muddle," *Boston Globe* editorial, May 6, 1920; untitled editorial, *San Francisco Daily News*, May 5, 1920. "Hoover Loses in California," *Boston Herald* editorial, May 6, 1920; "Senator Johnson's California Victory," *Outlook*, May 19, 1920, pp. 111–12.

102. Burner, *Herbert Hoover*, pp. 154–56; Bagby, *Road to Normalcy*, p. 159.

103. Hoover Memoirs, vol. 2, pp. 34–35.

104. Ibid., p. 35.

105. BSA letter to HH, Sept. 12, 1921, p. 1, Allen Papers, Box 446, HHPL.

106. Undated, unidentified article, "Ben Allen Tells Why He Disposed of His Interests in Sacramento Union," in ibid., Box 446.

107. Ibid.

108. Ibid.

109. See U.S. Department of Commerce interoffice memorandum, June 8, 1923, in ibid., Box 20.

110. Frank Parker Stockbridge, "President Hoover Describes His Contacts with the Press," *American Press*, 48, no. 7 (April 1930), p. 1.

2

Secretary of Commerce

Only days before Warren Harding's inauguration, reporters learned that Herbert Hoover had accepted the Secretary of Commerce post. He did so reluctantly and only at the urging of Charles Evans Hughes, the party's 1916 standard-bearer and soon-to-be Harding's secretary of state.[1] Newsmen found out that, instead of retiring from public life as he had intended, Hoover planned to return to Washington. For seven years, he attended to everyday details and set aside his presidential ambitions.[2] By accepting the cabinet post, Hoover rejected a $500,000-a-year position with mining company owner Daniel Guggenheim.[3]

David Lawrence wrote that the idea of Hoover as president displeased official Washington, but his appointment as Secretary of Commerce was welcomed. His expertise and organization were badly needed in the Commerce Department, which had grown into a confusing welter of loosely connected subagencies. Most newspapers and magazines praised his appointment.[4] The *New Republic* described Hoover as "easily the most constructive man in public life."[5] The *New York World* had cooled toward Hoover, and the newspaper described his appointment as political maneuvering by Harding. The *World* concluded:

In political circles which are unfriendly to the Administration there was a good deal of speculation as to the motive which prompted Mr. Harding at a rather late date in his Cabinet making to turn to Mr. Hoover. The view was expressed that it was an attempt to stave off criticism by getting at least one man with a sufficient popular following to offset the criticism aroused by the selection of Messrs. Daugherty, Mellon, and Fall and that Mr. Harding, if he could dodge Mr. Hoover and still get credit for having made him the offer would be just as well pleased.[6]

An accompanying article suggested that Harding had appointed Hoover at the behest of Sen. Hiram Johnson's "henchmen."[7] The *World* was wrong. Harding had offered Hoover the post in December. It was Hoover who had dragged out the process, while debating his options.

Being secretary of such a minor cabinet post was not apparently a base for building toward the presidency. It seemed to confirm that Hoover had only modest presidential ambitions. Had he harbored stronger aspirations, he would have waited to run for a U.S. Senate seat or for governor of California. Instead, Hoover attached himself to a Republican Administration under the tutelage of a figurehead president, and he was forced to accept the political ramifications of that decision, good and bad. Not only would he have to answer to Warren Harding, but newspapers and magazines would no longer see him as an apolitical humanitarian, but as a cabinet officer who would likely mouth the Republican line and follow policies established by Harding.

Because of who Harding was, this did not occur, of course. Harding allowed his appointees to run amuck, often making self-interested decisions on their own with little guidance or interest from Harding. Much more obligation fell upon the shoulders of the Cabinet appointees under Harding, than during most any other Administration in the twentieth century. Still, there were advantages to being in the Cabinet. Hoover had associated himself first with a corrupt Administration, but second and more importantly with the dominant Republican Party. The first turned out to be a disaster that he survived. The second was a wise decision that would eight years later make him a shoo-in for the presidency.

As a member of the Harding Administration, Hoover found life difficult. Because Harding paid scant attention to daily responsibilities,[8] Hoover was left to provide much of the direction for business, labor, and agriculture on his own. Still, Harding biographer Charles Mee, Jr., agreed with the *New York World* that Harding really only appointed Hoover to the cabinet as window dressing. Hoover was well known and respected, and Harding figured he would look good, if he appeared to rely on Hoover's counsel.[9]

On March 19, 1921, fifteen days after he took office, Hoover asked a group of 25 business, labor, and agriculture leaders to serve on an advisory committee for Commerce Department policies.[10] Hoover had taken over a department with oversight responsibilities ranging from foreign and domestic commerce to fisheries and steamboat inspection.[11] He chose two assistants to take care of daily administrative work and immediately streamlined the Commerce Department, reassigning some political appointees. When Congress refused to budget more money for his personal staff, he used his own money to hire two secretaries and three assistants.[12] In 1922 the number of home radio receivers increased twelve-fold. The increasingly complex industry was placed under Commerce Department control, widening the duties and responsibilities of the Cabinet officer in charge but also lodging him close to the inner workings of a powerful new medium.[13]

After the war, there was no longer a worldwide premium on U.S. finished products and agricultural goods. In the summer of 1921 the American economy floundered. Harding asked Hoover to chair the President's Conference on Unemployment to bring together business, academic, and labor leaders to discuss how to stimulate product demand. It was the first time that a president had called for a committee to respond to a downturn in the economy. Not surprisingly, the panel was Hoover's idea. The committee recommended that the government refine the collection of statistics and proposed that a federal agency be made responsible for public works contingency plans to be used in difficult economic times.[14] These changes helped future planners deal with recessions. Unfortunately, President Hoover was not one of those who benefitted from the committee's work. The depression of the 1930s was too great an economic downturn for such a plan to help much.

Hoover claimed in his memoirs that, despite his distaste for Harding's gambling and drinking and his dislike for Harding's advisors, he actually regarded the president fondly and got along well with him.[15] A conversation ten yeas later with his press secretary Theodore Joslin offers a more candid Hoover view, however. Hoover told Joslin that one day in 1921 he accompanied Harding to West Point, N.Y., with other members of the Administration. He added:

Harding asked [Charles Evans] Hughes [secretary of state] and me to sit in a game of poker with him, [Interior Secretary Albert] Fall, and a few others. We played for half an hour and then I begged off. Harding got so drunk that night he did not know what he was doing. I am not a prig, but I was so disgusted that I was fully determined to resign from the Cabinet upon my return to Washington. It was difficult indeed for me to reconsider my decision.[16]

As result of his distaste for Harding, Hoover decided he would operate his department independently and ignore Harding and his cronies as much as he could. Despite the heavy demands of the complex Commerce Department, Hoover took on many outside responsibilities. In 1922 and 1923 he was called upon to settle coal strikes nationwide. He found in favor of the miners, engendering considerable anger from obstinate mine owners.[17] Historian Joan Hoff Wilson points out that, in the mining text-book he wrote in 1909, Hoover actually espoused progressive labor pol-icies before most other managers in the industry did. He favored both compulsory arbitration and greater recognition of nonviolent labor or-ganizations.[18]

For her own part, Mrs. Hoover remained active in Washington social life, though she refused to observe the long-held rituals of regular social visits to other influential wives. Instead, shortly after arriving in Washing-ton, Lou Henry Hoover was elected president of the Girl Scouts and worked tirelessly for the organization, building its membership from 100,000 to one million and raising $2 million in contributions.[19]

Hoover's tenure as Commerce Secretary brought him into daily contact with the Washington press corps for the first time. He usually met infor-mally every afternoon with a few reporters, who agreed to use informa-tion he gave them only when permission to do so was granted. Alfred H. Kirchhofer, of the *Buffalo Evening News*, was one of the regulars in the Commerce Department in the 1920s. Others, according to Kirchhofer, were Roy A. Roberts, of the *Kansas City Star*; Jay G. Hayden, of the *De-troit News*; and Robert Choate, of the *Boston Herald-Traveler*, all of whom later became editors of their respective newspapers.[20]

Kirchhofer recalled 50 years later: "Those who went understood what was said was to be treated in confidence, and used only as specified. Everybody readily agreed to the procedure."[21] He continued:

By taking careful note of what was said at the private conferences with Mr. Hoo-ver, and relating some of this, for example, to what might come out of a presi-dential press conference, one would be able to better understand whatever did happen.

In this sense it might be said that Mr. Hoover was an interpreter for some of the Harding and later Coolidge policies, not in the sense of going over his su-perior's head but merely to assist him in getting his point across and clarifying it to a group of newspapermen anxious to know the objective truth.[22]

Kirchhofer's candid observation offers a rare insight into how Hoover interacted with reporters during this period. The relationship was cordial, but the reporters obviously were treated as messengers. With rumors of scandal leaking from the White House, Harding, despite his background as a journalist, provided little information to the press.[23] Often, reporters looked to politicians outside the administration. Hoover, always informed and always working industriously, was one of the few reliable adminis-tration sources, but he talked to reporters only on his terms.

Sometimes, the information flow from the Commerce Department made others in government suspicious. An incident in 1923 exemplifies this. J. Edgar Hoover (no relation) was special assistant to the attorney general in 1923. This was before he assumed his duties as head of the Bureau of Investigation in 1924 (later the FBI), but even in 1923 J. Edgar Hoover sought to keep close tabs on anyone sympathetic to the Soviet Union. In a letter marked "personal and confidential," J. Edgar Hoover wrote a rambling diatribe, almost undecipherable in places, to Lawrence Richey, a Herbert Hoover assistant. J. Edgar Hoover informed Richey that Willis Abbot, the editor of the *Christian Science Monitor*, appeared to have "connection[s] with radicals." An article concerning the Soviet Union published in the newspaper in December 1922 "show[ed] marked leanings that way," the assistant attorney general wrote to Richey. He added that Abbot had told those who complained to the *Monitor* that he could not refuse to publish the article, because Secretary of Commerce Herbert Hoover had "request[ed] or suggest[ed] that the *Monitor* publish it."[24] In a menacing closing that was typical of J. Edgar Hoover, he wrote: "You will, of course, treat the above information strictly confidentially but I would appreciate being advised as to any facts which you may be able to obtain upon the same as I have had several of my friends speak to me about it and I want to set them straight upon the entire matter."[25] Herbert Hoover's secretary Richard S. Emmet wrote a terse letter of response, which stated in part: "Mr. Hoover to my certain knowledge has never written any editorials, nor did he inspire this one."[26] Both J. Edgar Hoover and Richey used the terms "editorial" and "article" interchangeably. Apparently, nothing was ever made public in connection with the Justice Department inquiry, and there were no more inquiries from the Justice Department. However, the exchange was an indication of how people like J. Edgar Hoover disliked Hoover's close relationship with some reporters and editors and his propensity for providing them with stories.

Presidents of that era had only generally established how they or their Cabinet officers were to interact with reporters. Theodore Roosevelt twenty years earlier began the policy of giving reporters regular stories from the White House. Before Roosevelt, reporters relied upon the Congress for most news. By the 1920s, reporters had become accustomed to seeking out officials in the executive branch for stories, but still only gathering their news according to terms dictated by the president and his cabinet officers. Harding, though he was not attentive to the needs of reporters and met with them sporadically after he had been publicly chastised in print for his many weaknesses, was merely continuing press policies clearly established for many years. He did not care much whether Hoover set his own guidelines and talked freely with a few chosen members of the newspaper establishment either. What both Hoover and Harding failed to recognize was that the nature of reporting and White House coverage was changing. Reporters in Washington had risen in influence and prestige and found themselves less and less satisfied with handouts from government insiders or with a list of rules and guidelines as to how they could use background information.

Hoover's years in the Commerce Department, when he met regularly with only a handful of reporters, kept him insulated from these changes and convinced him that press relations should not stray from the one-sided approach that he had always found so successful. Often he did small favors for reporters and expected, in return, their allegiance and loyal camaraderie.[27] The *Washington Star*, a newspaper friendly to Hoover, observed on July 15, 1928, the day after Hoover resigned as Secretary of Commerce: "Under his administration the Department of Commerce became the most prolific source of readable news in Washington." The editorial observed that Hoover often refused to be quoted directly, but that he "not only made news but he made news available."[28] This approach worked well within the narrow confines of the Commerce Department, where Hoover could talk freely about all manner of political and governmental activities, but where news infrequently was made. When he became president and the central figure in government, he could not leak news and sidestep responsibility for its content, nor could he hold reporters to stifling rules and regulations.

Hoover himself occasionally wrote articles for newspapers and magazines.[29] However, as a steady stream of requests for these commentaries came to him, he was forced to turn down most.[30] Even Lou Henry Hoover wrote a piece reminiscing about her youthful experiences at a summer camp in California. The article, in exquisite prose and demonstrating an imaginative writing style far more polished than her husband's, appeared in the *American Girl*, the national Girl Scouts' magazine, in April 1924, while Mrs. Hoover was president of the Girl Scouts.[31]

SUPPORTIVE JOURNALISTS

Mostly, Hoover's image was boosted by journalists, who were also Hoover's close friends and advisors, or by other writers who seemed supportive of the commerce secretary and his ideas. Mark Sullivan, one of Hoover's most avid supporters in the 1920 primary campaign, continued to write freelance for important newspapers and magazines about Hoover and about Washington. Sometimes, Sullivan was identified as a trusted Hoover advisor and sometimes not.[32]

Sullivan, who had been close to Theodore Roosevelt and who frequently wrote for *Collier's* and later the *New York Herald Tribune*, served as an informal adviser to Hoover on press relations during this time. The Sullivans were regular Sunday-night dinner guests at the Hoover home, and Sullivan in the 1920s enjoyed as close a personal relationship with Hoover as any journalist of his time.[33] Though it is likely that most of the give-and-take between Sullivan and Hoover took place in personal conversations, Sullivan did correspond with Hoover occasionally. He offered his counsel on how Hoover might enhance his image and even went so far as to advise Hoover on public policy. Just three months after Hoover assumed his cabinet post, Sullivan wrote to Hoover to suggest that Chester County, Pennsylvania, would be a good place to make a political speech. Apparently, Hoover made the trip.[34] Later in the year, Sullivan advised Hoover to reexamine every foreign commercial treaty the United States had negotiated and report on "what ones of them, if any, should be denounced and what other changes should be brought about, in the light of America's changed relation to the world since the war."[35] Hoover brushed aside this suggestion with a polite acknowledgment.[36] It is likely, however, that Hoover's policy of reward and punishment toward newspapers and magazines was due, in part, to Sullivan's advice. Theodore Roosevelt had employed this same policy, and Sullivan was one of Roosevelt's favorites.

Another journalist friend was Edward Eyre Hunt, who had been on the Belgium Relief staff and had written a series of articles for distribution in the United States. Later during the Commerce Department years, Hunt wrote affirmatively about Hoover in *Outlook*, *Survey*, and the *Nation*, praising Hoover's organization skills and his scientific management. This enhanced Hoover's image with the public, while few readers realized that Hunt was a close personal friend.[37] Others in Hoover's inner circle included S. R. Winters, William Hard, Will Irwin, Arnold Margolin, Harold Stokes (who later became a Hoover Commerce Department aide), and, to a lesser extent, Richard Oulahan, of *The New York Times*.[38]

Hoover also used a clipping service to keep track of articles written about him and instructed his assistants to inform him of adverse newspaper publicity. He often went directly to publishers to complain both about Washington correspondents and about house editorials. He followed up on these articles with a vengeance. "Mr. Hoover is an avid reader of newspaper clippings. He has been accused of being thin-skinned. . . . But this is rather complimentary to the author," the *Star* concluded generously in its 1928 editorial that appeared just after Hoover stepped down as Commerce Secretary.[39] Only six months into his term at the Commerce Department, Hoover personally wrote to Frank Cobb, editor of the *New York World*: "You may cuss me out all you like about things I do commit—which may be aplenty—but for things I do not commit I deserve some consideration." He then corrected a quote about the foreign trade deficit that had appeared in the *World* a few days earlier.[40] This occurred only a year after Cobb and his newspaper had been first to endorse Hoover's 1920 candidacy, but it was clearly an indication that the *World* and Hoover were going their separate ways.

Sometimes, editors refused to give in to Hoover. Six weeks after the

Cobb letter, a Hoover outburst brought a lengthy explanation from Robert M. Lovett, editor of the *New Republic*, about the American Relief Administration, which Hoover still directed. Lovett offered an apology for any misunderstanding that might have arisen from a series of articles about the relief agency, but refused to bend to Hoover's complaints about inaccuracy and instead lashed back:

Instead of issuing any statement in modification of Miss Lane's and Captain Gregory's articles, or taking advantage of our willingness to publish anything which will give the American Relief Administration a better standing with certain sections of the community, Messrs. Baker and Page of the Association have busied themselves with assertions that I was a conscious liar and that the New Republic was venting a private grudge against you at the risk of ruining the cause of Russian Relief in America and adding enormously to the toll of death. Such statements have been made to the editors of the Nation, to the Civic Club of New York and in private correspondence by Mr. Page. Such statements do not hurt me or the New Republic in the least.[41]

Other editors cowered before Hoover's wrath. In 1925 the *Louisville Times* carried an editorial attacking Hoover for his lack of support for agricultural price supports.[42] He wrote personally to editor Robert W. Bingham that the "rather brutal editorial . . . was not justified." He said the misunderstanding may have arisen because a press release was too brief, and he then issued a longer explanation.[43] Bingham sent a telegram humbly apologizing, and the Washington correspondent who wrote the article visited Hoover to offer his explanation. "I should always feel you were actuated only by highest and most patriotic motives," Bingham cabled. "This incident moves me to say what ordinarily one might feel without expressing it and that is that no man in public life in my time has had my respect and confidence more fully than yourself."[44] Hoover graciously accepted the apology and concluded, "No one values more highly than I do the free expression of editorial opinion, so long as it is correctly informed."[45]

The Hoover files are replete with examples of Hoover or his assistants complaining to editors of magazines and newspapers or of Hoover complaining to associates about articles he disagreed with. There are more than 2,000 letters of complaints, responses, and clips of articles in question that Hoover and his assistants collected into a "misrepresentations" file during his seven years as Secretary of Commerce. Hoover also kept general clipping files during his years as Belgian Relief director and as Food Administrator. During his presidency, he expanded the clippings to include books and articles he considered particularly mean-spirited, classifying a special category of writing in his "smear file."[46]

Hoover bristled frequently at stories in newspapers and magazines, but

Calvin Coolidge largely ignored published criticism and marveled that negative stories so unsettled Hoover. "Do you mean a man in public life as long as you have bothers about attacks in the papers?" Coolidge asked Hoover once during the Coolidge presidency. "Don't you?" Hoover responded.[47]

Even tongue-in-cheek editorials brought severe responses. One such incident occurred in late 1924. Hoover expressed the opinion that radio should serve a higher purpose than constantly broadcasting modern jazz. The *Chicago Tribune* tweaked Hoover about for having old-fashioned tastes.[48] Hoover did not find the editorial amusing and promptly wrote to editor and publisher Robert R. McCormick. "[It] goes to show that you never can tell what an editorial writer is going to do," McCormick responded, advising Hoover to take the editorial in a humorous light. He added diplomatically: "We believe not only that you are working for the public welfare, which indeed is not unusual, but that you are accomplishing important results, which is almost unheard of."[49]

Unlike later presidents, Hoover relied heavily upon friendships with newspaper editors, publishers, and owners for good press relations instead of largely interacting with reporters. This began as early as 1921. As has been noted, only a handful of reporters visited him in the Commerce Department regularly. However, during this period, he stayed in contact with the most influential Republican newspaper publishers in the country and some maintained a cordial, if not servile, correspondence. The exchange with Bingham was typical of Hoover's reaction to an unfavorable story or editorial. He went right to the top. He considered a positive relationship with newspaper owners much more important than that of reporters. In return, friendly publishers placed their editorial and news pages at his disposal. In October of 1923 Harry Chandler, president and general manager of the *Los Angeles Times*, wrote to Hoover discussing the career of Hoover's political nemesis, Sen. Hiram Johnson of California. The same letter illustrates just how close the *Times*'s staff was to Hoover. Hoover wanted Robert Armstrong, *Times* Washington correspondent, to take a leave to serve as Director of the Mint. Chandler declined, saying that Armstrong was just too valuable to the *Times* to allow him to accept the temporary appointment.[50] But Chandler was willing to do anything else. A year later he wrote to Hoover:

Whenever there is anything THE TIMES can do to support or forward the fine work you are doing it goes without saying that we are glad to perform to the limit of our ability. Whenever you have an idea that we can render any service in your political affairs please write me or confer with Armstrong and he will use THE TIMES' wire.[51]

He flattered other editors and publishers and expressed his gratitude when they supported him in print. Hoover wrote to McCormick in 1924,

"There recently came to my attention an editorial in the *Chicago Tribune* which contained some friendly reference to my activities. . . . This character of support is very encouraging to a public official and I would not have you think me unappreciative."[52] It is indicative of Hoover and the times that he regarded the editorial as an encouragement that needed a note of thanks rather than a commentary designed to inform and motivate the reading public. Hoover wrote a similar letter to Clark Howell, editor of the *Atlanta Constitution*, after a favorable editorial appeared in the *Constitution* in December 1924.[53] A year later, Hoover became annoyed when he learned that a *Tribune* reporter was preparing an article about " 'Co-educational Courtships of Men in Public Life' or something like that," in Hoover's words.[54] He wrote again to McCormick:

She has seized upon my wife and myself as one horrible example.

I suppose I cannot ask that the whole reference to Mrs. Hoover and myself be suppressed, but truly the idea fairly sickens me. May I earnestly entreat that before publication the article be read by some friendly soul, and cut as far as possible to the public record—the fact of graduation together from Stanford, the collaboration on the translation of Agricola, etc. Of course, I would prefer that we be left out of the picture, altogether, as I have never grown sufficiently callous to feel anything but abhorrence for such public invasion of a man's domestic privacy.[55]

There is no record of McCormick's response, but the exchange shows not only that Hoover felt free to ask McCormick to squelch articles but also that Hoover was not ready for the very public life of a leader of a powerful nation. His abhorrence for prying journalism would not enhance his relationship with reporters later either.

Often Hoover felt free to ask that information about government activity be withheld. In 1927 he took charge of government relief for hapless victims of a Mississippi River flood, the worst flood in U.S. history until 1993. While touring the South, Hoover sent a telegram to *Christian Science Monitor* editor Lawrence Abbot, asking that the newspaper not publish anything that Hoover might have said that could be construed as criticism of the people of the South. A correspondent, whose name was not mentioned, had followed Hoover's tour closely, even sitting in on meetings. The secretary apparently had second thoughts about what the reporter might have heard and what he might write. "I would take it up with him personally but he has left," Hoover cabled.[56] There is no record of the response, but apparently there was compliance. Months later, the *Monitor* offered its new pages to Hoover. A friendly *Monitor* editorial board corresponding secretary wrote to him saying that the newspaper wanted to support him for president and that writer Harold Stokes, Hoover's former secretary, would be composing a series of articles on

Hoover's public record. Was Stokes a good choice or did he want someone else, the secretary wanted to know.[57] Hoover's press secretary George Akerson responded that it would not be right for Hoover to suggest a writer.[58] Even Hoover would not go that far!

Hoover sometimes suggested to publishers or editors who they should hire or promote. During the flood relief assignment, Hoover met a young reporter with the *Memphis Commercial Appeal*, Turner Catledge. On the scene for several weeks, Catledge offered valuable information to Hoover about the flood's effects and about logistics. Catledge was greatly impressed with Hoover's dedication and no-nonsense commitment to help flood victims, noting even that Hoover snubbed Republican politicians who came to the scene to make political grist from Hoover's visit.[59] Obviously, Catledge also favorably impressed Hoover, because upon his return to Washington, Hoover wrote to Adolph Ochs Sulzberger, publisher of *The New York Times*, recommending to him that *The Times* hire Catledge. Sulzberger sent the request to the managing editor Frederick T. Birchell, who filed it. A few months later Catledge joined the staff of the *Baltimore Sun*. Hoover persisted, however, and during a luncheon meeting in 1929 a few months after Hoover became president, he asked Sulzberger why he had not hired Catledge. Sulzberger investigated and a few weeks later Catledge joined the Washington bureau of *The Times*. Catledge did not learn of Hoover's role until years later, but the incident illustrates Hoover's relationship with Sulzberger and his tendency to influence the careers of reporters.[60]

Only the Hearst and Pulitzer newspapers remained aloof from Hoover during the Commerce Department era. Publisher William Randolph Hearst, who himself had sought the Democratic presidential nomination in 1904, controlled magazines, newsreels, the International News Service wire service, and 26 major newspapers from Atlanta to Detroit and from New York to Los Angeles. Though Hearst endorsed Hoover in 1928 against Al Smith, mostly he did not support the Californian after Hoover declared in 1920 that he was a Republican. Interestingly, though there is no correspondence with Hearst in the Hoover files during this period, there is a 1924 list of all Hearst newspapers nationwide that staffers apparently used to monitor editorial content.[61] The Pulitzer newspapers, after a brief interlude of support for Hoover in 1920, drifted away from him during his Republican years and bitterly opposed him during his presidency.

Hoover often fumed about news stories. Sometimes just the flow of news created friendly or hostile relations with reporters, editors, publishers, or other newsmakers. The 1918 Bolshevik revolution in Russia and surrounding territories, renamed the Soviet Union, reverberated throughout the capitalist world, creating a worldwide fear of bolshevism. At the same time, the Soviet Union contained millions of starving people ravaged first by World War I and then by civil war between the Whites, or conservative Czarist elements, and the Bolsheviks. By the end of 1921, the communist government under V. I. Lenin had subdued the White forces inside the Soviet Union, and Lenin turned his attention to feeding his starving people.

Though he had been Secretary of Commerce for nine months, Hoover still remained head of American Relief in Europe. In late 1921, a Chicago man named Walter Liggett formed a private organization, the American Committee for Russian Famine Relief, to aid starving Russians, and he asked for Hoover's support. This came just after the infamous Palmer raids by the Justice Department. On December 29, 1921, Henry C. Campbell, an executive with the *Milwaukee Journal*, wrote a letter to the Justice Department asking for information about the famine relief committee. Someone in the justice department, probably J. Edgar Hoover, wrote back to Campbell that the committee in question was one of several "officered and managed by well known communists or sympathizers. . . . These organizations are apparently opposed to the American Relief Administration [Hoover's Committee]."[62] The charges soon became public.

Hoover wrote to Liggett to explain that he could not be connected with the American Committee for Russian Famine Relief. Hoover advised Liggett:

I have obviously never considered [that] the question of religious or economic faith should enter into the field of charity. . . . It is useless, nevertheless, to try to disassociate from one's mind that this particular group of Russians despite the generosity of the American Government and the American people to their stricken countrymen, are still carrying on propaganda in the United States designed to undermine our Government and our institutions.

A matter of more immediate importance, in my conclusion that I cannot give the endorsement you ask, is my attitude toward the entrance of foreign governments into the United States and their stimulation of appeals for public charity. . . . American charity should be organized spontaneously by Americans and dispensed through absolute American agencies abroad.[63]

This Hoover hoped would end the matter, but a lengthy article appeared in *The New York Times* reporting that Harding had asked Hoover for a report on the Chicago organization, the American Committee for Russian Famine Relief. *The New York Times* article quoted from a December 3, 1921 letter written by Liggett, in which Liggett claimed that famine relief to the Soviet Union was hampered by prejudice against the Soviet government. The relief committee was seeking to align itself with the Russian Red Cross under American auspices, the article stated, and Idaho Gov. D. W. Davis had been asked to lend his name to Liggett's committee. Davis inquired about the committee and was given information by the Justice Department, the article stated. This information was apparently similar to what was included in the cable to Campbell. Davis refused to support Liggett's committee.[64] Liggett then sought and was given by Hoover's office a copy of the letter that the Justice Department had sent Campbell.[65]

Though Liggett and Hoover aides continued to correspond, this seemed to end Liggett's hope of attaching his organization to the Hoover relief efforts. The publicity obviously branded Liggett as a Bolshevik sympathizer. He may have been, but nothing except the spurious letter from the Justice Department seemed to support that. Hoover was obviously nettled by the negative newspaper publicity and the inquiries from Harding's office. The ever-wary Secretary of Commerce now had even more reason to be careful about newspaper stories and about groups wishing to help in relief efforts.

In early 1923, the nation suddenly, and what appeared to be mysteriously, experienced a sharp increase in the price of sugar from 2.6 to 6 cents per pound. Newspapers theorized that chicanery was involved, and many published editorials suggested that a pessimistic report from the Department of Commerce in February of 1923 had fueled sugar speculation.[66] Agents from the New York Coffee and Sugar Exchange investigated for two months, and generally it was learned that the problem derived from a variety of sources.

Sugar production had increased drastically in 1920 and 1921, especially in Cuba, and sent the postwar price of sugar plummeting. A poor crop in 1922 reversed the trend, and when the Department of Commerce issued a routine prediction on February 9, 1923, that there would be a small surplus of sugar by the end of 1923, speculators began buying up commodities.[67] By April investigators identified 23 speculators who had profited from the price increases. Hoover issued a statement saying that there actually was a surplus of sugar and not a shortage, but this did not slow the speculation. Reed Smoot, a Republican from Utah and chairman of the Senate Finance Committee, issued a public statement blaming greedy sugar refiners for gouging the public. By early May, both political parties called for a boycott of sugar until prices came down. Eventually, when the market normalized, prices dropped on their own, and it was generally agreed that supply and demand, aggravated by speculation, had caused the inflated sugar prices.[68] Again, Hoover and the Department of Commerce were blamed for the natural course of market trends. Hoover, it may be said, did bear some blame for the statement issued in February predicting a small sugar surplus and his inability to reassure the public that the problem was a short-term one. His statement in April that there really was a sugar surplus when prices had nearly doubled helped no one. Many newspapers that had been supportive of Hoover criticized him roundly when the public became agitated. A few writers, including William Hard, who wrote a supportive analysis for the *Nation*, absolved the

Commerce Department of blame. But, again, the ebb and flow of the news dragged Hoover into controversy, and he resented the criticism that naturally goes along with holding office.

Conversely, in 1924 Hoover headed a commission to explore the possibility of constructing the St. Lawrence Seaway to connect the Great Lakes with the Atlantic Ocean. The project was not completed until more than 40 years later, but Hoover correctly saw it as a great boon to U.S. commerce, and Calvin Coolidge appointed him to chair a commission to explore construction of such a seaway. Hoover wrote to the editors of the *New York Evening Post*, the *Des Moines Register*, and the *Chicago Daily News* asking for their editorial assistance.[69] He was not reluctant to stimulate positive news coverage, though he was greatly dismayed any time he incurred negative publicity.

The articles discussed here and the correspondence cited tell as much about the journalism of the time as about Hoover. Political reporting was becoming a profession in its own right, separate from the ambitions and ideologies of the editors and publishers, who sought to influence the nation's political process through their publications. Yet, this dichotomy in political intercourse did not shift with lightning swiftness, but took hold gradually over decades. The divergence of attitudes between Washington reporter and publisher accelerated during the Franklin D. Roosevelt Administration, when reporters were enamored with the suave and friendly Roosevelt, while the mostly Republican newspaper owners detested FDR.[70] Yet, this change began years before, and Hoover was part of the process even before he ascended to the presidency.

Still, many Washington reporters clung to nineteenth-century partisanship and unabashedly advised and supported their favorite candidates and officeholders. It was through this lens that Hoover saw the world of journalism. He did not acknowledge that the "new" reporter could be both critical and supportive. He could only be one or the other. Criticism and even questions or stories that Hoover considered invasive could not be tolerated. Those who found fault or who wrote about his private life were to be shunned and treated with contempt.

In some cases, Hoover had legitimate complaints about accuracy. In others, he simply could not handle criticism. Journalists were either for him or against him. Magazine and newspaper editors and publishers were to be cultivated or avoided. For Hoover, this concept of press relations never changed. When the country was relatively prosperous and questions posed were neither seriously threatening nor, on the whole, negatively phrased, Hoover's interpersonal relations with reporters remained quite cordial. Once readers became unhappy and clamored for more explanations about the nation's condition, particularly its economic plight, the buddy system dissolved. How could Hoover in 1930 write to all the newspapers and magazines that were criticizing him as he had during his years as commerce secretary? His policy of rewarding acclamation and of badgering those who would criticize fell apart in the 1930s. Hoover's cordial relations with reporters and editors in the Commerce Department years enhanced his image, but they also created an unstable foundation for press policy in later years. This could confound and dismay him after the Wall Street crash in 1929, when he regarded critical reporters, editors, and publishers as enemies who had turned on him when he needed them most.

From a practical point of view, because Hoover was extremely influential and helpful, reporters were usually friends like Hard and Sullivan. But even less friendly reporters were leaked information that was helpful to the Department of Commerce or the administration, and they were expected to use it in a way that would perpetuate a compromised but continuing relationship with Hoover.

THE COOLIDGE YEARS

In June of 1923 Harding, who had begun to learn of the treachery within his administration, decided to undertake a 1,500-mile train excursion through the Midwest to the Northwest and eventually to Alaska by steamer. On the way to Alaska, Harding asked Hoover, who had joined the party in Tacoma, "If you knew of a great scandal in our administration, would you for the good of the country and the party expose it publicly or would you bury it?" Hoover responded, "Publish it, and at least get credit for integrity on your side." Harding never raised the question again, Hoover noted in his memoirs.[71] In part, Harding's trip was an escape from the spreading scandal in Washington, and he never lived to see Washington again.

The Harding party returned from Alaska through Vancouver, British Columbia, where Harding addressed a cheering crowd of 60,000. He faltered midway through the speech and could not go on. That night, he collapsed during a speech at the Press Club in Vancouver. The train speeded to San Francisco skipping Portland where the president was to have delivered another address. Harding's doctor, Ray Lyman Wilbur, attributed his illness to ptomaine poisoning from crabmeat, and this diagnosis was widely reported for days until it was finally decided that Harding suffered a blood clot to the brain. Harding died on August 2, 1923, in a hotel in San Francisco.[72] Wilbur wrote a lengthy article for the *Saturday Evening Post* that appeared on October 13, 1923. He explained that he penned the article because "my colleagues asked me to make a public record of some personal experiences not covered in our brief but descriptive bulletins." In the article, Wilbur claimed that Harding died of pneumonia.[73] This led to more confusion and to speculation that Harding was poisoned. Such rumors never were laid to rest, but the preponderance of evidence suggests that Harding died of natural causes.

The Harding trip and illness caused more stir among Washington reporters than had been seen in years. Only because of the vigilance of an Associated Press reporter, Stephen Early, was the Harding death even reported in a timely manner. Other reporters had retired for the evening, but Early continued his watch at the hotel. He and his editor did not believe optimistic press releases. Ironically, Early later would become Franklin Delano Roosevelt's press secretary and in 1945 would announce to the world the death of FDR.[74] Harold Phelps Stokes, who would join Hoover's staff a few months later, wrote a 17-part series of articles for the *New York Post* on Harding's Alaskan trip that was published beginning on July 30 and continuing through August 20, 1923, three weeks after Harding's death. The feature articles reported the details of the trip, but were delayed for three weeks, so that Stokes's first story on July 30 actually reported on the July 5 ship's departure from Tacoma. The series had obviously been planned before Harding was stricken, but the coincidence of Harding's death provided Stokes with an avid reading audience.[75]

Calvin Coolidge was sworn in as president that night by his father, a justice of the peace, at the family farm in Plymouth. Vermont, after reporters had driven to the farm to inform him of Harding's death.[76] The nation, still unaware of the great scandals plaguing the Harding White House, mourned the dead president. The new president could have chosen a different cabinet, but he did not. Albert Fall, Secretary of the Interior, had resigned in March and eventually went to prison. Attorney General Harry Daugherty resigned later and escaped prison, because a jury could not agree on a verdict.[77] Coolidge, who had no direct knowledge or participation in the scandals, escaped taint, as did Hoover. By the time the 1924 election rolled around, the public had forgotten the Harding administration escapades and overwhelmingly reelected Coolidge over John Davis, a colorless Wall Street lawyer. Republican dominance in the White House continued for another four years, but Hoover's ambitions remained stalled. His name had been mentioned for the vice presidency, but Charles Dawes, author of a respected German reparations plan in 1923 was chosen.

Hoover's department oversaw or regulated a myriad of public programs, and he often wandered beyond the purview of his assigned duties while he was Secretary of Commerce. Harding and Coolidge often called upon him to resolve thorny problems. He coordinated health and educational agencies for children, designating May Day as "Child Health Day."[78] Radio increasingly dominated his time with petty, nettlesome details. For instance, when evangelist Aimee Semple McPherson acquired a radio station and the station wandered from its frequency, Hoover was forced to ask her to keep to the assigned frequency. McPherson responded angrily that Hoover was interfering with her doing God's work, but the secretary prevailed.[79]

Foreseeing perhaps that Americans would turn to a new broadcast medium, Hoover, as Secretary of Commerce, with responsibility for broadcast regulation, spoke before a camera in Washington in April 1927, while his image was recorded on the screen of a small television set in New York. This experiment by Dr. Herbert E. Ives in cooperation with Bell Telephone Laboratories and the American Telephone and Telegraph Co. was believed to be the first television broadcast ever. Only a few weeks after the first transatlantic radio broadcast, communications entered a new era "as fascinating and stupendous in its potentialities as the radio or the telephone," observed *The New York Times*. "In time millions of people may watch and listen to a Presidential inauguration, a championship football game, or even the clash of armies on a battlefield," the *New York World* accurately prophesized.[80] While the coming Great Depression and World War II interrupted the commercial progress of television for 20 years, Americans who heard of Hoover's face appearing on a small screen knew in the 1920s that they would someday be seeing on television all that they heard then over the radio. For just a few moments on an April day in Washington, Hoover had stepped into broadcast history annals as a subject for a pioneering television show.

On a more imminent topic, Hoover recognized a need for new and better housing nationwide and formed a volunteer organization. "Better Homes in America," comprised mostly of women. The organization sought to improve local zoning ordinances, to lower lending rates, to encourage year-round construction, and to install uniform construction codes. About 30,000 persons became members.[81] In 1922, Hoover expressed his personal philosophy for individual accomplishment in a book entitled *American Individualism*.[82]

His years with various relief organizations, the Food Administration, and the Department of Commerce continually reminded Hoover of the importance of positive publicity. In 1925 he appointed George Akerson, a newspaperman, as a full-time assistant. A 1912 Harvard cum laude graduate from Omaha, Akerson had worked his way through the hierarchy of the *Minneapolis Tribune* from the time of his graduation from Harvard. He met Hoover while covering Washington from 1921 to 1923 but left for Minnesota in 1923 to assume the duties of assistant managing editor. He returned to the *Minneapolis Tribune*'s Washington bureau in 1925 for a few months before accepting a position on Hoover's staff. Harold Phelps Stokes, who joined Hoover's staff in 1924 after a distinguished career with the *New York Evening Post* and the *Washington Evening Post*, left the Commerce Department in 1926 to join the staff of *The New York Times*.[83] Christian Herter, also a Hoover aide, had been editor of *Inde-*

pendent and *Sportsman's* magazines before joining the Commerce Department.[84]

Akerson's appointment not only continued to recognize the need for a former newsman on the staff to maintain good press relations but also provided a ready-made press secretary when Hoover ascended to the presidency. Akerson, however, eventually left Washington in 1931 on less than perfect personal terms with Hoover. In his memoirs Hoover personally thanked 28 persons who helped him during his Commerce Department years,[85] including four of his six secretaries. Among his personal secretaries, only Richard Emmet's and George Akerson's names do not appear.[86]

By 1927 Hoover had convinced Americans he was both a great humanitarian and someone who could take care of the nation's business efficiently and cost-effectively. In the spring and summer of 1927 when heavy rains caused the Mississippi River to overflow its banks, Coolidge asked Hoover to step in once again and use both his organizational skills and his compassion for the needy. In April a Mississippi Flood Committee, appointed by Coolidge, took over providing relief, setting up refugee camps, and eventually providing help for victims to return to their homes. Federal direction of widespread calamity relief was unprecedented and, at Coolidge's urging, Hoover chaired the committee. He spent three months circling the flood area in a railcar directing rescue and relief with thousands of volunteers and government workers under his direction. Before Hoover took charge, 200 persons had drowned in the floods. After the committee began its work, only three Delta residents were lost.[87]

The committee combined Red Cross resources with independent donations from around the country and created 150 refugee camps, which metamorphozed into small communities, not unlike the tent cities that sprung up around the country during the Great Depression.[88] These tent cities housed an aggregate total of over one million people and benefitted from Hoover's organization and the government's care. At one point in late April, southern Louisiana residents waited in fear as engineers studied whether levees in the Delta might burst, sending flood waters roaring into New Orleans. Finally, millions of acres of sugar plantations were deliberately flooded to relieve the pressure on the levees and save New Orleans.[89] Later Hoover used his engineering background to suggest ways in which levees could be built to minimize the impact of such floods in the future.[90]

The terrible flooding brought Hoover to where he was most useful, to the homes of those desperately in need of organization and help. Southerners who had only known Hoover by reputation came to know him personally. On April 30 he spoke to Americans nationwide, but particularly Southerners, via the National Broadcasting Company radio network. He described over the air the devastation the flooding had engendered and explained what relief measures were being undertaken. Following

Hoover's talk, jazz singer Al Jolson hosted a 15-minute benefit concert over the same stations.[91] This was one of the first nationwide emergency broadcasts ever heard in the United States. The NBC network had just been formed.

A few weeks later Hoover accepted an invitation from the *Birmingham News* to write in his own words what relief workers had accomplished and what remained to be done. "The American people ought to know that everything humanly possible is being done," Hoover wrote. "At the various places we visited there was a multitude of actions of heroism and devotion of people to the South. Some day they will make an epic to thrill all America. The South has done and is doing its great and full share."[92]

While overseeing the rescue and relief efforts in the South Hoover spent weeks in close quarters with many newspersons, with whom he had not had contact in the past. This left a lasting impression on many, including hundreds of reporters and editors from the South who began to see Hoover as something more than a representative of the Republican Party. As has been mentioned, Hoover met Turner Catledge for the first time as Catledge covered the flood for the *Memphis Commercial-Appeal*.[93] At Hoover's instigation, Catledge joined the Washington staff of *The New York Times* two years later. He became the managing editor of *The New York Times* before his career was over. Theodore Joslin, a Washington reporter with the *Boston Transcript*, also wrote flood stories emphasizing Hoover's role.[94] Joslin in 1931 became Hoover's second presidential press secretary. It was Hoover's work not his writing or broadcasts, however, that brought him close to the people and reminded all Americans of why he was one of the most respected men in America. The *Commercial-Appeal* carried a complete biography of Hoover in mid-May, reviewing his career and explaining to Tennesseeans, particularly a new generation who knew Hoover only as Secretary of Commerce, how Hoover had always identified with relief efforts.[95]

Despite his pleas for no publicity, flood stories emphasized Hoover's role at every turn. His name was in the news more often than Coolidge's.[96] Genuine bipartisan expressions of admiration for Hoover poured in from all parts of the nation. "Once again the American people have turned to their handyman, Mr. Hoover," editorialized *The New York Times Magazine*. "Hoover is never afraid of trouble. The harder a job is the more he relishes it."[97] T. H. Alexander, a writer for the *Atlanta Journal*, told readers that Hoover was concerned about everyone, both black and white, and had grown up learning to have empathy for all suffering victims.[98] Tuskegee, Alabama, Mayor Albon Holsey wrote a front-page article for the *Pittsburgh Courier* several months after the flood, recalling fondly how Hoover had touched the people in his community.[99]

The country could not hear enough about Hoover. Hoover's journalist friends dusted off their typewriters and once again churned out biographical articles about the hero of World War I and the Great Mississippi flood. Even before he undertook his flood relief efforts, Ruth Crawford was recalling for Californians Hoover's meteoric rise to success in a March article appearing in the special features section of the *San Francisco News*.[100] In April Anne Hard, who along with her husband had been personal friends with the Hoovers for over 30 years, told *New York Herald Tribune* readers that Hoover was truly a humanitarian "who cannot endure the sight of human suffering."[101] Husband William Hard wrote in the *American Review of Reviews* seven months later that a new Hoover had emerged, one associated with both compassion and efficiency. "I have observed and reported, sometimes admiringly, sometimes critically Mr. Hoover's activities," William Hard wrote in introducing his article. He was cheating somewhat on the truth.[102]

On May 5, 1927, M. E. Hennessy, editor of the *Boston Globe* took the extraordinary step of going on the air to support Hoover, telling Boston radio listeners that "if Mr. Coolidge should decide to retire from the Presidency he would wish to be succeeded in the White House by Hoover." Hennessey added, "The President is indeed fortunate in having a man like Hoover in his Cabinet to deal with the relief problem along the Mississippi."[103] Vernon Kellogg wrote a biographical article about Hoover in *Outlook* magazine, telling readers that he had known Hoover for 35 years, since they were neighbors in Palo Alto. "I have known him especially in those activities where for the first time in history the highest statesmanship, leadership, and executive ability have been applied as vigorously to save human lives as they ever hitherto have been applied by men and nations to carry on life-extinguishing war," Kellogg wrote.[104] William Hard told Consolidated Press Syndicate readers in July 1927 that Hoover was "the busiest man in Washington" because "there seems to be no limit at all to the variety and intensity of his interests."[105] L. C. Speer of *The New York Times* echoed that observation in a biographical interview six months later.[106]

Will Irwin had the greatest impact upon Hoover's popularity, however. Soon after the Mississippi flood, Irwin, who accompanied Hoover in his relief work, began work on a biography about Hoover. It was published by the Century Company in early 1928.[107] A straightforward but highly complimentary discussion of Hoover, it was the first major, book-length Hoover biography since Rose Wilder Lane's effort in 1920. Excerpts were published in the *New York Herald Tribune, Cincinnati Enquirer*, and *Des Moines Register* in April 1928.[108] Because of Hoover's increased popularity, the heavily publicized and promoted book[109] met with favorable reviews and public interest. The reviewers generally only mentioned the quality of Irwin's work in passing and concentrated on musing about what a great career Hoover had enjoyed. *The New York*

Times noted, "There is nothing in Mr. Irwin's biography which will lose Mr. Hoover a single vote."[110] Added Geoffrey Parsons, of the *New York Herald Tribune*:

It has been the unusual fate of Herbert Hoover, call it good luck or misfortune as you will, to become a myth before becoming known as a man. That is to say, he lived an extraordinarily able and successful carer as an engineer up to the age of forty without attracting the least public attention. . . .

The effect of this volume of reminiscences is to make the personal doubts seem ludicrous. By all the past here is a great public servant, peculiarly fitted to handle the problems of the present day. Unless there is a hopeless incompatibility between democracy and the engineering tradition—which is to say, between the art of public leadership and the modern breed of silent, organizing doers—Mr. Irwin has written the life of a great President.[111]

In February 1928 the *New York Telegram* carried excerpts from the book[112] followed by excerpts from a biography about Al Smith, the apparent Democratic nominee for president.[113] George Barr Baker, a long-time co-relief worker with Hoover in Europe and in the Food Administration, published his memoirs in the spring of 1928 adding more personal reminiscences about Hoover to the public record.[114]

The most impressive example of Hoover's reach among journalists appeared in the *New York Post*. The Irwin book, written by a long-time friend, was reviewed in the *Post* by Robert M. Field, another long-time admirer and co-biographer with Rose Wilder Lane on a series appearing in Field's *Sunset* magazine in 1920. Not surprisingly, Field found the Irwin book fascinating. "Evidently the writing was a labor of love. It has the fine touch that only goes into a congenial task," Field wrote. "For the unvarnished story of Herbert Hoover is the very striking record of a simple, great-hearted American."[115] A journalist friend of Hoover wrote a book about him that was given rave reviews by another journalist friend. What more could Hoover ask?

For several months after the Mississippi flood, journalists friendly to Hoover and even those not generally predisposed to favorable comments about the Secretary of Commerce heaped praise on him. Frank R. Kent, Washington bureau chief of the Democratic *Baltimore Sun*, told his readers in December that Hoover's Cabinet work was drawing "genuine praise" from Congress.[116]

It appeared that Hoover might be a strong candidate to succeed Calvin Coolidge in 1932. For the moment Hoover had to decide whether he would continue in his Cabinet post during a new Coolidge term. He had served two Republican administrations for more than six years and his two sons had grown to manhood in Washington. Herbert, now 53 years old, and Lou Hoover had to look toward the future and a life of their own with no children to raise, with or without political ambitions.

Then in August of 1927, Calvin Coolidge had a surprise of his own, and once again Hoover's future direction was, more or less, decided for him.

NOTES

1. David Burner, *Herbert Hoover: A Public Life* (New York: Knopf, 1979), p. 157; Herbert Hoover, *The Memoirs of Herbert Hoover: The Cabinet and the Presidency 1920–1933* (New York: Macmillan, 1952) [hereafter referred to as Hoover memoirs, vol. 2], p. 36.

2. For a discussion of Hoover's agricultural policies during his Commerce Secretary era, see Joan Hoff Wilson, "Hoover's Agricultural Policies 1921–1928," *Agricultural History*, 51, no. 2 (April 1977), pp. 335–61; Gary H. Koerselman, "Secretary Hoover and National Farm Policy: Problems of Leadership, in ibid., pp. 378–95. For a general philosophical discussion of the Hoover contribution during this period, see Ellis W. Hawley, "Herbert Hoover, the Commerce Secretariat, and the Vision of an 'Associate State,' 1921–1928," *Journal of American History*, 61, no. 1 (June 1974), pp. 116–40.

3. Eugene Lyons, *Our Unknown Ex-President: A Portrait of Herbert Hoover* (Garden City, N.Y.: Doubleday, 1948), p. 201.

4. David Lawrence, "Hoover as Cabinet Member Pleases Official Washington," *Sacramento Union*, Feb. 27, 1921. See also Harold Phelps Stokes, "Hoover's Strength to Have Early Test," *New York Post*, Feb. 25, 1921, p. 1; "Revitalizing a Department," *New York Times* editorial, Feb. 25, 1921; "Hoover Named for Commerce Post in Cabinet," *Washington Herald*, Feb. 25, 1921, p. 1; "Mr. Harding's Cabinet," *Washington Post* editorial, Feb. 25, 1921; "Hoover Accepts Place in Cabinet; Keeps Relief Post," *The New York Times*, Feb. 25, 1921, p. 1.

5. "Hoover," *New Republic*, March 9, 1921, p. 29.

6. "Hoover Accepts; Gets Free Hand to Make Big Job," *New York World*, Feb. 25, 1921.

7. "Johnson Henchmen Backing Hoover," *New York World*, Feb. 25, 1921.

8. For a complete discussion of the Harding presidency, see Francis Russell, *The Shadow of Blooming Grove: Warren C. Harding in His Times* (New York: McGraw-Hill, 1968), pp. 437–603; and Charles L. Mee, Jr., *The Ohio Gang: The World of Warren C. Harding* (New York: M. Evans, 1981), pp. 117–233.

9. Mee, *Ohio Gang*, pp. 126–28.

10. Hoover memoirs, vol. 2, p. 41.

11. Ibid., p. 42; Burner, *Herbert Hoover*, pp. 160–62.

12. Dorothy McGee, *Herbert Hoover: Engineer, Humanitarian, Statesman* (New York: Dodd, Mead, 1959), pp. 196–97.

13. Burner, *Herbert Hoover*, p. 163. This study will confine its discussion of radio largely to how Hoover was perceived by a public that listened to him on the radio during his presidency. For a more complete discussion of radio and Hoover during his Commerce years in the 1920s, however, see Louise Margaret Benjamin, "Radio Regulation in the 1920s: Free Speech Issues in the Develop-

ment of Radio and the Radio Act of 1927," Ph.D. dissertation, University of Iowa, 1985; Philip Rosen, *The Modern Senators* (Westport, Conn.: Greenwood Press, 1980); Erik Barnouw, *A Tower in Babel* (New York: Oxford University Press, 1970); and C. M. Jansky, Jr., "The Contributions of Herbert Hoover to Broadcasting," *Journal of Broadcasting* vol. 1, p. 241 (1956–57).

14. Burner, *Herbert Hoover*, pp. 164–65; McGee, *Herbert Hoover*, pp. 197–98; Hoover memoirs, vol. 2, pp. 44–46.

15. Hoover memoirs, vol. 2, pp. 47–50. Early biographer Eugene Lyons seems to have accepted this Hoover analysis as well. See Lyons, *Unknown Ex-President*, pp. 226–27.

16. Joslin Diary, July 27, 1931, entry, Joslin Papers, Box 10, HHPL.

17. Burner, *Herbert Hoover*, pp. 175–77.

18. Joan Hoff Wilson, *Herbert Hoover: Forgotten Progressive* (Boston: Little, Brown, 1975), pp. 33–34.

19. Hoover memoirs, vol. 2, p. 188.

20. Alfred H. Kirchhofer oral history with Raymond Henle, director of Hoover oral history project, April 4, 1969, Buffalo, N.Y., HHPL oral history files, p. 4.

21. Ibid.

22. Ibid., pp. 4–5. Also see Leo Rosten, *The Washington Correspondents* (New York: Harcourt, Brace, 1937).

23. See John Tebbel and Sarah Miles Watts, *The Press and the Presidency: From George Washington to Ronald Reagan* (New York: Oxford University Press, 1985), pp. 391–402.

24. J. Edgar Hoover letter to Lawrence Richey, March 22, 1923, Commerce Papers, Newspapers and Magazines, *Christian Science Monitor*, Box 438, HHPL.

25. Ibid.

26. Richard S. Emmet letter to J. Edgar Hoover, March 27, 1923, in ibid.

27. For instance, at the request of *The New York Times* correspondent Richard Oulahan, Hoover provided an autographed copy of his book on American individualism. See Christian Herter to Oulahan letter of December 21, 1922, Commerce Papers, Box 456, HHPL. On another occasion a Hoover assistant interceded for Oulahan with the Commissioner of Patents for Information Oulahan was seeking. See George Akerson personal letter to Thomas E. Robertson, Commissioner of Patents, February 12, 1927, in ibid.

28. *Washington Star* editorial, July 15, 1928.

29. For one early example, see Herbert Hoover, "To Break the Vicious Circle," *The Nation's Business*, February 1921, p. 17, in which Hoover outlines what needs to be done for industry in the United States to continue to expand.

30. See correspondence in Commerce Papers, Newspapers and Magazines, HHPL.

31. Lou Henry Hoover, "Our Loveliest Camp," *American Girl*, April 1924, pp. 11, 12, 32.

32. See, for instance, Mark Sullivan, "Strange Mixture of Good and Bad Friends of Harding," *San Francisco Journal*, March 5, 1924; Sullivan, "Will Mr. Coolidge Be Renominated?" *World's Work*, October 1923, pp. 620–26.

33. Hoover memoirs, vol. 2, p. 187.

34. MS to HH, May 26, 1921, Commerce Papers, Mark Sullivan File, Box 589, HHPL.

35. MS to HH, Sept. 23, 1921, in ibid.

36. Richard S. Emmet, Hoover's secretary (for Hoover) to Mark Sullivan, Sept. 26, 1921, in ibid.

37. Craig Lloyd, *Aggressive Introvert: A Study of Herbert Hoover and Public Relations Management 1912–1932* (Columbus: Ohio State University Press, 1972), pp. 61–62.

38. See "Hoover Needed in Commerce Department, Asserts Forbes," *Washington Herald*, Nov. 28, 1924; "An Interview with Secretary H. C. Hoover," *Radio News*, October 1924, p. 472; William Hard, "Sugar Cain," *Nation*, 116, no. 3020 (May 23, 1923), p. 596; Hard, "Giant Negotiations for Giant Power," *Survey*, March 1, 1924, pp. 577–80; Arnold Margolin, "Lenin and Hoover," *Our World* (December 1923), pp. 55–57; Richard Oulahan, "Coolidge to Dominate Party Convention/Main Republican Task Is to Find Suitable Vice President," *The New York Times*, June 1, 1924, special features section, p. 1.

39. Ibid.

40. HH to FC, Aug. 29, 1921, Commerce Papers, Newspapers and Magazines, *New York World*, Box 444, HHPL.

41. RML to HH, Oct. 5, 1921, Commerce Papers, Newspapers and Magazines, *Louisville Times*, Box 443, HHPL.

42. "The World Be Damned," *Louisville Times*, Jan. 20, 1925, p. 6.

43. HH to RB, Jan. 27, 1925, Commerce Papers, Newspapers and Magazines, *Louisville Times*, Box 442, HHPL.

44. RB to HH telegram, Feb. 3, 1925. Also see HH to RB letter, Feb. 5, 1925, both in ibid.

45. Ibid.

46. See, for instance, Hoover letter to editor Oswald Garrison Villard, Aug. 8, 1921; Villard response of Aug. 12, 1921; Richard S. Emmet letter to Villard, Aug. 25, 1921; letter from Villard to Edgar Rickard, March 23, 1923; Hoover letter to Christian Herter, March 16, 1923; all in Commerce Papers, Newspapers and Magazines, *Nation* File, Box 443, HHPL; letter to the *New Republic* of June 5, 1922, Commerce Papers, Newspapers and Magazines, *New Republic* File, Box 136, HHPL; Herter to Rickard letter, April 7, 1923, about a *Minneapolis Star* article, Commerce Papers, Newspapers and Magazines, *Minneapolis Star*, Box 442, HHPL; Hoover letter of April 27, 1925, to Fred Essary, Washington correspondent for the *Baltimore Sun*, Commerce Papers, Newspapers and Magazines, *Baltimore Sun*, Box 438, HHPL; Christian Herter letter to the editor of the *Bayonne (N.J.) News*, August 2, 1921; letter to the editor of the *Aberdeen (Idaho) Times*, April 25, 1923; Herter letter to the editor, *Fort Wayne Gazette*, August 2, 1921; the latter three in Commerce Papers, Box 437, under appropriate newspaper file headings.

47. Tebbel and Watts, *Press and Presidency*, p. 410.

48. "Et Tu, Herbert!" *Chicago Tribune* editorial, December 23, 1924, p. 8.

49. RRM letter to HH, Dec. 28, 1928, Commerce Papers, Newspapers and Magazines, *Chicago Tribune* File, Box 438, HHPL. For more on the jazz controversy see "Secretary Hoover Considers Ways and Ideas for Making Radio Worth Listening in Order That It Cannot Live on Endless Jazz Diet," *New York World*, Nov. 30, 1924.

50. HC to HH letter, Oct. 6, 1923, pp. 1–2, Commerce Papers, Newspapers and Magazines, *Los Angeles Times* File, Box 441, HHPL.

51. HC to HH letter, Jan. 5, 1925, in ibid.

52. HH to RRM letter, Dec. 6, 1924, Commerce Papers, Newspapers and Magazines, *Chicago Tribune* File, Box 438, HHPL.

53. HH to CH letter, Dec. 18, 1924, Commerce Papers, Newspapers and Magazines, *Atlanta Constitution* File, Box 438, HHPL.

54. HH to RRM letter, Jan. 5, 1925, Commerce Papers, Newspapers and Magazines, *Chicago Tribune* File, Box 438.

55. Ibid.

56. HH to LA cable, June 11, 1927, Commerce Papers, Newspapers and Magazines, *Christian Science Monitor* File, Box 441, HHPL.

57. BIM to HH, Aug. 19, 1927, in ibid.

58. GA to BIM, Aug. 26, 1927, in ibid.

59. Turner Catledge oral history interview with Raymond Henle, director of Herbert Hoover oral history project, Sept. 15, 1969, in New York, N.Y., p. 3, HHPL oral history files.

60. Ibid., pp. 14–17.

61. "Hearst Papers" list, June 1, 1924, in Commerce Papers, Newspapers and Magazines, Hearst File, Box 440.

62. Justice Department telegram to Henry C. Campbell, Dec. 30, 1921, Commerce Papers, Walter W. Liggett File, HHPL, Box 126.

63. HH to WL, Jan. 23, 1922, in ibid.

64. "President to Get Report on Agencies for Russian Relief," *The New York Times*, Feb. 10, 1922, p. 1.

65. Department of Commerce telegram to Walter W. Liggett, Jan. 16, 1922.

66. See, for instance, "Oh, Sugar!" *Atlanta Georgian*, April 6, 1923; "Why Sugar Goes Up," *Birmingham (Ala.) Age-Herald* editorial, April 6, 1923; "Big Sugar Brokers May Reveal Leak," *New York Herald*, April 17, 1923; "The Sugar Hold-Up," *Phoenix (Ariz.) Herald*, April 17, 1923; "Sugar Price Boosted on Hoover's Report," *New York American*, April 30, 1923.

67. For a complete explanation of how the sugar controversy unfolded see "Sugar Facts and Prices," *New York Herald* editorial, April 20, 1923; "By Threat and Intimidation," *Austin (Tex.) Statesman* editorial, April 16, 1923; "The Sugar Steal," *Wichita (Kan.) Eagle* editorial, April 7, 1923; W. S. Cousins, "Sugar Consumer Must Pay for Exchange Rule," *San Francisco Call*, April 7, 1923, p. 1.

68. "Smoot Sees Robbery Plot by Sugar Men," *Washington Herald*, April 6,1923; "In Justice to Mr. Hoover," *Steubenville (Ohio) Gazette* editorial, May 25, 1923; "Boycotting Sugar," *Indianapolis Star*, May 16, 1923; William Hard, "Sugar Cain," *Nation*, 116, no. 3020 (May 23, 1923), p. 596.

69. Burner, *Herbert Hoover*, p. 181.

70. See Graham J. White, *FDR and the Press* (Chicago: University of Chicago Press, 1979).

71. Hoover memoirs, vol. 2, p. 49; also see Russell, *Shadow*, p. 582; Mee, *Ohio Gang*, pp. 220–21.

72. Hoover memoirs, vol. 2, pp. 50–51; Russell, *Shadow*, pp. 588–92; Mee, *Ohio Gang*, pp. 220–26.

73. Ray Lyman Wilbur, "The Last Illness of a Calm Man," *Saturday Evening Post*, 196, no. 15 (Oct. 13, 1923), p. 64.

74. W. Richard Whitaker, "The Night That Harding Died," *Journalism History*, 1, no. 1 (Spring 1974), pp. 16–19.

75. Harold Phelps Stokes, "A Correspondent's Diary of Harding's Alaskan Trip," installments 1 through 17, *New York Post*, July 30–Aug. 20, 1923, p. 1.

76. Tebbel and Watts, *Press and Presidency*, p. 403.

77. Hoover memoirs, vol. 2, pp. 54–55.

78. Lyons, *Unknown Ex-President*, p. 232; McGee, *Herbert Hoover*, p. 201.

79. Lyons, *Unknown Ex-President*, pp. 232–33; Richard Norton Smith, *An Uncommon Man: The Triumph of Herbert Hoover* (New York: Simon and Schuster, 1984), p. 100; Burner, *Herbert Hoover* (New York: Simon and Schuster, 1984), p. 100; Burner, *Herbert Hoover*, p. 163; Hoover memoirs, vol. 2, p. 142.

80. Newspapers quotes and accompanying information taken from "Television Makes Its Bow," *Literary Digest*, April 21, 1927.

81. Lyons, *Unknown Ex-President*, p. 201.

82. Martin Fausold, *The Presidency of Herbert C. Hoover* (Lawrence: University of Kansas Press, 1985), pp. 17–19; Smith, *Uncommon Man*, p. 43; McGee, *Herbert Hoover*, p. 192; Burner, *Herbert Hoover*, p. 112.

83. *Who's Who in America, 1930–1931* (Chicago: Marquis Who's Who, 1930), p. 158; also see Lloyd, *Aggressive Introvert*, p. 60; "Secretary Hoover Is Human Dynamo; Known Here as 'Great Nordic Monsoon,' " *Washington Post*, Dec. 2, 1928; 'Human Dynamo Is Akerson, Herbert Hoover's Secretary," *New York World*, Nov. 16,1928; "Akerson May Be Hoover Secretary," *Minneapolis Journal*, Jan. 13, 1929; "G. E. Akerson Funeral Today at Bronxville," *New York Herald Tribune*, Dec. 23, 1937.

84. Lloyd, *Aggressive Introvert*, p. 60.

85. Hoover memoirs, vol. 2, p. 185.

86. Hoover lists all of his Commerce Department personal secretaries in his memoirs, vol. 2, p. 43. Hoover's relationship with Akerson will be discussed in detail in chapter 5.

87. See Frederick Simpich, "The Great Mississippi Flood of 1927," *National Geographic*, 52, no. 3 (September 1927), pp. 243–89. For a complete discussion of Hoover's role in the Mississippi River flood relief, see Bruce A. Lohof, "Herbert Hoover, Spokesman of Humane Efficiency: The Mississippi Flood of 1927," *American Quarterly*, 22, no. 3 (Fall 1970), pp. 690–700; also see Hoover memoirs, vol. 2, pp. 123–31; Burner, *Herbert Hoover*, pp. 193–96; McGee, *Herbert Hoover*, pp. 204–5; Smith, *Uncommon Man*, p. 101; Lyons, *Unknown Ex- President*, pp. 233–34.

88. "Can the Mississippi Be Tamed?" *Literary Digest*, 93, no. 6 (May 7, 1927); "The Receding Flood's Bequest: A Rich Legacy of Anecdote," *Literary Digest*, 93, no. 8 (July 16, 1927), pp. 42–43.

89. "Consider Levee Blast to Save New Orleans; Would ruin Rich Region," *New York World*, April 27, 1927, p. 1; "New Orleans Safe, Hoover Declares," *Birmingham News*, May 10, 1927, p. 1.

90. Lohof, "Herbert Hoover," pp. 693–98; Hoover memoirs, vol. 2, p. 126; McGee, *Herbert Hoover*, p. 205.

91. "Hoover Pictures Flood Conditions over Air Tonight," *New York American*, April 30, 1927, p. 1; "Hoover to Radio Flood Conditions," *Springfield (Mass.)*

Republican, April 30, 1927, p. 1; "Relief Concert Planned on Air," *Louisville Courier Journal*, April 30, 1927, p. 1.

92. Herbert Hoover, "Secretary Hoover Tells Story of Efforts to Aid Those in Overflow Area," *Birmingham News*, May 9, 1927, p. 1.

93. For examples of Catledge's coverage, see "Hoover Will Spend Millions in South after Flooding Over," *Memphis Commercial-Appeal*, April 27, 1927, p. 1; "North Parish People Trembling in Boots," *Memphis Commercial-Appeal*, April 29, 1927, p. 1.

94. For an example of Joslin's writing, see Theodore Joslin, "Will Ask Congress to Solve Flood Problems," *Boston Transcript*, April 27, 1927.

95. "Nation Turns to Hoover in Time of National Disaster," *Memphis Commercial-Appeal*, May 9,1927, p. 1.

96. For examples of flood coverage, see Arthur Hachten, "Mississippi Now 60 Miles Wide as New Floods Swell Current," *San Francisco Examiner*, April 25, 1927, p. 1; "Nation Can End Menace of Flood, Hoover Declares," *New Orleans Times-Picayune*, April 28, 1927, p. 1; "Hoover Urges Relief Need," *Los Angeles Times*, April 25, 1927, p. 1; "New Orleans Alarmed as Water Rises," *Chicago Tribune*, April 29, 1927, p. 1; "Control of Situation New, Hoover Finds; Calamity of Worst Sort," *New York World*, April 28, 1927, p. 1; "Hoover Finds Relief under Way on Visit to Semi-submerged City," *Louisville Courier Journal*, April 27, 1927, p. 1; "Relief Workers Say Disaster Is Growing Hourly," *St. Louis Post-Dispatch*, April 27, 1927, p. 1; "Between Hoover and High Water," *Collier's*, July 16, 1927, pp. 9–10; Owen P. White, "—and the floods came," *Collier's*, July 9, 1927, p. 4; "Troops Ring Area Doomed by Blast," *Chicago News*, April 30, 1927, p. 1.

97. "Again Hoover Does an Emergency Job," *The New York Times* magazine, May 15, 1927, p. 6.

98. T. H. Alexander, "Herbert Hoover Wins Hearts of Folks in Flood District; 'He'd Make a Fine President,' Both White and Black Declare," *Atlanta Journal*, May 1, 1927, features section, p. 1.

99. Albon L. Holsey, "Hoover 'Discovers' South While Handling Flood Situation," *Pittsburgh Courier*, Jan. 21, 1928, p. 1.

100. Ruth Crawford, "How I Got That Way As Told to Ruth Crawford By Herbert Hoover," *San Francisco News*, March 15, 1927, special topics section, p. 1.

101. Anne Hard, "Herbert Hoover," *New York Herald Tribune* Sunday magazine, April 10, 1927, p. 8.

102. William Hard, "The New Hoover," *American Review of Reviews*, November 1927, pp. 22–28.

103. M. E. Hennessy radio script, May 5, 1927, Commerce Papers, Reprint File, 1927, HHPL.

104. Vernon Kellogg, "Herbert Hoover as I Know Him," *Outlook*, 147, no. 7 (Oct. 19, 1927), pp. 203–7.

105. For an example of the handling of the Consolidated Press story see William Hard, "Hoover is Still Capital's Busiest Man," *Cincinnati Times-Star*, July 12, 1927, p. 1.

106. L. C. Speer, "The Sort of Man Herbert Hoover Is," *The New York Times* magazine, Jan. 29, 1928, p. 3.

107. Will Irwin, *Herbert Hoover: A Reminiscent Biography* (New York: Century, 1928).

108. Will Irwin, "The Mystery of Herbert Hoover," page 1 in all three newspapers throughout the month of April 1928.

109. See, for instance, paid advertisement, "Meet Herbert Hoover the Man" in *The New York Times* book review section, April 8, 1928.

110. "Will Irwin Writes Friendly Life of Hoover," *The New York Times* book review, May 6, 1928.

111. Geoffrey Parsons, "Hoover: The Man behind the Myth," *New York Herald-Tribune* book review, April 8, 1928.

112. "The Life of Herbert Hoover," *New York Telegram* features section, Feb. 14, 1928, p. 1.

113. Norman Hapgood and Henry Moskowitz, *Up from the City Streets: Alfred E. Smith, a Biographical Study in Contemporary Politics* (New York: Harcourt, Brace, 1928). Excerpted parts of the book may also be found in "When Smith Rushed to Power in New York," *World's Work* magazine, December 1927, pp. 183–85.

114. For advance chapters on the book, see "The Great Fat Fight," *Saturday Evening Post*, May 12, 1928, p. 12.

115. Robert M. Field, "Herbert Hoover and His Career As Observed by Will Irwin, Who Knew Him 'When,' and Does Now," *New York Post* book review, May 19, 1928.

116. Frank R. Kent, "Hoover's Work in Cabinet Is Given Praise," *Baltimore Sun*, Dec. 10, 1927, p. 1.

3

The Campaign and Aftermath of the 1928 Election

Just weeks after Herbert Clark Hoover completed his flood relief stewardship, president Calvin Coolidge traveled to Rapid City, South Dakota, for a fishing vacation. As he prepared for his departure, a lengthy article appeared in *The New York Times*. Written by Senator William Cabell Bruce, a Democrat from Maryland, the article implied that if Coolidge campaigned for reelection and sought a third term, he would be violating the spirit of the Constitution. Actually, it would have been a second term. Coolidge had served only 19 months of the remainder of Harding's four years.[1]

It is unclear whether Bruce's article had any impact, but upon his arrival in Rapid City, Coolidge in his usual mysterious and taciturn manner told accompanying reporters to meet him at the high school at noon the next day, August 2. He offered no explanation for the meeting. At the appointed hour he handed each reporter a slip of paper containing this handwritten message: "I do not choose to run for president in nineteen twenty-eight." He refused further comment then, and never really elaborated on his decision, even after he left office.[2]

The announcement came on the fourth anniversary of Harding's death and 19 months before the end of Coolidge's elected term. Many in the Republican Party had considered the possibility of Coolidge stepping down, but he had not indicated any inclination to leave office and, Bruce's article in *The Times* notwithstanding, conventional wisdom placed him in the presidency for four more years.

Newspaper and magazine editors and reporters were caught by surprise, too, but immediately writers speculated on what Coolidge's decision would mean. "The political world has been counting so confidently on Mr. Coolidge's renomination that other candidates had been little thought of," the *Literary Digest* commented.[3] Added the *New York World*: "Washington next winter will be the scene of a political battle such as this country has not seen in recent years."[4] The *Wichita Eagle* also looked ahead to a tumultuous race, but discounted Hoover's chances. Editorial writers predicted that Hoover "may appeal to the Southern immigration, particularly because of his recent visits to the Mississippi flood sections [but] it means nothing politically."[5] Hoover confidant Mark Sullivan, writing for the *New York Herald Tribune*, predicted a Hoover-Smith race and told readers that if Al Smith were nominated, Southern states would turn to Hoover.[6]

Coolidge's unexpected missive stunned editors, reporters, and readers. Most political observers agreed that he meant what he said and that his political career was ending, though there was speculation that political pressure might force him to change his mind.[7] The stock market, which had been on a steady upturn for three years, dropped precipitously.[8]

On the day of the announcement, Hoover had been vacationing with a group called the Bohemian Club, camping out among the California redwoods. He remembered years later that within an hour of Coolidge's announcement more than a hundred newsmen and public officials descended upon his retreat, demanding that he announce his candidacy.[9] However, he remained uncommitted for six months, while one Republican candidate after another entered the race.

Vice President Charles Dawes, who in 1923 had chaired a German reparation-payments advisory committee, appeared to be Hoover's major competitor. The reparations committee drew up the Dawes Plan, which linked currency stabilization with reparations payments. Dawes was awarded the Nobel Prize for peace in 1925 for his contribution. Still, vice presidents were not highly regarded until thirty years later, and Dawes commanded little popular support. Other candidates included such recycled hopefuls as former Secretary of State Charles Evans Hughes, the 1916 standard bearer; World War I hero John J. Pershing; and 1920 hopeful Frank Lowden, former governor of Illinois. Long-shot possibilities were Senators George Norris, of Nebraska; James E. Watson, of Indiana; Charles Curtis, of Kansas; and Guy D. Goff, of West Virginia.[10]

All these potential nominees either had tried and failed in the past or were relatively unknown or unpopular. "Are there any more great men?" *Outlook* magazine asked in an October editorial. The magazine's editors concluded that there was one: Herbert Hoover.[11] Only Hoover, with just a minor foray into presidential politics in 1920, was new to voters, was well-known, and was highly regarded inside and outside Washington. Yet, few regulars within the Republican Party supported the Commerce Secretary. In his memoirs Hoover speculated that Harding's successful nomination, engineered by backroom politics, had encouraged Republican senators to choose another of their own in 1928.[12] More likely, Hoover's progressive, internationalist record and his close association with the Wilson Administration worried many party stalwarts, particularly the isolationists.

Though popular with the public and newsmen, Hoover realized that he would need overwhelming popular support to overcome the misgivings of party regulars. That was clear from the 1920 campaign. Only weeks after Coolidge's announcement, Hoover began assembling a staff of experts on newspapers and magazines and on public relations. He would continue to add to that staff as the primary and general election campaigns moved along. The staff stimulated positive articles in newspapers and magazines.

After Coolidge's decision to step down, Hoover was forced to deal with the usual political skulduggery engendered by both journalists and politicians. They revived the leftover red herrings from the 1920 campaign: Hoover had cheated the Chinese while he was an engineer there, and he was really a British citizen. The supportedly aggrieved Chinese came forward early in the campaign to say that they were quite fond of Hoover and he had never acted unethically toward them. When a London clerk revealed that Hoover was on the voting rolls in his district, U.S. Secretary of State Frank Kellogg ordered a full investigation and later affirmed Hoover's U.S. citizenship. Sometimes, anyone residing in Britain at that time had his name added to the voting rolls, citizen or not, and Hoover had lived in London just before and during the earlier part of World War I, it was explained. Hoover was listed as a voter in Britain, but it was a bureaucratic mistake.[13] Later in the campaign, the Democrats produced a doctored photograph that purported to show Hoover dancing with a black woman while he was in Mississippi directing flood relief. The photograph was circulated in the South, where racism divided society into two cultures,[14] but it was ignored and had little impact.

Hoover remained a noncandidate until February. "The time will come, and that shortly, when Secretary Hoover will throw aside the veil and reveal to an astounded Nation that he is willing to take the nomination. This will come after a solemn body of eminent citizens from all parts of the country have appeared with a plea that he permit them to present his name," wrote sarcastic *New York World* columnist Charles Michelson, a Hoover antagonist.[15]

Despite the *World's* earlier biased prediction of a wild scramble for the

Republican nomination, it was the *Outlook* that turned out to be correct. Republicans had run short of credible names. Eight years of Harding-Coolidge mediocrity showed that the nation's dominant party could not find regular organization candidates with powerful leadership qualities. Frank Kent, writing for *Plain Talk* magazine, noted:

If . . . Herbert Hoover becomes the Republican nominee for President, it will mark an interesting departure from the beaten political track. For one thing it will be the first time in twelve years the Republicans have nominated a first grade man for the Presidency. . . . With the exception or Hughes and Roosevelt, the Republican Party has not since anyone can recall nominated a really strong man.[16]

Hoover so overshadowed his opponents early in the race that Charles Cheney, Washington bureau chief for the *Minneapolis Journal*, wrote in December 1927: "Republicans who do not like Herbert C. Hoover are beginning to wonder how he can be stopped. . . . Unless some of the large delegations can be tied up to favorite sons, there is prospect now that Hoover will make a runaway race of it by next April."[17] A few weeks later, Albert Fox, of the *Washington Post*, added: "He is widening the gap every day and every hour."[18]

In February, with supporters in Ohio needing a commitment to place Hoover's name on the primary ballot, the Commerce Secretary advised Coolidge that he was opening a primary campaign. "I did not deliver prior to the convention a single speech or issue a single press statement having any political connotation. As far as I was concerned the party should make its decision on the basis of my public record," Hoover recalled 34 years later.[19]

In 1924, after a lengthy deadlock and 104 ballots, John Davis was named the compromise Democratic standard-bearer. The Davis nomination finally broke a deadlock between Al Smith, governor of New York, and William Gibbs McAdoo, the former Secretary of the Treasury. In September 1927 McAdoo announced that he would not be a candidate in 1928. The overwhelming favorite, Smith glided through the primaries to the June 30 nomination at the Democratic convention in Houston.[20] At Smith's urging, Franklin D. Roosevelt, the 1920 vice presidential nominee, sought the Democratic nomination for governor of New York in Smith's place.

Newspaper reporters competed energetically to obtain exclusive interviews with the enigmatic Hoover. One reporter caused momentary embarrassment for his newspaper and angered Hoover mightily just as the primary campaign was getting underway. In late February, Hoover traveled to Florida for a vacation at the home of friends. Even as he prepared for the primaries, Hoover still attended to his duties as Secretary of Commerce, and he wanted a brief rest before campaigning began. On February 19 the *Miami Herald* carried an interview story written by Earl Adams, a correspondent from the *Herald*'s Kay West bureau. The article quoted Hoover and Mark Sullivan liberally. A furious Hoover, who by then was in Savannah, Georgia, fired off a telegram to the *Herald* denouncing the story. The telegram read:

Purported interview with me published this morning is faked from beginning to end, both in direct or indirect quotation through Sullivan. Not a single paragraph represents the fact or opinion held. No discussion was held either directly or indirectly with either your or any other press representative. As a piece of sheer mendacity on part of your correspondent I have never seen the equal.[21]

Sheepish *Herald* editors published a front-page story in the *Herald* the next day admitting that Adams had made up the interview, an extraordinary step by the editors considering that newspapers in the 1920s rarely ever conceded in print that a story had erred. The correction story, 20 paragraphs long, quoted from Hoover's telegram and from one sent by Sullivan, who also denied talking with Adams. "The Herald has been represented at Key West for more than a year by Earl Adams . . . until last evening there has been no reason whatever to doubt, in the slightest way his veracity," the article stated. The editors explained how they had assigned Adams the story, how he had wired at first that Hoover declined all interviews, and how Adams later mailed a copy of the purported interview. Adams included a note with the copy telling editors that Hoover had asked that it not be published until after he had left town. Apparently, Adams naively thought Hoover would never see or hear of the interview. "Under the circumstances, of course, all the Miami Herald can do is to admit that it was imposed upon by its own employee, apologize to Secretary of Commerce Hoover, Mr. Sullivan and to readers of The Herald and to express its sincere regret for the occurrence," the editors wrote. The explanation and apology went on for several paragraphs more.[22] The incident became even more bizarre when the *Herald* editors later declared that Adams had indeed actually been given the interview and Adams was later rehired.[23]

Other than providing an amusing campaign anecdote that reporters probably chuckled about for years to come, the incident illustrates a few points. First, it showed how newspapers feared Hoover. The article first refers to Hoover as "Hon. Herbert Hoover" and begs his forgiveness. The humble apology appears even more deferential, considering that the newspaper rescinded its retraction later. Even if the interview were faked, the harm done was not that great. The interview did not credit Hoover or Sullivan with any damaging or outrageous statements. Certainly, the editors had reason to be embarrassed and Hoover to be miffed, if it were a made-up interview, but novice reporters can be overeager, especially when tempted by a scoop with the most sought-after person in the country. The editors should have double-checked, but Hoover wanted to be left alone and probably would not have responded to inquiries about the authenticity of the interview anyway. The furor was more a typical example of Hoover's ability to cow news media than it was a usual case of problematic news reporting.

Second, the tone of Hoover's cable leaves no doubt that he felt the newspaper had intentionally tried to embarrass him, a standard Hoover feeling of persecution when dealing with the press. A few moments of thought from someone who had handled reporters regularly for 14 years would have provided the conclusion that the interview had to be the result of an ill-considered decision by an eager reporter. Yet, despite the overwhelmingly favorable publicity Hoover received before he reached the White House, he always felt that, beyond his trusted circle, journalists and newspapers were treacherous.

Third, the circumstances of the interview reflect a strange Hoover fetish for privacy, though he was seeking the most public job in the nation. He was a declared candidate and an obvious front-runner for the Republican nomination, tantamount to a guarantee of the presidency. Yet, just days after he revealed his formal candidacy, he refused to speak to any reporters or issue any statements while in Key West. Certainly, such an approach to news flow contributed to consternation among reporters and the controversy over whether the interview was phony or not. A few well-chosen words released to reporters would have avoided the entire situation.

As Hoover formally entered the race, newspapers and magazines confidently predicted a Smith-Hoover race. "Governor Smith's nomination on an early ballot . . . is as certain as anything in politics, and while Secretary Hoover's case is not so obvious, he is, at present, running away easily with the Republican standard," wrote Charles Willis Thompson for *Commonweal* magazine.[24] "Never has the outlook been so clear and so stirring four months before the nominees were announced," wrote Silas Bent in *Century* magazine.[25] Humorist Will Rogers, writing for the Hearst newspapers, conceded that Hoover would cut into Smith's popularity in the South. But, Rogers asked, would Southerners vote for Hoover?[26] When primary opponents suggested that Hoover could not carry Kansas, the Hoover campaign committee trotted out famed Emporia, Kansas, editor William Allen White, who said:

We are for Curtis first, last and all the time and will proudly hail his nomination, but to say that Kansas under Curtis' leadership would not be for Hoover in November is deeply unjust to Curtis. If Hoover wins, our Republicans will compliment Curtis by piling up a majority for Hoover, if for no other reason, to prove the loyal quality of Curtis' leadership. But there are other reasons; Kansas naturally likes the Hoover kind of man.[27]

Smith and Hoover provided contrasting styles, opposite backgrounds, and diametrically opposed political and ideological philosophies. Smith, the first Roman Catholic nominee for president in the nation's history and a New York machine politician, privately flaunted the nation's Prohibition laws, keeping several bottles of liquor at his Albany mansion. It was clear that he felt uncomfortable addressing rural or small-town audiences. Hoover, despite his world travels and his international reputation, was billed as the small-town conservative Protestant candidate who supported Prohibition. In his excellent study of the 1928 election, historian Allan J. Lichtman wrote, "Herbert Hoover represented a public philosophy founded on an evocation of traditional values and a celebration of modern technology."[28] Smith, in contrast, was the "indigenous urban liberal, isolated from the mainstream of progressive politics in the United States."[29]

Though he remained off the campaign trail, Hoover won every primary except for Indiana, Ohio, and West Virginia, where Watson, Frank Willis, and Goff were favorite-son victors.[30] Entering the June convention in Kansas City, Hoover held a commanding delegate lead with 400 of the 1,089 total. Curiously, though, Hoover approached Coolidge in May and offered him the support of the 400 delegates, if Coolidge wanted to change his mind. The president merely responded, "If you have 400 delegates, you better keep them." Hoover remembered: "I could get no more out of him."[31]

The Kansas City convention included the usual hoopla, but without the contentiousness that had marked the 1920 convention. Hoover won the nomination on the first ballot. He chose Curtis as his vice presidential candidate and a few days later submitted his resignation as Commerce Secretary to Coolidge to concentrate full-time on the campaign.

As usual, reporters practically outnumbered delegates at the convention, but the coverage was fairly staid given the predictability of the outcome. The much-ado-about-nothing atmosphere prompted a memorable column by renowned author H. L. Mencken. Writing for the liberal *Nation* magazine, he commented in his usual acerbic manner:

At one stroke Lord Hoover was nominated, the outcast garbage-hauler grabbed his niche in history, and the Mellon legend blew up with a bang. . . . From end to end of it I can't recall seeing a chief actor who looked honest, even in the modest sense that a police sergeant looks honest, or hearing a sensible word. It was all unmitigated bilge, discharged in roaring streams from red, raw throats, and projected into the ether by the faithful radio.

. . . Clowns inside and out. Every tattered phrase in the lexicon of political balderdash was in their speeches. They roared, fumed, and sweated, but all it came to in the end was sound and fury, signifying nothing. . . . The choice of the preposterous Curtis as the virtuous Lord Hoover's running mate rubbed in the fraud and fustian of the whole proceedings.[32]

Ironically, except for the personal insults to Hoover and Curtis, Hoover, who despised showmanship himself, probably agreed with Mencken. Mencken remained a caustic adversary of Hoover's, and after the Wall Street crash he wrote about the 1928 campaign:

He was nominated and elected in 1928 mainly by professional blacklegs of the worst sort, and the methods they employed on his behalf, obviously with his full knowledge and apparently with his eager consent, made his campaign one of the most disgraceful in American history.[33]

THE 1928 GENERAL ELECTION

The nomination prompted another spate of positive Hoover biographies in books, newspapers, and magazines. Will Irwin's Hoover biography, for instance, was off the presses and drawing many of the curious.[34] For an older generation, uncomfortable with the flippant attitudes and loosened morals of the Roaring Twenties, a couple such as Herbert and Lou Hoover, pulling together for so many years and achieving the American dream, seemed to be a reassuring phenomenon in American politics. Hoover campaign staffers set out not only to remind Americans how well off they were but also to emphasize that Hoover was a small-town man with traditional values.

As both Lichtman and Craig Lloyd point out, Hoover's campaign organization was a menagerie of long-time associates, party leaders, advertising executives, and newspaper people who, despite their political inexperience, guided a highly organized public relations campaign under Hoover's well-schooled and close direction.[35] As head of Belgium Relief, the U.S. Food Administration, and the Commerce Department, Hoover had learned the value of public relations and public awareness. The 1928 campaign was no different from his other public experiences: well constructed, well staffed, and informational with little emphasis upon style. Hoover rarely spoke for the record, confining his election wisdom to a few prepared public speeches.[36] He hired public relations expert Bruce Barton to promote his campaign.[37] Not surprisingly, Republican prosperity was the key theme. On Aug. 11, in an epic speech at Stanford University Hoover told his audience: "We in America today are nearer to the final triumph over poverty than ever before."[38]

Alfred H. Kirchhofer, one of the correspondents who regularly visited the Commerce Department in the early 1920s, had risen to the post of editor of the *Buffalo Evening News* by 1928 and was a member of board of directors of the American Society of Newspaper Editors. Just after the convention, Hoover aide Roy A. Roberts, who was also a correspondent for the *Kansas City Star* and president of Washington's elite press club, the Gridiron Club, asked Kirchhofer to coordinate publicity for the campaign. Kirchhofer was to work behind the scenes quietly, while former Gov. Henry J. Allen, of Kansas, served as titular director of publicity. Kirchhofer declined the request, citing his responsibilities to the newspaper, but Hoover's staff contacted Kirchhofer's publisher, and Kirchhofer soon departed for New York with a leave of absence from the newspaper.[39]

Kirchhofer met with Hoover on July 3, just three weeks after the convention. Hoover explained that Edward Anthony would direct publicity for New York and would generate public relations material for the campaign. Hoover gave Kirchhofer little direction except that Kirchhofer was not to criticize Smith's wife, and there were to be no releases about Smith's Catholicism or about Prohibition without Hoover's prior approval.[40] There was no other guidance. Kirchhofer recalled: "I gathered at my interview with Mr. Hoover that a general plan for the campaign had been set. This turned out to be so, and it only remained to fit the pieces together as the days and weeks moved toward election."[41]

Throughout the primary and general election campaigns, Hoover's committee expended much energy appealing to special interest ad hoc groups and writing press releases about endorsements from such groups. Sensing that some non-Catholic urban ethnic groups were nervous about Smith, the committee churned out press releases heralding endorsements from such diverse groups as American Latvians, Swedes, Danes, and Jews.[42] Newly enfranchised women, voting in their third presidential election since the enactment of the Nineteenth Amendment, were not forgotten either. "The women want Mr. Hoover in the White House. He is the only candidate that women won't mind being bossed by," said Mrs. Anna M. Parks, of Binghamton, N.Y., as quoted in a press release.[43] The condescending phraseology certainly suggests that men must have written the press release.

Aviator Charles Lindbergh, who attained instant stardom in 1927 with his first transatlantic, nonstop air flight to Europe, endorsed Hoover, much to the dismay of the Democratic *Baltimore Sun*, which labeled his endorsement a naive mistake.[44] J. C. Penney, president of the famed department store chain and a lifelong Democrat, backed Hoover, saying that he preferred Hoover's position to Smith's on farm relief and prohibition.[45]

Besides many distinguished editors, publishers, and writers who openly supported Hoover, other working journalists quietly joined organizations working for his election. The name of Mrs. William B. Meloney, editor of the *New York Herald Tribune* Sunday magazine, was buried among a list of distinguished women working for Hoover's election, according to a press release from the Republican National Committee.[46] Later, Mrs. Meloney also worked behind the scenes during Hoover's presidency, informing him of what was happening in New York journalism that might affect him. Col. L. G. Ament resigned as general manager of the *New York Telegram*, a Scripps-Howard newspaper, to become a Hoover presidential aide, though the *Telegram* was Democratic. William H. Hill, publisher of the *Binghamtom [N.Y.] Sun*, served as chairman of Hoover's New York State campaign. A close Hoover insider, Hill was the focus of a *Syracuse Herald* article in 1932 in which the *Herald* alleged that Hill was the only man who could drop in on Hoover unannounced "and sit on the arm of the president's chair."[47]

Roy W. Howard, chairman of the board of Scripps-Howard newspapers, one of the nation's oldest and largest newspaper chains at the time, visited with Hoover over lunch in Washington in January of 1927.[48] A month later, Howard asked Hoover to spare time for an interview with Ned Cochran, the Scripps-Howard chief political editorial writer. In June 1928 the chain's foreign editor, William P. Simms, traveled through Europe to develop favorable foreign policy stories and editorials on Hoover's behalf. Howard asked Akerson to be sure to arrange a meeting with Hoover in Washington for Simms to background himself with Hoover. "And lastly, this has more of a time element in it than a request for a photograph," Howard concluded. The latter was a veiled warning not to brush off his correspondent.[49] Akerson responded positively within three days. "How is that for service?" he cabled Howard.[50] The newspaper magnate, a Democrat, issued a glowing endorsement of Hoover on October 4, 1928, the text of which was circulated to media around the country by the Hoover-Curtis campaign.[51] William Allen White, writers Arch Shaw and, of course, Mark Sullivan, and reporters will Irwin and William Hard also wrote articles for newspapers and magazines that supported Hoover.[52] The *New York Sun*, which had been close to Smith, endorsed Hoover.[53]

As with Harding and Coolidge, Hoover enjoyed the editorial support of a large majority of the nation's newspapers. In mid-October a straw poll of daily newspaper editors by *Editor & Publisher*, a newspaper trade magazine, revealed that 720 editors thought Hoover would win to 180 for Smith. Twenty-six were listed as "doubtful of the outcome," meaning that they did not know. Though not an exact survey of editorial endorsement, the magazine poll was a clear indication of Hoover support by editors, who usually linked their endorsements with the candidate they thought would win. Smith lost the favor of many Southern newspapers, which either refrained from any endorsement or switched to Hoover. Taking the editors' responses and using a complicated mathematical computation, *E & P* calculated how Hoover and Smith would do at the polls state by state. Based on the responding editor's opinions, *Editor &*

Publisher predicted Hoover would poll 16.3 million votes to Smith's 12.9 million and 387 electoral votes to 126.[54] Their predictions of an overwhelming Hoover victory proved accurate, though they underestimated drastically the total number of votes cast and gave Smith 39 more electoral votes than he actually polled.

The *Literary Digest* predicted that Hoover would win by a two-to-one margin.[55] The magazine had asked readers to respond with their preferences, and 2.7 million did answer.[56] The *Digest*'s unscientific poll proved to be highly accurate, leading editors to assume incorrectly that there was necessarily a correlation between reader response and the upcoming election results. This assumption would prove fallible in the 1936 Alfred E. Landon–Franklin D. Roosevelt election. Neither the *Editor & Publisher* straw poll nor the *Literary Digest* reader survey had any scientific value. Their accuracy in 1928 was simply an indication that the results were easily predicted.

The New York Times reported that the nation's foreign-language newspapers were divided in their support of the candidates:

A strong leaning toward Mr. Hoover in the Scandinavian groups and among the Finns; predominant pro-Smith sentiment among the Czechs, Slovaks, Slovenes and Croatians, and a sharp division of political opinion among the Italian, Polish, German, Jewish and several other foreign-born groups are shown by a countrywide survey of the foreign language press in the United States.[57]

Ironically, the newspaper that most ferociously opposed Hoover in 1928 was the *New York World*, the first newspaper ever to endorse him for president in January 1920. His eight years with Republican administrations had turned the *World* against Hoover. Herbert Baynard Swope, executive editor for the *World*, served as Smith's campaign publicity director,[58] and Washington bureau chief Charles Michelson churned out stories that sought to boost Smith and embarrass Hoover. Michelson in 1929 became the publicity director for the Democratic Party and a hated figure among Republicans. Hoover otherwise enjoyed overwhelming support from newspapers and even won endorsements from Hearst-owned papers. Correspondents in Washington in the 1920s usually complemented the political attitudes of editors back home, though increasingly Washington reporters were selected for their news gathering prowess, rather than their political leanings. Still, the bevy of friendly stories about Hoover and the overwhelming pro-Hoover sentiment in Washington stories suggests a strong favoritism for Hoover over Smith. Certainly, there is no evidence to suggest that most Washington reporters favored Smith, as is asserted by Hoover biographer David Burner.[59]

Hoover wrote his own speeches, relying on assistants only for research information.[60] During the campaign, Kirchhofer urged Hoover to speak publicly more often. Hoover answered: "I can make only so many speeches. I have just so much to say. I write a speech as I build a bridge, step by step, and that takes time."[61] Hoover himself monitored newspapers and magazines; if a particularly effective argument were published, he brought it to the attention of the publicity bureau and asked that it be reproduced and distributed.[62] Kirchhofer hired other reporters and writers to provide literature, the reporters obviously seeing no conflict in accepting pay from both a newspaper and a campaign publicity organization.[63]

Smith tried but failed to picture himself as the antithesis to Hoover. In fact, he sought to appeal to everyone and reached practically no one. He hoped to illustrate that he was the candidate of both the Democratic South and of the urban North, while he argued that his knowledge and respect for business gave him a kinship with small-town America and with corporate leaders. Smith selected John J. Raskob, a converted Republican and a wealthy industrialist, to manage his campaign and to underscore his interest in business.[64] Historian Arthur Schlesinger points out that this attempt at dividing Hoover's support and enhancing his own appeal succeeded only in alienating many on both sides.[65]

The Hoover-Smith campaign awakened passions in American voters and generated voter enthusiasm. The 1920 election had revolved around the League of Nations issue and resulted in the election of Harding, who has proved to be the weakest president of the twentieth century. The 1924 election had been a foregone conclusion, with the divided Democrats practically conceding to Coolidge before the campaign began. Not since Woodrow Wilson had come from behind to narrowly edge out Charles Evans Hughes in 1916 had the country been so galvanized by two credible candidates.

The campaign seemed to center around four issues: the personalities and contrasting backgrounds of the candidates, Smith's Catholicism, Prohibition, and the state of the nation's economy. Of the four, prosperity was the overwhelming influential issue, though Smith's Catholicism and the personal contrast between the two brought more discussion and debate in newspapers and magazines. Editors and reporters did not pay as much attention to Prohibition, because Smith was clearly wet and Hoover clearly dry. Either the opinion makers agreed or disagreed, and by 1928 the pros and cons of the Eighteenth Amendment had been debated for nearly ten years. Usually, even if the editorial board disagreed with the Prohibition stance of the candidate, they overlooked that position and supported the candidate with whom they agreed on other issues. In October 1928 the *Chicago Tribune*, headquartered in the hometown of the nation's most notorious bootleggers, observed: "We disagree emphatically with Mr. Hoover's present view of prohibition, but the problem presented by prohibition and its attempted enforcement is insoluble in this campaign."[66]

Smith's Catholicism, however, was another matter. Newspapers usually tried to argue that religion was not a factor in their editorial endorsements of the candidates, and probably this was true in many cases. But the 1920s were not far from the day when East Coast newspapers looked the other way as businesses refused to hire Irish Catholics like Smith. Protestant values were dominant still in the 1928 election. A backlash against modernism and changing national values contributed to a revitalization of the Ku Klux Klan in the 1920s in the South and even in states as far north as Indiana and Michigan. The Klan frequently organized torchlight parades during the 1928 campaign and marched down the streets of small communities, wearing white robes made from bedsheets and pointed hats designed from pillowcases. Klan members invoked the word of God against Smith and predicted that the Pope would sit in the White House, if Smith were elected. Few Southern newspapers denounced these tactics, though they did not implicitly endorse them.

At various times in the nation's history Quakers had experienced religious bigotry themselves. As a member of that gentle faith, Hoover genuinely detested intolerance. He resented those Protestants who attempted to trade on Smith's religion as an issue and denounced a Virginia Republican organization that circulated anti-Catholic statements.[67] He did not hesitate to complain when Catholics sought to use Smith's religion as an anti-Hoover device, however.[68]

Smith and his admirers contributed to the controversy by emphasizing his Roman Catholic support or verbally attacking those who made Catholicism an issue. In June the *Chicago Tribune* reprinted an article from an Italian Catholic newspaper in Florence in which Italians expressed support for Smith. The *Tribune* article brought a chorus of complaints about interference from Italy in an American election and was used as "evidence" of Smith's support from Rome. A month later, the newspaper, *Unita Cattolica*, attacked the *Tribune* and declared that it would publish no more articles about Smith. "Those who wrote us may rest assured that we have no intentions to interfere with such politics," the newspaper stated. *Tribune* writer David Darah assured readers that the *Tribune* had had no ulterior motives in reprinting the article and, in fact, *Unita Cattolica* had published five articles in June and July supporting Smith.[69]

On September 20 Smith told an Oklahoma City audience that "un-Democratic and un-American Secret Propaganda" was being used against him, referring to scurrilous undercurrents about his Catholicism. "It is dishonest campaigning. It is un-American," Smith told the mostly Protestant audience. "I here emphatically declare that I do not wish any member of my faith in any part of the United States to vote for me on any religious grounds." He asked that people not vote against him for religious reasons either.[70] Newspapers at this time usually published stories that reacted to campaign rhetoric rather than to set the agenda themselves. As long as candidates did not give credence to religious bigotry, the issue did not capture many headlines. When Smith chose to speak against religious bigotry in Oklahoma, newspapers picked up on the theme, which dominated discussion just weeks before the election. Smith was not wrong in facing up to the issue squarely, but the timing was probably not good and seemed to lend credence to religion as an issue.

Newspaper editorial reaction to Smith's speech was interesting, especially commentary from Southern newspapers. The *Nashville Banner* did not even acknowledge that Smith had addressed the Catholic issue in his epic speech but instead focused on that part of the speech addressing the evils of big business. "The press and the orators of a colossal, tremendously fortified special capitalistic class are silent in this campaign as to its menace and methods," the newspaper observed. "In high duty and constancy he [Smith] is making a great fight for Tennessee; and Tennessee, in justice and good faith should make a great fight for him." The Democratic border-state newspaper found that supporting such a populist message was much more appealing than arguing for religious tolerance. Hoover won Tenneesse in November.

The pro-Smith *Louisville Courier Journal* editorial staff applauded the attack against intolerance as "one of the most important of the campaign" because, the newspaper argued, it was far more important to protect the Constitutional separation of church and state than it was to win the election.[71] Smith's speech may have been "impolitic," but it was right and necessary, argued the *Richmond Times Dispatch*.[72] "How do you like it?" the *Norfolk Virginian Pilot* demanded of Smith's opponents in white robes. "How does it sit on your Democratic stomach, this business of kukluxing an exceptionally qualified Democratic leader out of the presidency because he did not take the precaution of being born a Protestant?"[73] The *Clarksburg (W. Va.) Telegram* dismissed the Smith speech as politicking:

There are some who think it was a mistake for Governor Smith to bring this up in his Oklahoma speech. Perhaps it was . . . but it was not a new move. . . . Voters should be wary of these phases of the whispering campaign and not let the questions of "intolerance" or "bigotry" upset their mental equilibrium.[74]

The *Hammond (La.) Vindicator* saw Smith's speech as a smokescreen and declared that Smith's four successful campaigns for governor of New York were accomplished thanks to the voters in the "alien city of New York." Smith rarely carried upstate New York counties, the newspaper argued, indicating that Catholics and Jews had put him in office. People opposed him not because of bigotry but because of the issues and he "had better prepare to take the worst drubbing ever given a presidential candidate," the newspaper concluded.[75]

Northern and western newspapers generally applauded the Smith speech, even if some did not support his candidacy. "Altho [*sic*] a few political preachers are doing the best they can to divide the American people politically along religious lines, there is little reason to believe they will get very far with it," concluded the Albuquerque *New Mexico State Tribune*.[76] Added the *Omaha World-Herald*: "Since Alfred E. Smith is a Catholic he is a Christian. A good many other Christians seem to lose sight of that. Why then, do other Christians abuse and revile him for his religion's sake? What must Jesus think of such Christians?"[77] The Republican *Portland Oregonian* editorialized: "The strictly political issues are weighty enough of themselves to decide the choice between Hoover and Smith, and they should so divide adherents of any creed as to leave no opening for party division on the line of religion."[78] The *Chicago Daily News*, a conservative Republican newspaper but one located in a very Catholic community, editorialized: "In his speech at Oklahoma City Gov. Smith's expressions were characteristically frank, vigorous and plain. His theme was simple and his handling of it was masterly."[79] Added the *Washington Post*: "Although his courage is universally commended, serious question is raised as to his political wisdom in engaging in controversies with individuals [religious bigots publicly denouncing Smith]."[80]

Smith not only attacked bigotry but named persons who had, he said, been bringing it into the campaign. This required the inevitable response from those attacked, allowing them more newspaper and magazine space than they normally would find and so somewhat defeating Smith's aim in making the speech. Newspapers, for instance, scrambled to interview Protestant Bishop James Cannon, Jr., one of those named in the speech. Bishop Cannon used the attention to assert that Smith drank heavily in the governor's mansion and that he, Cannon, was "attempting to preserve democracy in the South" by opposing Smith.[81]

Interestingly, one of the reporters who covered Smith's speech in Oklahoma City was Theodore Joslin, of the *Boston Transcript*, who later became Hoover's press secretary. Joslin told his readers that Smith bored the crowd with the speech which "at times was noble and at other times childish."[82]

The Catholic issue, then, dominated the pages of the nation's periodicals at a time when Smith desperately needed to establish more positive, issue-oriented coverage. It was a desperate gesture. The Catholic controversy was not the dominant issue of the campaign, as has been noted. A review of newspapers and magazines reveals that readers were urged to keep the Catholic issue out of the campaign. That, at least, was the public editorial posture. It appears, too, that the vehemence with which dailies attacked religious bigotry in the campaign depended upon whether the newspaper supported or opposed Smith. Newspaper support of Smith in the South split, perhaps more over his urbane, New York background than over his Catholicism, however. That Smith's religion was a controversial topic in the end tells us much more about the people who voted in 1928 than it does about the Republicans, Herbert Hoover, or the outcome of the election.

RADIO'S INFLUENCE

Smith campaigned vigorously, speaking to crowds wherever he went. Hoover confined his public utterances to a handful of prepared formal speeches in West Branch, Newark, Elizabethton, Boston, New York, and St. Louis. All speeches were carried live across the nation by radio over the National Broadcasting Company and the Columbia Broadcasting System networks. Eighty-four stations carried his Palo Alto speech on August 11, a formal acceptance of the convention nomination.[83] Hoover's final speech just before the election, also in Palo Alto, was delivered strictly over the radio with no live audience. It was the first time a presidential candidate delivered an address to the nation only over the radio.[84] The network stations varied in size from WEAF in New York to WNAX in Yankton, S.D. Four short-wave transmitting stations also picked up the signal and carried it to U.S. possessions such as Alaska, Hawaii, Guam, and the recently acquired Virgin Islands. The ceremonies began at 4 P.M. Savvy Hoover supporters had already learned something about the appeal of radio, and they had calculated when listeners were most likely to tune in. Four P.M. Pacific Time would catch evening audiences at 7 P.M. on the East Coast and 6 P.M. in the Central time zone. The radio broadcast of the speech was advertised to newspapers as the "largest hook-up in the history of broadcasting."[85]

Radio had come a long way since the first commercial broadcast in Pittsburgh of the 1920 Cox-Harding election results. Americans had chosen to include the new broadcast medium as part of their daily lives. Hearing Hoover's and Smith's voices on the radio made the election more exciting and more personal. Radio covered both nominating conventions live on 75 National Broadcasting Company stations and 50 Columbia Broadcasting System outlets. M. H. Aylesworth, president of NBC, announced on June 1 that the conventions would "have the right of way over all other programs during the hours the conventions meet." CBS announced that transmitters would be placed all around the convention floor so that listeners could pick up the sounds of the convention excitement.[86] Hoover stayed in Washington during the Republican convention, as was the practice for nominees in those days, and learned first of the convention's choice as he listened to live coverage on the radio.[87]

NBC commanded $11,500 an hour for 49-station advertising and CBS $4,000 an hour for 17 stations.[88]

Yet, neither Hoover nor Smith electrified radio audiences. Hoover was a shy person whose voice sounded timid and distracted over the radio. He read his addresses word-for-word from sheets of paper, and his monotone voice was flat and emotionless. Though his words were well chosen and his points intelligently argued, Hoover tended to put his audiences to sleep.[89] Hoover did not have a deep resonant voice suited for radio. He never learned to use radio adequately and to employ the dramatic voice inflections that capture the listener's attention.[90] Smith had a heavy New York City twang, which did not appeal to Southern and rural listeners particularly, and he had a hesitant speaking style over the air.

The Hoover committee did not ignore radio's impact, however. Not only did they arrange for speeches to be aired in what would later be known as "prime time," but they employed party faithful all over the country to present Hoover's stands on issues to local listeners. Each night these radio supporters, known as "Hoover minute men," took to the air to explore one particular issue of the campaign for five to ten minutes. Known as the Eastern Speakers Bureau, these supporters were supposedly counseling listeners with their own impressions of Hoover and his ideas on the issue of the day. John Calvin Brown was named director of the speakers bureau. The Republican National Committee described him as "a political debater of wide experience and the author of several books on International Economy." The minute men went on the air in stations in twenty-eight states and the District of Columbia, beginning on September 26 with a discussion of Prohibition and continuing nightly with other issues until the campaign ended.[91]

Interestingly, more than three-quarters of the stations were in small communities, which essentially meant that the Republicans were preaching to the faithful. The National Committee created what was called a Radio Division of the Republican National Headquarters and named Paul Gascoigne as director.[92] Hoover minute "men" were not always men. They included such Republicans as Hamilton Keen, GOP candidate for Senator of New Jersey; F. Trubee Davison, assistant secretary of war; Yale professor Charles M. Bakewell; and the school superintendent in Altoona, Pa.; as well as several women prominent in their communities.[93] Days before the election both candidates used famous stage actors and actresses in dramas that promoted their respective campaigns. Such actors and actresses as Helen Hayes, Roger Pryor, Helen MacKellar, and Ann Sutherland participated in the Smith drama. Hoover's cast included, among others, Frieda Hempel, Marie Sundelius, Charles Wagner, Francine Larrimore, Pauline Lord, Raymond Hitchcock, Walter Huston, and Marion Green.[94] On election night 100 stations nationwide broadcast the returns, compared with 16 in 1924 and one in 1920.[95] In February 1929, *Sunset* magazine carried excerpts from all of Hoover's campaign radio broadcasts, beginning an era of print relying on broadcast for its news.[96]

All this demonstrated the strong attention that radio had garnered in eight short years of commercial broadcasting and what a factor it would be in presidential politics for the next two decades. Summarizing from a *New York Times* article, the *Literary Digest* noted that radio had changed presidential politics. Radio will debunk politics, Robert J. Duffus of *The Times* said. "Campaign speakers can no longer pretend to be misquoted in the newspapers for the radio instantly exposes that sort of duplicity," the *Digest* added. The *Digest* credited radio for perking up interest among women and increasing voter registration.[97] "When one sets out to measure the effect of radio broadcasting on the election, he is trying to measure something for which no measuring stick has yet been invented," observed the *Buffalo Courier-Express*.[98] The *Richmond Times Dispatch* philosophized:

When Andrew Jackson was the Democratic candidate a hundred years ago, he was forced to wait for weeks before he knew whether he or his opponent would be the next President of the United States. The situation to-day is quite different. When Hoover and Smith spoke in the 1928 campaign, audiences ran literally into the millions.[99]

The *Omaha World-Herald* concluded:

The radio has made our national politics national in fact, rather than provincial or sectional. Why under these circumstances must we any longer undergo the quadrennial agony of four and five months' campaigns? A month with radio is equal to six months of the old-fashioned campaigning.[100]

Grudging post-election acknowledgment of radio's role in the campaign came from *Editor & Publisher*. A newspaper trade magazine, *Editor & Publisher* somewhat mirrored the collective wisdom and hopes of the nation's publishers and editors. *Editor & Publisher* philosophized:

Nothing could be more puerile than to question the power of radio in the recent campaign—it was indeed an election conducted in major part upon the air.

Far be it from EDITOR & PUBLISHER to attempt to build a dam of pebbles and sand to hold back the sweeping radio tide.

In a much less enlightened vein, the editorial then called upon wire services to stop allowing radio to read from copy on the air, because such practices hurt the immediacy of newspapers, which had spent millions over the years building up the wire services.[101]

Presidential election night in a pre-computer newspaper newsroom was an experience not to be missed. Voters in a presidential year choose

a chief executive and a large number of local, state, and national representatives. When typewriters and copyboys were the vehicles for transmitting news, editors paced and reporters drummed their fingers
impatiently waiting for the polls to close and the votes to be counted.
Then, a hellish onslaught of vote tally results burned the newspaper telephone lines, fueling a cacophony of clacking typewriters and general
mass confusion. In the election of 1928 Americans cast over 36 million
votes, more than in any previous U.S. election. As there were no exit
polls or computer analyses, headlines had to wait until the votes were
counted. Still, the count was not close, and morning newspaper editors
had plenty of time to fashion headlines announcing Hoover's victory.

Hoover collected 21.4 million votes, or 58 percent, to Smith's 15 million, or 40.7 percent, with a few votes scattered among minor party
candidates. Hoover won nearly every state, including Florida, Tennessee, Texas, Virginia, and Kentucky, breaking the Democrats' post-
Reconstruction grip in the South, while Smith collected only 87 electoral
votes nationwide.[102] Newspapers across the country hailed the Hoover
victory with banner headlines.[103]

Republican newspapers were exultant. The *Washington News* said
Hoover owed no one anything. He had run a campaign free of political
entanglements and promises so now he could be "president of all the
people."[104] Democratic newspapers were philosophical. Wrote the *New
York World* editorial writers:

Where so many millions have contributed to the result, with the returns decisive
as to the outcome, it is impossible to-day to attempt any estimate of the relative
weight of all the elements which gave Mr. Hoover his victory. . . . [There was] a
common factor in all of them: a deep-seated aversion to change.[105]

Comment came from all manner of political analysts, including Mark Sullivan, who told *New York Herald Tribune* readers that Hoover's personal
qualities won the election. The euphoria was dampened somewhat by
the independent *New York Post*, which cautioned readers that Hoover
had actually polled one million votes less than Calvin Coolidge. Despite
smashing the Solid South, Hoover had only carried New York by 104,000
votes, the newspaper noted.[106] Still, even opposing editors found little to
criticize about the election process or about Hoover's campaign.[107]

After the lackluster 1920 and 1924 campaigns, the 1928 presidential
election generated an electric excitement not seen by Americans in years.
"The interest taken in this year's Presidential election has rarely been
equalled. Its [bipartisan] range and intensity are explained by the fact
that the United States is not a politically minded country," observed *The
New York Times* early in the campaign.[108] Just before the election, *The
Times* praised newspapers for their campaign coverage, especially the

Associated Press. Newspapers had allowed both Smith and Hoover to air their views on the news pages regardless of the particular daily's political allegiance, *The Times* concluded. Such fair treatment could not have been expected from partisan newspapers in the past, *The Times* added, remarking that journalism was entering a new era.[109]

In the end, it was not campaign organization, newspaper endorsements, Smith's Catholicism, prohibition, or the urban-rural division that elected Hoover. He won because his past successes made him popular and because the Republican Party, of which he was the standard-bearer, was given credit for full employment and prosperity at the time. "This balderdash about prosperity is the sum and substance of Mr. Hoover's official campaign," sniffed the *New York World* on the eve of the election.[110] Middle-class Americans had benefitted greatly from prosperity in the 1920s and business was never better. If the nation's economic system were about to collapse, few seemed to recognize that possibility. The Republicans had dominated the White House and Congress for 32 years, since William McKinley's resounding election over William Jennings Bryan in 1896.

Catholic or not, urbane or not, wet or not, Smith faced an overwhelming burden. That Hoover ran a nearly flawless campaign despite his relative inexperience in election politics and that he was one of the most qualified presidential candidates the party had fielded since its inception in 1856, only left Smith less room to maneuver and explains the landslide electoral college victory. Except for farmers and the poor, Americans in 1928 were generally well satisfied with their lot and with Republican tutelage. Hoover's decision in 1920 to declare himself a Republican paid large dividends in the campaign of 1928.

But the emphasis upon economic well being and upon Hoover's image as a small-town purveyor of the American dream would once again build a weak foundation for the future. Prosperity and a positive image elected Hoover, just as the Great Depression and negative imagery would defeat him. The Hoover celebration drowned out some other minor headlines. Franklin D. Roosevelt had barely won the governor's mansion in New York, by 25,000 votes, announced the New York newspapers. A small headline in *The New York Times* read: "Vote Booms Stocks; Public Buys Heavily in Jubilant Market."[111] As time progressed, those headlines turned out to be more important than the ones announcing Hoover's victory.

NOTES

1. Sen. William Cabell Bruce, "The Case against a Third Term Stated," *The New York Times*, July 31, 1927, special features section, p. 1.

2. Herbert Hoover, *The Memoirs of Herbert Hoover: The Cabinet and the Presidency 1920–1933* (New York: Macmillan, 1952), p. 190 [referred to hereafter

as Hoover memoirs, vol. 2]; David Burner, *Herbert Hoover: A Public Life* (New York: Knopf, 1979), p. 190; Dorothy McGee, *Herbert Hoover: Engineer, Humanitarian, Statesman* (New York: Dodd, Mead, 1959), p. 212; Gene Smith, *The Shattered Dream: Herbert Hoover and the Great Depression* (New York: William Morrow, 1970), p. 50; and John Tebbel and Sarah Miles Watts, *The Press and the Presidency: From George Washington to Ronald Reagan* (New York: Oxford, 1985), p. 413.

3. "The Republican 'Free-For-All,' " *Literary Digest*, 46, no. 11 (Sept. 10, 1927), p. 6.

4. Quoted in ibid.

5. Ibid., p. 7.

6. Ibid.

7. For a summary of press reaction, see "The Coolidge Renunciation," *Literary Digest*, 94, no. 7 (Aug. 13, 1927), pp. 4–5.

8. Ibid.

9. Hoover memoirs, vol. 2, p. 190.

10. For a discussion of the candidates, see Martin L. Fausold, *The Presidency of Herbert C. Hoover* (Lawrence: University of Kansas Press, 1985), pp. 21, 24; Burner, *Herbert Hoover*, pp. 198–99; and Hoover memoirs, vol. 2, pp. 190–91.

11. "Hoover and the Politicians," *Outlook*, Oct. 19, 1927, p. 291.

12. Hoover memoirs, vol. 2, pp. 192–93.

13. Hoover memoirs, vol. 2, pp. 205–6. See also Mark Sullivan, "Hoover Status As Resident Cleared," *New York Herald Tribune*, Dec. 25, 1927, p. 1; Sullivan, "Hoovers Are Old American Family," *Hartford (Conn.) Courant*, Dec. 25, 1927, p. 1; Sullivan, "Hoover's Residence in Europe," *Des Moines Register*, Dec. 25, 1927, p. 1.

14. Richard Norton Smith, *An Uncommon Man: The Triumph of Herbert Hoover* (New York: Simon and Schuster, 1984), p. 104.

15. Charles Michelson, "The Political Undertow," Dec. 24, 1927.

16. Frank R. Kent, "Can Hoover Be Ditched Again?" *Plain Talk*, March 1928, p. 313.

17. Charles B. Cheney, "Hoover's Political Enemies Fear Runaway Race, Seek Means to Hold Him Back," *Minneapolis Journal*, Dec. 13, 1927, p. 1.

18. Albert W. Fox, "Hoover Is Seen Far Out in Front for Nomination," *Washington Post*, Jan. 16, 1928, p. 1.

19. Ibid., p. 191.

20. Arthur Schlesinger, Jr., *The Age of Roosevelt: The Crisis of the Old Order, 1919–1933* (Boston: Houghton Mifflin, 1957), p. 125.

21. HH telegram to *Miami Herald*, Feb. 19, 1928, Campaign and Transition, Newspapers and Magazines, *Miami Herald* File, Box 442, HHPL.

22. "Hoover Repudiates Herald Interview," *Miami Herald*, Feb. 28, 1928, p. 1.

23. See " 'Tightening' of Press Relations Irks Washington Correspondents," *Editor & Publisher*, 52, no. 8 (July 6, 1929), p. 50.

24. Charles Willis Thompson, "Smith and Hoover," *Commonweal*, Feb. 8, 1928, pp. 1030–31.

25. Silas Bent, *Century* magazine, as quoted in "Smith against Hoover," *Montgomery (Ala.) Advertiser* editorial, Feb. 27, 1928. *Literary Digest* also predicted

early victories for Smith and Hoover. See "A Smith-Hoover Contest Looming," *Literary Digest*, May 5, 1928, p. 12.

26. Will Rogers, "Hoover Has Moral Backing in South! How about Vote?" *San Francisco Examiner*, March 11, 1928.

27. Hoover for President Committee press release, April 28, 1928, Campaign and Transition, Box 183, HHPL.

28. Allan J. Lichtman, *Prejudice and the Old Politics: The Presidential Election of 1928* (Chapel Hill: University of North Carolina Press, 1979), p. 7.

29. Ibid., p. 12.

30. Burner, *Herbert Hoover*, p. 198.

31. Hoover memoirs, vol. 2, p. 193.

32. H. L. Mencken, "Clown Show," *Nation*, 126, no. 3286 (June 27, 1928), p. 713.

33. H. L. Mencken, *American Mercury*, undated article, 1928 clippings file, HHPL.

34. See, for instance, Sarah Comstock, "A Woman of the West Knocks at the White House Door," *New York Post*, June 16,1928; picture layout entitled "Mrs. Herbert C. Hoover—A Study of the Perfect Hostess," *New York Journal*, June 15, 1928. For Herbert Hoover biographies see "How Will Irwin Got Revenge on Hoover," *Des Moines Register*, June 9, 1928; "The Education of Herbert Hoover," *Collier's*, June 9, 1928, pp. 8–9; "The Human Side of Herbert Hoover," *New York World*, June 18, 1928 (also reprinted in *A.R.A. Association Review*, June 1928, p. 1); Marie Mattingly Meloney, "Hoover in Victory," *New York Herald Tribune* Sunday magazine, June 24, 1928, pp. 1–3.

35. Ibid., pp. 8–9; and Craig Lloyd, *Aggressive Introvert* (Columbus: Ohio State University Press, 1972), pp. 153–55.

36. Burner, *Herbert Hoover*, p. 201; and Hoover memoirs, vol. 2, p. 198–99.

37. Lloyd, *Aggressive Introvert*, p. 154.

38. Burner, *Herbert Hoover*, p. 201.

39. Alfred H. Kirchhofer oral history interview with Raymond Henlie, archivist, HHPL, in Buffalo, N.Y., April 4, 1969, pp. 6–7.

40. Ibid., p. 8.

41. Ibid.

42. See Hoover for President press releases of April 17, Aug. 28, Sept. 20, Sept. 29, Oct. 4, 1928, Campaign and Transition, Boxes 183–187, HHPL.

43. "Women Won't Mind Being Bossed by Hoover," Hoover for President Press Release, New York State Committee, March 22, 1928, Campaign and Transition, Box 184, HHPL.

44. "Lindbergh's Decision," *Baltimore Sun* editorial, Oct. 4, 1928.

45. "Chain Store Head, Democrat, for Hoover on Farm Record," Hoover-Curtis Campaign Committee press release, Aug. 31, 1928, Campaign and Transition, Box 184, HHPL.

46. Republican National Committee press release, August 13, 1928, Campaign and Transition, Box 204, HHPL.

47. Robert W. Lillard, "Billy Hill of Binghamton, Pal of Herbert Hoover," *Syracuse Herald* Sunday magazine, April 10, 1932, p. 3.

48. GA to RH telegram, Dec. 30, 1927, Campaign and Transition, Scripps-Howard File, Box 441, HHPL.

49. RH to GA telegram, Jan. 30, 1928; RH to GA letter marked "personal," June 20, 1928, both in ibid.

50. GA to RH telegram, June 23, 1928. See also G. B. Parker acknowledging cable of same date, GA to RH letter, same date, and RH to GA letter of July 2, 1928, all in ibid.

51. Republican National Committee press release, "No 'Bull' about Hoover, Declares Roy W. Howard," Campaign and Transition, Box 188. See also "Scripps-Howard Editors Vote Unanimously to Support Herbert Hoover for President," *Washington News*, undated, 1928 clippings file, HHPL.

52. Lloyd, *Aggressive Introvert*, p. 153.

53. "Hoover for President," *New York Sun* editorial, Aug. 27, 1928.

54. "Editors Pick Hoover to Win with 387 Electoral Votes to Smith's 126," *Editor & Publisher*, 61, no. 21 (Oct. 13, 1928), pp. 3–4.

55. See *Literary Digest* editions of October 13 and 27 and Nov. 24, 1928. Also see Republican National Committee press release of Oct. 26, 1928, Campaign and Transition, Box 190, HHPL.

56. The *Digest* drew much attention and praise from newspapers for its "accurate" poll. See especially "Digest Poll Close to Election Results," *The New York Times*, Nov. 8, 1928, p. 1.

57. "Foreign-Tongue Press Divides on Candidates," *The New York Times*, Nov. 4, 1928, p. 1.

58. Ronald Steel, *Walter Lippmann and the American Century* (Boston: Little, Brown, 1980), p. 245.

59. Burner, *Herbert Hoover*, p. 254.

60. Ibid., p. 9.

61. Ibid.

62. Ibid., p. 17.

63. Ibid.

64. "Raskob to Leave General Motors," *New York American*, July 24, 1928, p. 1; Schlesinger, *Age of Roosevelt*, p. 126.

65. Schlesinger, *Age of Roosevelt*, p. 128.

66. "The Issue in This Campaign," *Chicago Tribune* editorial, Oct. 4, 1928.

67. Hoover memoirs, vol. 2, pp. 207–8.

68. Burner, *Herbert Hoover*, pp. 205–6.

69. David Darrah, "Catholic Paper to Print No More Articles on Al," *Chicago Tribune*, Aug. 4, 1928, p. 1.

70. For exact quotes see "Smith in Kluxdom," Salem, Oregon, *Capitol Journal*, Sept. 21, 1928.

71. "American Speaks," *Louisville Courier-Journal* editorial, Sept. 22, 1928.

72. "Smith in Ku-Kluxia," *Richmond Times Dispatch* editorial, Sept. 22, 1928.

73. "The Mask Is Off," *Virginia-Pilot* editorial, Sept. 23, 1928.

74. "The Religious Phase," *Clarksburg (W. Va.) Telegram* editorial, Sept. 25, 1928.

75. "There's Quite a Difference," *Hammond (La.) Vindicator* editorial, Sept. 28, 1928.

76. "Religion and Politics," *New Mexico State Tribune* editorial, Sept. 21, 1928.

77. "Patriot and Christian," *Omaha World* editorial, Sept. 22, 1928.

78. "Religion No Political Issue," *Portland Oregonian* editorial, Oct. 1, 1928.

79. "Gov. Smith Denounces Intolerance," *Chicago Daily News* editorial, Sept. 22, 1928.

80. "Judging the Candidates," *Washington Post* editorial, Sept. 28, 1928.

81. "Bishop Cannon Again Attacks Governor Smith," *Richmond Times Dispatch*, Sept. 22, 1928, p. 1.

82. Theodore Joslin, "Signal Failure for Smith at Oklahoma City," *Boston Transcript*, Sept. 21, 1928, p. 1.

83. For a text of the acceptance speech see "Address Accepting the Nomination," *Public Papers of the Presidents of the United States, Herbert Hoover 1929* (Washington: U.S. Government Printing Office, 1974), Supplement 1, pp. 499–520.

84. For complete texts of all of Hoover's campaign speeches see "Addresses during the Campaign," in ibid., Supplement 2, pp. 521–611.

85. Republican National Committee press release, Aug. 4, 1928, pp. 1–4, Campaign and Transition, Box 185, HHPL.

86. "Radio Will Give Fullest Details of Conventions," *Christian Science Monitor*, June 2, 1928, p. 4.

87. "Hoovers Hear Nomination News by Radio in Washington," *Christian Science Monitor*, June 15, 1928.

88. *Literary Digest*, Dec. 1, 1928, p. 13.

89. For examples of Hoover speeches, see the audiovisual collection, radio speeches for 1928, in HHPL.

90. For a complete discussion of both Hoover's and Coolidge's speaking styles, see James. D. Barber, "Classifying and Predicting Presidential Styles: Two 'Weak' Presidents," *Journal of Social Issues*, 24, no. 3 (1968), pp. 51–80.

91. Republican National Committee Speakers Bureau press release, Sept. 19, 1928, pp. 1–2, Campaign and Transition, Box 166, HHPL.

92. Ibid.

93. Republican National Committee press release of Oct. 26, 1928, listing radio speakers for the evenings of Oct. 27–29, 1928, Campaign and Transition, Box 190, HHPL.

94. "Stage Stars Take Part in Smith and Hoover Dramatic Broadcasts," *New York Herald Tribune*, Nov. 4, 1928, section 4, p. 22.

95. "100 Stations Radio Election Returns," *The New York Times*, Nov. 7, 1928, p. 1.

96. "Hoover Broadcasts on the Home," *Sunset Magazine*, 62, no. 2 (February 1929), p. 23.

97. "Radio 'Debunking' the Campaigns," *Literary Digest*, Dec. 1, 1928, p. 13.

98. As quoted in ibid.

99. Ibid.

100. Ibid.

101. "Radio and Elections," *Editor & Publisher* editorial, 61, no. 25 (Nov. 10, 1928).

102. Schlesinger, *Age of Roosevelt*, p. 129.

103. See, for instance, "GOP Sweeps Nation by Record Majority; Solid South Smashed," *New York Journal*, Nov. 7, 1928, p. 1; "Hoover Wins by Landslide," *San Francisco Chronicle*, Nov. 7, 1928, p. 1; "Landslide Elects Hoover," *San*

Francisco Examiner, Nov. 7, 1928, p. 1; "Hoover and Curtis Win in Landslide," *Christian Science Monitor*, Nov. 7, 1928, p. 1; "Hoover Sweep Sets Record," *New York Telegram*, Nov. 7, 1928, p. 1; "Hoover Sweeps in with 432 Votes," *New York Post*, Nov. 7, 1928, p. 1; "Hoover Wins, Sweeps the Nation: Smith Loses State; South Broken; Roosevelt Leads for Governor," *The New York Times*, Nov. 7, 1928, p. 1.

104. "He Can Be Himself," *Washington News* editorial, Nov. 8, 1928.

105. "A Conservative Landslide," *New York World* editorial, Nov. 8, 1928.

106. "How Hoover and Smith Ran," *New York Post* editorial, Dec. 22, 1928.

107. For a roundup of newspaper editorial opinion, see "Clean Triumph by Republicans Hailed in Press" and "Southern Press Dissects Break in Sectionalism," *New York Herald Tribune*, Nov. 8, 1928; and "Views of Newspapers of All Sections on the National Result," *The New York Times*, Nov. 8, 1928.

108. "The Candidates," *The New York Times* election summary, Sept. 28, 1928, special features section, p. 1.

109. "The Press and the Election," *The New York Times* editorial, Nov. 4, 1928.

110. "In Conclusion," *New York World* editorial, Nov. 5, 1928.

111. "Vote Booms Stocks; Public Buys Heavily in Jubilant Market," *The New York Times*, Nov. 8, 1928, p. 3. See also"Stocks Bound on Buying Rush," *New York Telegram*, Nov. 7, 1928, p. 1.

4

Lost Opportunities

No person ever entered the presidency with more justification for the usual early optimism than Herbert Hoover. He had made few commitments, had accumulated an unblemished public record, and had risen from Belgian relief administrator to president in just 14 years. He could look forward to Republican majorities in the House (100) and Senate (17). Americans were contented and as optimistic about the future as probably they had been at any time in the nation's history. Hoover finally had the power and authority to change Americans' lives for the better, and he fully intended to attack the job with all the enthusiasm and know-how he had at his vast disposal.

But first he had to confront prying reporters. Three days after the election, Elihu Root, a former New York senator and the Secretary of State under Theodore Roosevelt, wrote to Hoover to congratulate him and to advise him to stay away from Washington until after the inauguration. Hoover wrote to Root:

I agree with you that I should keep entirely out of Washington and also that I should keep in the background as much as possible. It was partially with this in mind that I have undertaken the South American journey, and I am proposing to stay in Florida or somewhere away from Washington until March 4th.[1]

He also asked Root for suggestions on Cabinet appointments.[2] Illustrating his distaste for official Washington and for politics and demonstrating his reluctance to intrude on Coolidge's last four months in office, Hoover undertook a "Good Neighbor" tour of South America just two weeks after the election. Intrusive U.S. foreign policies practiced during the previous three decades had severely strained United States–Latin American relations. Hoover, who regarded foreign affairs as one of his strongest areas of expertise, sought to ease relations. On November 19 the Hoovers bid farewell to friends in Palo Alto and boarded the battleship *Maryland* in San Francisco. Later during the six-week tour, the party switched to the *Utah*.

The president-elect did assuage much of the discord with South American governments,[3] and generally newspapers and magazines applauded his gesture. He returned from South America to Washington on January 6, 1929, for three weeks of discussions with Republicans, Democrats, and private businessmen about Cabinet appointments and legislative strategies. On January 29, 1929, he met with Smith for 25 minutes to rehash the campaign. The two exchanged pleasantries during a lighthearted get-together.[4] Then Hoover left for Key Biscayne to vacation at the Florida home of J. C. Penney, where he stayed until just before the inauguration.[5]

Never a great admirer of the Coolidge administration, Hoover kept only two Coolidge Cabinet appointees, Andrew Mellon, Treasury, and James J. Davis, Labor. Henry L. Stimson, the governor of the Philippines, was named Secretary of State; James W. Good, War; William D. Mitchell, attorney general; Walter F. Brown, Postmaster-General; Charles F. Adams, a descendent of presidents John Quincy Adams and John Adams, Navy; Ray Lyman Wilbur, president of Stanford, Interior; Arthur Hyde, Agriculture; and Robert P. Lamont, an engineer like Hoover, Commerce.[6]

George Akerson, Lawrence Richey, and French Strother left the campaign staff to become members of Hoover's personal staff.[7] Akerson assumed the post of press secretary, and newspapers fussed more over his appointment than any of the others. Some writers observed that Akerson even looked like Hoover. The *Boston Globe* carried a picture of Mrs. Akerson and their three sons.[8] Though his Cabinet was a coterie of experts with minimal party influence, Hoover's personal staff and confidants consisted of long-time friends and associates. They were not formally part of the staff, but Mark Sullivan, William Hard, and Will Irwin continued to correspond frequently with Hoover and to visit the White House.

Edgar Rickard returned to private business in New York, leaving the relief administration, but continued to look after the president's personal finances. An engineer and long-time Hoover associate, Rickard had been one of the first to join Hoover in Europe during the Belgian Relief days.

He had served briefly as Acting Food Administrator after the war, when Hoover left for Europe to once again direct aid to the starving. In New York in the 1930s and 1940s, Rickard served as either director or officer of the Pejepscott Paper Company, the Hazeltine Electronics Corporation, and the Pitney-Bowes Company.[9] He kept up a steady correspondence with Hoover, but did not join the Administration. Lewis Strauss, a Wall Street financier and a former secretary to Hoover during the Belgian Relief Days, provided informal advice to Hoover on the nation's finances. Strauss was in 1959 an unsuccessful Cabinet nominee under Dwight D. Eisenhower.

Both Rickard and Strauss thought Hoover should not have appointed Akerson as press secretary. "He [Strauss] feels, and I agree, that George is likely to misrepresent the Chief in regard to individuals George dislikes or has reason to dislike," Rickard noted on January 3, 1929, in his diary.[10] It is unclear whether Rickard or Strauss ever voiced those feelings to Hoover. Rickard noted later in his diary: "Agree with Strauss, but hesitate to mention to Chief, as George has done a fine job and the Chief has implicit confidence in him."[11]

In the same entry, Rickard wrote of Strauss: "Lewis Strauss is going to be a big factor in New York finance. Wish he was not a Jew."[12] Hoover personally was a tolerant man. The Hoovers had refused to sign a restrictive covenant attached to their S Street residence in Washington that forbade Jews or blacks from purchasing the property, a typical covenant for that time period.[13] People like Rickard who advised Hoover were not as tolerant. In fairness to Rickard, though, his attitude was perhaps more reflective of most influential businessmen and leaders of the time than Hoover's.

Good died a few months after taking office, and Patrick Hurley replaced him as Secretary of War. Walter Trohan, long-time Washington bureau reporter for the *Chicago Tribune* after the Hoover presidency and a close Hoover associate from 1933 to 1964, recalled that Hurley spoke contemptuously of Hoover behind Hoover's back. "He said he had a face as flat as the bottom of a beer glass. He didn't like Mr. Hoover at all," Trohan said. The Cabinet and the men around Hoover were a mixture of efficient administrators, hacks, close Hoover friends, and mediocre politicians sometimes with divided loyalties to each other and to the president. As was usual in the 1920s, they were all men, all white, and almost all from upper-income backgrounds. But in the final analysis, Hoover's presidency rested largely upon Hoover, the Great Engineer, who unlike Coolidge and Harding liked to attend to most all details himself anyway.

The letter to Root in November contained another Hoover observation that would prove to be an ominous foreshadowing of his press relations. He wrote:

As usual, it is very difficult to deal with the press in these matters [trip to South America]. The youngsters who are detailed to inform the American public seem to think they have a divine mandate to invent something sensational every day and one is constantly torn between trying to furnish them with something that is true and trying to evade them and allow them to invent on their own responsibility.[14]

Hoover, who had benefitted from more positive press than any American since Theodore Roosevelt, still saw reporters only as nuisances. His handling of press matters in South America only underscored his disdain.

Just days after his return, a scathing article appeared in the January 12, 1929, edition of *Editor & Publisher*. George H. Manning, the magazine's Washington correspondent, wrote that the 18 reporters and seven photographers aboard the *Maryland* and the *Utah* were indignant over censorship of their news stories while aboard ship. All stories had to be submitted to Hoover aide George Barr Baker before they could be sent to shore by radio. Baker asked for five copies of each story. "While the deletion of stories was not frequent or at great length, the atmosphere almost of intimidation which prevailed imposed psychological conditions which are regarded by the correspondents as far more important," Manning wrote. He told readers that many correspondents stopped writing stories because attempts to radio them to shore were futile. "No similar censorship has been attempted by government officials within the memory of the oldest Washington man," Manning wrote. He quoted a *Baltimore Sun* editorial that asked: "By what authority was censorship established over the news writers who accompanied the President-elect?" Manning said that when the ship stopped in Bolivia and three reporters— Edward Price Bell of the *Chicago Daily News*, Rodney Dutcher of NEA, and William Phipps Simms of Scripps-Howard—had not returned from shore by departure time, they were left behind. This despite a well-known antipathy for Americans in the area, Manning noted. The latter suggested that callous government officials may have left the reporters in a dangerous situation. In fact, the reporters were dining in comfort with the port commander, who had assured them the ship would not leave for hours. The three were forced to catch the ship by chartering rickety planes and flying in poor weather.[15]

The article was overblown and whiny, particularly the discussion of the three hapless reporters left behind. It was their responsibility to return to the ship in time. They had no complaints. Mentioning the incident to Manning and having him present their side may have been a way for the three reporters to deflect criticism from their home offices. Baker's scanning the correspondents' stories before the copy could be radioed from the ship was a more serious breach of the constitutional guarantee of free news flow. The incidents suggest that an independent press was not something that Hoover apparently took seriously when he was in charge of the transmission facilities.

Walter Strong, publisher of the friendly *Chicago Daily News* and Edward Price Bell's boss, met with Hoover in Washington just after the South American trip. At the urging of *Daily News* Washington correspondent Paul Leach, Strong suggested to Hoover that he "make more of an effort to know better the regular reporters who would be covering the White House for the next four years and possibly a second four." Hoover responded stiffly that he had always chosen his friends and confidants and would continue to do so as president. Strong pressed on, reminding Hoover that his favoritism toward Irwin and Sullivan rankled some reporters.[16] During the Latin American tour, 25 newsmen had accompanied Hoover, but only Irwin and Sullivan were invited to breakfast with the Hoovers every morning.[17] The pair were old friends, Hoover answered, and had never violated his confidence.[18]

A month later, J. Frederick Essary, *Baltimore Sun* Washington correspondent, wrote a column from Miami Beach near Hoover's Florida retreat for *Editor & Publisher*. He outlined his impressions of relations between Hoover and reporters. Essary told *Editor & Publisher* readers: "How Herbert Hoover will deal with the press of the country, once he enters the White House, is a question that is troubling him and one to which as yet he has found no answer." Hoover was more remote than he had ever been, Essary noted. He said Hoover had not given the slightest indication of liberalizing White House press policy from the Coolidge Administration and that written questions would have to be submitted at press conferences with no personal give-and-take for the record. "There will be no direct quotations of the new President . . . following press conferences, without a specific authorization," Essary wrote. While in Washington in January, Hoover had seen a myriad of politicians but few reporters or editors (Strong being one exception) and had given out almost no information to the 20 reporters posted near his Florida retreat, Essary complained. Reporters were disappointed.[19]

William Hard responded in the *Washington Star* on February 24, a week later, that Hoover was doing his best to please reporters. In language that suggested that Hoover had dictated to Hard what to say, Hard not only conceded that Hoover had close friends among the correspondents and that these reporters were treated deferentially, but he also contended that this "constituted the effective total of his whole 'genius for publicity.' " Hard correctly noted that those reporters who in early 1929 criticized the President-elect for being "a news clam" were the same ones who had accused him at other times of being "a news hound." Hoover had not told reporters anything since his election, because he had not assumed office and had done nothing for which he could call a press conference, Hard wrote. Then, in a telling explanation he added:

When he has done nothing to tell, he cannot and will not talk to the press and he seems to have two reasons.

In the first place, it seems to make him exquisitely unhappy to stand up before a crowd of men, many of whom are strangers or semi-strangers, and try to "sell" them a lot of unachieved ideas, a lot of incompleted purposes.

In the second place, his few experiments in that direction since the time of the Republican national convention of last June have yielded a large crop of what seem to him to be misunderstandings and misinterpretations and distortions and perversions of his views.

Because of this, Hoover confided only to friends and understanding correspondents, Hard told his readers, but this would change after the inauguration. Hard also wrote that sympathetic correspondents were at a distinct disadvantage to other reporters because Hoover had forbidden them to speculate on Cabinet appointments and other Hoover Administration decisions.[20]

Hoover's concept of press relations as enunciated through Hard's column suggests a flawed perception of why reporters covered Washington and what their roles were in informing the public. If he found fault with their reporting—and probably much that he had said and done was badly twisted or misinterpreted—Hoover felt he then was well within his rights simply to refuse to meet with reporters. The White House was not the Commerce Department nor the Food Administration office. Hoover now had to handle reporters of all political persuasions and attitudes and answer their questions, because he was the nation's chief policy maker. This did not sit well with him. The President-elect was stepping into a firestorm that he could have prevented, but he saw no need to change the press policies that had been successful since the Belgian Relief days.

For the moment, however, editors and editorial writers were not nearly so concerned about Hoover's treatment of Washington correspondents as they were the impending inauguration. The breach between Hoover and reporters would be forgotten for the moment. In its New Year's Eve 1928 edition, a *Washington Star* headline described Hoover as the "outstanding figure in American Affairs in 1928."[21] In March 1929, the Sunday editorial page of the *New York Herald Tribune* bannered the next day's inauguration with the declaration that Hoover's presidency would be the "Earth's Greatest Opportunity."[22] Only Elmer Davis of *Harper's* magazine worried that possibly all was not well. "All Mr. Hoover has to do is keep up the present show of prosperity," Davis summarized. He added:

The suggestion that prosperity may not last forever, despite the admittedly superior virtue of the American people, is customarily denounced as the work of an enemy of prosperity, who hates the human race and wants everybody to be poor and miserable. . . . Let it be hastily repeated that I hope that I am wrong. . . .

But I observe, even since the election, symptoms of doubt and uneasiness among men who know a good deal about prosperity.[23]

THE INAUGURATION

Monday, March 4, was a cold, rainy day, but large crowds waited patiently in the drizzle for the new president to arrive at the podium and speak to the nation. Sound motion pictures had only come to theaters two years before. Newsreel companies were still experimenting with sound newsfilm. Pathé, a popular newsreel company, captured the inauguration for distribution in moving picture theaters. Pathé's classic newsreel footage of the ceremonies employed no narrator, but simply presented moving pictures accompanied by the subjects' voices and other natural background noise, such as crowd cheers. This to modern viewers gives the feel of a home movie. The film contained long, lingering shots of the happy crowds cheering from the sidewalks as Hoover's open vehicle passed by, the president seated next to Coolidge. Lengthy visuals focused on the color guard and on uniformed soldiers who participated in the inauguration parade. Hoover's speech was recorded on film and shown in theaters almost in its entirety. Once again, Hoover had accidentally made media history by serving as the subject of the first inaugural shown on sound newsreel. But once again, his delivery was not impressive. He spoke too fast, the words spilling over each other into a monotonous flow, and his voice was emotionless and uninspired. His words and thoughts were well conceived and incisive. He addressed the problems and complexities of prohibition at length, for instance, and offered confidence and optimism for the future of the nation. He also spoke of a need for improved education, about the relationship between business and government, about public health issues, about world peace, and about the responsibilities of political parties.[24]

The inauguration festivities were simple and unadorned, as one might expect of the Hoovers. Framed with a picture of an aerial view of the city of Washington, the official program bore only portraits of Hoover and Curtis accompanied by a sketch of an eagle inside a wreath. The words at the top of the program read: "Official Program, Inauguration Ceremonies, Washington, D.C., March 4, 1929." The program's second page contained only a framed picture of Hoover, and the third page a 15-paragraph biography of the new president.[25]

The next day Hoover was hard at work in his office, as he was for nearly every one of the succeeding 1,460 days of his presidency. Biographer David Burner has carefully chronicled Hoover's first few months in office, pointing out that Hoover used his presidential powers to bring about many positive changes. He replaced Mabel Willebrandt as assistant attorney general. Mrs. Willebrandt had been guilty of excessive campaign tactics and had used heavy-handed methods in pursuit of Prohibition laws and prison reform. The Hoovers showed their support for civil rights by hosting Dr. Robert Morton of the Tuskegee Institute in the executive mansion and later other black guests. The president pardoned a black man who had been convicted on shaky evidence of shooting a white woman, and he employed more blacks in government than ever before.[26] In May he appointed a National Commission on Law Observance and Enforcement to study prison and law enforcement reform. Strong, the *Chicago Daily News* publisher, incidentally had told Hoover that Chicago was in the hands of gangsters.[27]

But his relationship with reporters was uneven. Weeks before Hoover took office, journalist and long-time friend Mark Sullivan sent the president a two-page memo in which he outlined a suggested approach to White House press relations. Sullivan told Hoover that he had no obligation to hold any press conferences and should consider discontinuing them any time he chose to do so. "Consequently the initiative should not be on the President for managing the conferences, nor policing them, nor fixing the conditions as to who may participate in them," he wrote. Sullivan also recommended that Hoover set down rules that helped Hoover, not the reporters, and that he make the correspondents themselves discipline colleagues who did not follow the rules. He advocated direct quotations only from written statements and some indirect quotes, attributed to "the White House." Anything else should be for background use by the correspondents with no provision for publication, Sullivan told Hoover.[28]

Following most of Sullivan's ideas, Hoover held his first presidential news conference the day after the inauguration, a Tuesday, and a second one three days later. Regular conferences were held on succeeding Tuesdays and Fridays. As Essary had predicted in his February article for *Editor & Publisher* and as Sullivan had recommended, Hoover required that all questions be submitted in writing before press conferences. At the first meeting, Hoover told the more than 200 reporters gathered in his office that press relations had inched forward since the days of Theodore Roosevelt and that he hoped they would improve even more during his administration. He asked for a committee of correspondents to meet with him informally over dinner that night to work out acceptable press conference guidelines, thus putting the onus on the reporters, as Sullivan had suggested.[29] During the first two regular press conferences, Hoover read written answers to several pre-submitted questions about foreign and domestic issues. To many of the queries, he simply said he did not have any responses worked out yet. At the private dinner meeting with correspondents on March 5, it was agreed that reporters could quote him directly from press conferences with the provision that the comments be preceded by the phrase "in reply to a question from representatives of the press the president stated today." This Hoover insisted upon, because he said he did not want the public to think he was constantly offering opinions on a plethora of subjects on his own. The direct-quote provision apparently was the only concession that Hoover made during the private meeting.[30]

Still, *Editor & Publisher* was greatly pleased. "EDITOR & PUBLISHER, in the name of free press and intelligent public opinion, rises to thank Mr. Hoover for this courageous and noble stand and congratulate the people and the newspapers," the magazine commented. The *Editor & Publisher* editorial also asked that Washington correspondents exorcise from all press conferences "press agents, lobby lizards, and that type of venal tipster who write confidential letters about public affairs to 'clients.' "[31]

Apparently, this was one of Hoover's great fears. In June, he did issue such a ban saying that stock tipsters, who used press conferences for financial gain had become a serious problem. Reporters were asked to sign statements that they were not connected directly or indirectly with any brokerage firm and that they had no special interest in any legislation before Congress. The pledge brought approval from newspapers, even the *New York World*.[32] It is unclear if any such tipsters existed among the White House press corps. Certainly, Hoover needed to be certain that none did, but forcing reporters to sign pledges probably engendered more mutual distrust at the wrong time, even if editors back home approved.

In the same March edition of *Editor & Publisher*, the magazine allowed George Barr Baker to respond to criticism of censorship during the South American trip. Baker wrote that any censorship that might have occurred was innocent and unintentional.[33] Journalist Ray Tucker wrote in the *North American Review* that Hoover had put an end to one-sided press relations.[34] Days later, Manning, who had excoriated Hoover only two months before, praised his new press guidelines as "the best method for getting the news to them [reporters] that they have enjoyed under any President."[35] Manning and his editors apparently were more concerned in March 1929 about pleasing the president than making constructive headway in press relations. The direct-quote authorization for which the magazine's editors were so thankful was a step forward for correspondents, but the requirement that questions still be submitted in writing was so stultifying that it made the concession seem useless, especially as months and years of the depression dragged by. Hoover and most reporters believed a reasonable compromise had been struck. The angry moments brought on by bad times would prove them wrong.

Meanwhile, Hoover worked the luncheon circuit to retrieve his popularity among newsmakers. Five weeks after taking office, the president enjoyed an evening of fun at a Gridiron Dinner, where Washington reporters spoofed him about his efficiency and the issues of the day.[36] Hoo-

ver responded in kind with a tongue-in-cheek speech in which he
thanked reporters for "assist[ing] me beyond my greatest hopes by their
suspicious research work."[37] The next week he was the featured speaker
at the Associated Press's annual luncheon in New York. He asked the
news people gathered at the luncheon, mostly editors, to spend less time
glorifying criminals and more time playing up the roles of law enforcement officials, an obvious reference to the embellished headlines that
made public heroes of such bootlegging mobsters as Chicago's Al Ca-
pone. Hoover told the luncheon audience:

A surprising number of our people, otherwise of responsibility in the community,
have drifted into the extraordinary notion that laws are made for those who
choose to obey them. And in addition, our law-enforcement machinery is suffering
from infirmities arising out of its technicalities, its circumlocutions, its involved
procedures, from inefficient and delinquent officials.[38]

The Hoover luncheon speech brought a swift reaction from newspaper
magnate William Randolph Hearst, who wrote a lengthy editorial in support of Hoover's arguments and, for unknown reasons, gave the piece to
a reporter from the non-Hearst *Kansas City Star*, instead of a staffer at
one of his own 28 newspapers. The *Star* carried the editorial on page
17, and Hearst newspapers then reproduced a lengthier version a week
later.[39] The *Denver Post* devoted its entire front page and two and one-
half inside pages to comment on and reaction to the Hoover address.[40]

BELL'S MISSION

Hoover still knew how to generate good publicity and how to calm
angry press people. Indignant news reporters and editors relaxed for a
time. The Hoovers even hosted Mr. and Mrs. Adolph Ochs at the White
House. The president spent a day with *The New York Times* publisher,
according to *Time* magazine, chatting about journalism. Ochs, "usually a
Democrat" in the words used by *Time*, had supported Hoover in the
1928 election.[41] Hoover favored Anne O'Hare McCormick, of the *Times*,
with an exclusive interview two weeks later in *The New York Times* magazine. O'Hare praised Hoover in the article for his leadership and his
efficiency.[42] In late May, Hoover and Stimson hosted a dozen distinguished foreign editors at a White House reception.[43] In July Hoover traveled to Chicago to help celebrate the dedication of a new printing plant
for the *Chicago Daily News*.[44] The friendliness even crossed party lines,
as Akerson joined a local country club through the efforts of Paul Anderson, White House correspondent for the Pulitzer-owned *St. Louis Post-
Dispatch*. Anderson intervened on Akerson's behalf with the club
president.[45]

Despite the concerted effort to sooth reporters and editors, White House correspondents were once again upset with the administration by the middle of July. The White House and several cabinet departments had wrangled with reporters and photographers about "unauthorized" stories and pictures written and photographed without the approval of official sources. One United Press correspondent, Al Reck, was fired for publishing an interview Treasury Secretary Andrew Mellon claimed he had not authorized. Drew Pearson, stringer for the *Baltimore Sun* who would in the 1930s become a popular Washington gossip columnist; Lawrence Sullivan, UP White House correspondent; various *Washington Post* editors; and Theodore Wallen, *New York Herald Tribune* bureau chief, all came in for criticism by the White House for publishing "unauthorized" pictures or stories.

Editor & Publisher correspondent George H. Manning once again charged that the White House was choking off reporter enterprise and making White House correspondents "mere disseminators of administration propaganda."[46] John Martin, managing editor of *Time*, wrote to Hoover asking whether it was true that Hoover had ordered leaks plugged in connection with stories that had appeared in *Time*.[47] Angry reporters also learned that they would have no access to Hoover while he visited a newly built presidential fishing retreat along the Rapidan River in Virginia, 33 miles from Washington. Hoover left word that he was to be left alone at Rapidan, and that the Secret Service was to prevent reporters from even following the president as he was driven from Washington to the camp.[48]

But the strangest interaction with a reporter in the early months of Hoover's Administration involved Edward Price Bell, a 25-year veteran of the *Chicago Daily News*. Bell was one of the unlucky reporters left behind while dining with the port captain in Bolivia during the South American tour. Normally Bell covered Europe from the *Daily News*'s London bureau. In late 1927 the *Daily News* combined 50 of Price's articles, all interviews with world leaders, into a special book published through the newspaper's Personal Service Bureau. Publisher Walter Strong sent a complimentary inscribed copy to Hoover in late October 1927 just as Hoover was preparing for the upcoming spring primaries.[49]

Apparently impressed, Hoover secretly asked Bell to undertake a diplomatic mission for him in the spring of 1929. Bell met with British Prime Minister Stanley Baldwin to set up a fall conference in Washington between Hoover and Foreign Minister Ramsay MacDonald. *Editor & Publisher* reported later that Bell's mission had occurred on April 1, 1929, but correspondence between Bell and Hoover clearly indicates that Bell did not meet with Baldwin until late April. Bell filed a series of confidential reports on his meeting with Baldwin and other British officials and on his impressions of how Hoover was perceived in official British government circles.[50]

Word leaked to London Papers in June that Bell had acted as an emissary between Hoover and Baldwin. Dawes was reported to be bringing an invitation from Hoover to MacDonald. U.S. newspapers picked up the story. An article in *Editor & Publisher* asserted that the summit meeting was entirely Bell's idea and that he had orchestrated the diplomatic initiatives with Hoover's approval. Bell was quoted liberally about U.S.–British relations in the article.[51]

Bell boarded a Liverpool-to-New York steamer in late June. While en route, he wrote a long letter of apology and explanation to a miffed Hoover. Bell advised Hoover that he would wait for a call from the president at a New York Hotel before traveling West. He blamed the publicity he had garnered on "irresponsible reports and personal chatter" and told Hoover it was probably best that he not come to the White House. In the letter Bell denied that he had represented himself as an envoy empowered to commit Hoover to a meeting, that he had not leaked information about Dawes coming to London, and that he had worked hard to "prepare official and popular opinion in Great Britain" to accept Hoover and to eagerly anticipate Dawes's visit. Bell told Hoover that he had succeeded admirably in the last goal, until press reports began to twist around the purpose of his mission. To make certain Hoover would meet with Bell, Bell wrote that he had some special messages from MacDonald that he had to deliver orally to Hoover personally. He praised Hoover and MacDonald as "two honest men [who] would give his right arm [sic], aye, I daresay, his life, to build unshakable foundations for world peace."[52]

Hoover apparently declined to meet with Bell, so Bell wrote another letter when he arrived in New York giving the details of what he claimed had to be delivered in person. MacDonald told Bell that he would not reopen the German reparations payment question, that he trusted Hoover, and that Canadian Prime Minister Mackenzie King should be included in the conference. The rest of the letter contained gossip about British officials and U.S. and British reporters.[53]

MacDonald did meet with Hoover in October 1929, but not King.[54] The two set up a five-power conference on disarmament that opened on January 20, 1930, in London with more than 360 reporters from around the world on hand.[55] Bell desperately wanted to be involved diplomatically in the conference, if only as an advisor to Secretary of State Stimson, who represented the United States. Two weeks after the conference opened, Bell wrote to Stimson and sent a copy of the correspondence to Hoover with a cover letter. He informed Stimson that he would be available at the Carlton Hotel anytime Stimson wanted to meet with him, and he pointed out that he would be writing only commentary and not covering the conference because "my work is entirely exclusive."[56] He wrote to Hoover:

I could help the Secretary substantially, I feel, if he only would let me. Of course, he does not really know me. He probably ranks my judgment and my influence with the judgment and the influence of some other correspondents here. If he does, I am surprised that he lets me get anywhere near him; I am surprised, indeed, that he does not instruct the hall porter to throw me out of the Ritz.[57]

Stimson, burdened with delicate negotiations on complex armament issues, wanted no part of Bell or his advice. Nevertheless, Hoover wrote to the Secretary of State two weeks after Bell's correspondence:

I fancy that you do not think so much of his usefulness, but on the other hand his reflections here are of very considerable importance, and he might be made use of there if you have a minute of time to talk to him. I hesitate to impose any further burdens on you, but we need to bear in mind that he is the only correspondent of the Chicago press who gives us any support at all.[58]

Stimson wrote a polite response to Hoover on March 11. He told the president that he had met twice with Price in February, that he had fully briefed him on the negotiations, and that he had personally reviewed a speech that Bell had delivered in London. The speech was reproduced in its entirety in the *London Observer*. Stimson had then taken the time to write to Bell to tell the reporter that Baldwin had spoken to Stimson favorably about the speech. "Thus I think I have done everything I can think of to make him feel that I appreciated his opinion and his labors," Stimson concluded in his letter to Hoover. That ended Bell's role. The London Naval Conference did reach agreement on arms reduction on April 22, 1930, with France and Italy only partially accepting the accord. The Senate reluctantly approved the Naval Limitation Treaty in July.[59] The agreement followed the Kellogg-Briand Pact signed on August 27, 1928, in which 15 of the world's most powerful nations voted, in effect, not to go to war over their differences. Both agreements lasted only a few years. Hitler began to rearm Germany in 1934, and Europe marched steadily toward another war. Bell in 1932 wrote an article for *Current History* magazine in which he greatly exaggerated his role in the conference, suggesting that the multipower parley was due almost exclusively to his efforts.[60]

But, more importantly, Hoover once again demonstrated that reporters, in his mind, were to be used as tools to achieve his ends, not as independent guardians of the public welfare. Bell used Hoover's distrust and suspicion of reporters to inveigle his way into the president's good graces, arrogantly trying to separate himself from the rest of the press corps. In his 25 years of associating with important foreign officials, Bell had forgotten why he was sent to London.

When Strong sold the *Daily News* to Frank Knox in the summer of

1931, Bell's lack of perspective was not lost on Knox. Bell knew his job
was in jeopardy. He dispatched a telegram to the White House pleading
with Hoover to vouch for him when Hoover met with Knox in August of
1931. "My future connection is probably in the balance," Bell wired Hoover.[61] Three days later, he wrote a one-page letter to Hoover asking his
advice on what he ought to do about Knox. *Time* reported that Knox,
who had been with the Hearst organization, liked to fire older employees,
Bell wrote. Bell told Hoover it was in the president's own interests to
protect Bell. He criticized fellow *Daily News* European correspondent
Paul Scott Mowrer as "a half-mad, egotistical and impertinent, doctri-
naire, and really anti-American." He added: "He hates you. In fact, he
hates anybody who has any sense."[62] Thus, if Hoover did not protect Bell,
he would be left to be criticized daily in print by Mowrer, Bell inferred.
By November 1931 Bell knew that he was finished at the *Daily News*. He
wrote Hoover again, asking him to find a job for him in government
service or with some other news organization.[63]

Bell left the *Daily News* a few months later to become a freelance
correspondent. He toured the globe interviewing world leaders for *Literary Digest* in 1934 and 1935 before the magazine ceased publication.
Bell wound up his career as political editor of the *Saturday Spectator* in
Terre Haute, Indiana, for two years before his death in 1943.[64] Hoover
must have realized that he had made a mistake in involving Bell in the
diplomatic process. He had only been seeking to use Bell to solidify his
influence with the *Chicago Daily News* and with Strong, but Bell, in his
arrogance, thought Hoover really was interested in his opinions on foreign affairs and apparently clung to that perception for years after the
conference.

By the fall of 1929 a pattern had emerged in press-presidential relations. Hoover maintained strong links with influential magazine and
newspaper editors and with friendly but pliable correspondents, but his
up-and-down relationship with the White House press corps had gone
awry once again. In September he abruptly canceled one of his regular
press conferences, saying that he felt it unnecessary to meet, because he
had nothing to say.[65] This angered and baffled reporters, who wondered
what Hoover was up to and what the future might hold for them as they
tried to generate stories. When the infuriated reporters lashed out at
Hoover, *Plain Talk* magazine accused them of being frivolous and easily
influenced by a few free drinks at a political gathering.[66]

Henry Suydam, Washington correspondent for the *Brooklyn Eagle*, responded to the magazine's criticism. Remarking that even most editors
and reporters outside Washington had "a general prejudice against" the
Washington press corps, Suydam pointed out that such sweeping criticism was illogical. Most of the 500 correspondents covering Washington
focused on news relating to their own small circulation areas back home,

and the 75 national correspondents were all of different character and disposition, Suydam wrote. Generalizations were inaccurate and foolish, he added. Suydam made note of many other universal problems for Washington reporters including constant interference from managing editors back home, lack of "exclusive interviews," the incessant need to reproduce the same stories already sent out by the wire services, and the daily pressure for new story ideas. Suydam pointed out that Hoover's reticence for speaking with reporters only further aggravated correspondents' usual woes. "The writer has had one private audience with the President since March 4, but what was said on that occasion did not appear in print in the form of an interview," Suydam revealed. The one meeting to which he referred was probably the March 5 dinner with Hoover in which correspondents ironed out press conference guidelines.[67]

To add to the president's disappointment, a farm-support bill had stalled in Congress, and other legislation introduced by Hoover on various topics ranging from court reform to education had not moved toward progress. Obstinate regular congressional Republicans were paying the maverick Hoover back. As early as June 1929 stories began to circulate that Hoover would be challenged by Coolidge in 1932 with the backing of regular Republicans.[68]

Still, these nettlesome matters were typical presidential headaches and comprised nothing that Hoover had not expected. Though the honeymoon was over, journalists generally praised Hoover on his first months in office.[69] He had even popularized a new game called "Hoover Ball," so that friends and staffers could join him in jovial exercise. Participants tossed a heavy medicine ball back and forth over a volleyball net. Correspondent William Hard joined the friendly game one day in May, only to sprain his ankle and wind up on crutches.[70]

But now Hoover was neither the Great Engineer nor the Great Humanitarian, nor even the newly elected candidate. He was president of the United States, and he was leading the country during peace and prosperity, undertaking the distasteful task of dealing with reporters while seeking to move the country in a positive direction.

Then, on October 23, 1929, brokers watching their stock market ticker tapes noticed an alarming trend toward a huge stock sell-off. No one knew for certain what was happening, but the world was about to plunge into a deep hole, derailing one of the most meteoric public careers in the history of the country and dragging the presidency and the country into depression.

NOTES

1. HH to ER, Nov. 16, 1928, Campaign and Transition, General Correspondence, Elihu Root File, HHPL.

2. Ibid.

3. Herbert Hoover, *The Memoirs of Herbert Hoover: The Cabinet and the Presidency, 1920–1933* (New York: Macmillan, 1952), pp. 212–15 [referred to hereafter as the Hoover memoirs, vol. 2]; Dorothy Horton McGee, *Herbert Hoover: Engineer, Humanitarian, Statesman* (New York: Dodd, Mead, 1959), pp. 218–21.

4. "The Hoover-Smith Meeting," *Washington Post* editorial, Jan. 30, 1929.

5. David Burner, *Herbert Hoover: A Public Life* (New York: Knopf, 1979), p. 210.

6. For biographies of all the Cabinet members, see "The Cabinet of President Hoover," packet of January 1929 articles from the *Christian Science Monitor*, Campaign and Transition, January 1929 Reprint File, HHPL. See also "The Cabinet/Eight New, Two Old," *Time*, 13, no. 10 (March 11, 1929); Burner, *Herbert Hoover*, pp. 209–10.

7. Burner, *Herbert Hoover*, p. 209.

8. "Harvard Man to Stand between Hoover and Public," *Boston Globe*, Dec. 2, 1928, features section, p. 1. See also Thomas Carens, "Hoover's Right Hand Man," *New York Herald Tribune*, Sunday magazine, Jan. 13, 1929, p. 1 (also appearing same day in *Minneapolis Journal*); "Secretary to Hoover Is Human Dynamo; Known Here as 'Great Nordic Monsoon,' " *Washington Post*, Dec. 2, 1928; "Human Dynamo Is Akerson, Herbert Hoover's Secretary," *New York World*, Nov. 16, 1928; Delos Lovelace, "The Man to See, to See Hoover," unidentified article in January 1929 clipping file, HHPL.

9. *Who's Who in America, 1950–1951* (Chicago: Marquis Co., 1950), pp. 2302–3.

10. Edgar Rickard diary entry, Jan. 3, 1929, Rickard Papers, HHPL.

11. Ibid.

12. Ibid.

13. Burner, *Herbert Hoover*, p. 215.

14. HH to ER, Nov. 16, 1928, Campaign and Transition General Correspondence, Elihu Root File, HHPL.

15. George Manning, "Charge Press Censorship on Hoover Good-Will Trip to South/Washington Correspondent Corps Reported Indignant at Deletions in Copy and General Atmosphere of Intimidation—Three Correspondents Forced to Risk Lives in Air," *Editor & Publisher*, Jan. 12, 1929, p. 12.

16. Paul R. Leach oral history interview with Raymond Henle, director of Herbert Hoover oral history project, in Washington, D.C., March 14, 1969, oral history files, HHPL.

17. McGee, *Herbert Hoover*, p. 218.

18. Leach oral history.

19. J. Fred Essary, "Hoover Sensitive to Criticism, Will Tighten Relations with Press," *Editor & Publisher*, Feb. 16, 1929, p. 8.

20. William Hard, "Hoover Passing through New Relationship with the Press," *Washington Star*, Feb. 24, 1929, feature section, p. 1.

21. "Herbert Hoover Outstanding Figure in American Affairs in 1928," *Washington Star*, Dec. 31, 1928, p. 15.

22. "Earth's Greatest Opportunity," *New York Herald Tribune*, March 3, 1929,

editorial section, p. 1. For other insight, also see S. T. Williamson, "Washington's One Day of Days," *The New York Times* magazine, March 3, 1929, p. 1.

23. Elmer Davis, "If Hoover Fails," *Harper's* magazine, 946 (March 1929), pp. 412–13.

24. Pathé newsfilm, March 4, 1929, audiovisual archives, HHPL; "Inaugural Address," *Public Papers of the President of the United States: Herbert Hoover 1929* (Washington: U.S. Government Printing Office, 1974), pp. 1–12.

25. Official Inauguration Program, March 4, 1929, Reprint file, March 1929, HHPL.

26. Burner, *Herbert Hoover*, pp. 216–17.

27. Ibid., p. 219.

28. MS to HH undated memo from February or March 1929, President's Personal File—Mark Sullivan, pp. 1–2.

29. "The President's Press Conference of March 5, 1929," in *Public Papers of the President: Herbert Hoover 1929*, pp. 12–13.

30. "The President's Press Conference of March 8, 1929" in ibid., pp. 16–17.

31. "The Great White Light," *Editor & Publisher* editorial, 61, no. 42 (March 9, 1929), p. 44.

32. "Stock Tipsters," *New York World* editorial, June 6, 1929; see also "President Hoover Bars Stock Tipsters from His Press Conferences," *Commercial and Financial Chronicle*, June 15, 1929.

33. George Barr Baker, "Baker Philosophizes on Charge of Good-Will Censorship," in ibid., p. 6.

34. Ray T. Tucker, "Mr. Hoover Lays a Ghost," *North American Review*, June 1929, pp. 661–69.

35. George H. Manning, "Hoover's Press System Best Instituted by Any President, Capital Writers Say," *Editor & Publisher*, 61, no. 43 (March 16, 1929), p. 3.

36. "Hoover Efficiency Chief Target of Gridiron Club at Annual Dinner," *Editor & Publisher*, 61, no. 48 (April 20, 1929), p. 50.

37. "Addresses of President Hoover at the Dinners of the Gridiron Club—April 13, 1929, Speech," reprint file of April 1929, HHPL; also see Theodore Joslin, *Hoover after Dinner: Addresses Delivered by Herbert Hoover before the Gridiron Club of Washington, D.C., with Other Informal Speeches* (New York: Charles Scribner's Sons, 1933).

38. "President Hoover Calls on Nation's Press to Aid Cause of Law Enforcement," *Editor & Publisher*, 61, no. 49 (April 27, 1929), pp. 9–11.

39. William Randolph Hearst, "We Need Laws We Can Respect," *Kansas City Star*, April 23, 1929; also in *San Francisco Examiner*, May 3, 1929, p. 1. For details of Hearst giving the story to the *Kansas City Star* see *Time*, "The Press" section, "Hearst v. Hoover," 13, no. 19 (May 13, 1929).

40. *Denver Post* coverage, April 23, 1929, p. 1; see also "Denver Post Takes Up Hoover Crusade," *Editor & Publisher*, 61, no. 49 (April 27, 1929), p. 44.

41. "The Presidency/Speech No. 1," *Time*, 13, no. 17 (April 29, 1929), p. 9.

42. Anne O'Hare McCormick, "The Dawn of the 'Hoover Era,' " *The New York Times* magazine, May 12, 1929, p. 1.

43. "Foreign Editors Meet Hoover," *Editor & Publisher*, 62, no. 2 (June 1, 1929), p. 54.

44. "Chicago Daily News Plant Dedicated," *Editor & Publisher*, 62, no. 8 (July 13, 1929), p. 11.

45. GA to PA letter of appreciation, July 10, 1929, George Akerson Papers, Box 15, HHPL.

46. " 'Tightening' of Press Relations Irks Washington Correspondents," *Editor & Publisher*, 52, no. 8 (July 6, 1929), p. 50.

47. JSM to HH, June 14, 1929, Press Secretary File—*Time* magazine, President's Personal File, HHPL.

48. George H. Manning, "White House Is Best News Source for Rapidan Camp 100 miles away," *Editor & Publisher*, July 13, 1929.

49. WS to HH, Oct. 28, 1927, Commerce Papers, Newspapers and Magazines, *Chicago Daily News*, Box 438.

50. "Private and confidential" letters from EPB to HH, May 2, 1929, and May 15, 1929, Presidential Papers—Individuals, Edward Price Bell File, Box 1031, HHPL.

51. Ben Kartman, "MacDonald Visit Newspaperman's Idea," *Editor & Publisher*, 62, no. 4 (June 22, 1929), p. 13.

52. EPB letter to HH marked "personal," June 30, 1929 (received by White House July 8, 1929), pp. 1–2 in ibid.

53. EPB to HH letter, July 9, 1929, pp. 1–2, in ibid.

54. "Five-Power Disarmament," *Time*, Sept. 16, 1929; "Momentous Steps toward Disarmament," *The New York Times*, Sept. 22, 1929; P. W. Wilson, R. V. Oulahan, "The Reasons for MacDonald's Coming," *The New York Times*, Oct. 6, 1929; "European Tremors at MacDonald's Visit," *E & P*, undated article, reprint file, HHPL; "Peace & Disarmament," *Time*, Sept. 30, 1929, p. 25.

55. "Elaborate Preparations Are Made by Press for Covering London Naval Parley," *Editor & Publisher*, 62, no. 35 (Jan. 18, 1930), p. 3.

56. EPB to HS, Feb. 12, 1930, Price file, HHPL.

57. EPB to HH, Feb. 12, 1930, in ibid.

58. HH to HS, Feb. 25, 1930, in ibid.

59. Hoover memoirs, vol. 2, pp. 348–52.

60. Edward Price Bell, "The Origin of Premier MacDonald's Visit to America," *Current History*, November 1932, pp. 167–72.

61. EPB to HH telegram, Aug. 21, 1931, in ibid.

62. EPB to HH, Aug. 24, 1931, in ibid.

63. EPB to HH, Nov. 7, 1931, in ibid.

64. *Who Was Who in America*, vol. 3, p. 56.

65. George H. Manning, "President Cancels a Press Conference," *Editor & Publisher*, Sept. 7, 1929.

66. As quoted in "Suydam Answers Magazine Article Attacking Washington Writers," *Editor & Publisher*, 62, no. 26 (Nov. 16, 1929), p. 16.

67. Ibid.

68. "With Their Eyes on '32," *Collier's*, June 15, 1929.

69. See especially a roundup of newspaper opinion in "Six Months of Hoover's Presidential Engineering," *Literary Digest*, Sept. 21, 1929, p. 14. Also see Richard V. Oulahan, "Hoover's First Half Year As President," *The New York Times*, Sept. 1, 1929, special features section, p. 1; Arthur Sears Henning, "Hoover Keeps Politicians on Merry Go Round," *Chicago Tribune*, July 7, 1929.

70. "The Presidency," *Time*, 13, no. 19 (May 13, 1929), p. 3.

5

The Crash

During his second term as secretary of commerce, Herbert Hoover repeatedly warned Calvin Coolidge about wild stock market speculation
and counseled a slowdown in domestic investment.[1] Coolidge disagreed;
in fact, in the spring of 1927 the Federal Reserve Board actually dropped
its discount rate to 3.5 percent, fueling more speculation.[2] Weeks after
entering the White House, Hoover met privately with newspaper and
magazine editors and publishers and asked them to initiate a campaign
against dangerous stock manipulation. Many responded with editorials,
but eager investors just kept pushing the value of stocks higher. Readers
were more fascinated by Hoover's call for a war against bootlegging gangsters than by a campaign against reckless stock speculation.[3]

Hoover's proposals for restraint were also brushed aside by business
leaders. Walter Trohan, *Chicago Tribune* Washington bureau reporter
during the Franklin D. Roosevelt years and a long-time Hoover associate,
remembered: "He [Hoover] told me that in the summer of 1929 he called
the Wall Street people in and told them the market was due to crash. I
asked him why he didn't publicize that. He said that wasn't his way."[4]
About the same time, Hoover told his friend and personal financial manager, Edgar Rickard, to liquidate much of Hoover's personal holdings.[5]
Despite the strong market, Hoover was nervous.

On October 23, 1929, the market dropped precipitously, but it rebounded briefly before Black Tuesday, October 29, when another unprecedented sell-off brought worry and panic to the market. Stock prices
continued to slide, until industrials were off by 60 percent by the end of
November.[6] The market crash was a most dramatic event, and it preceded
the Great Depression. Speculators had pyramided their investments. That
is, they paid 10 percent of the cost of stock and then borrowed the rest.
The original stock served as collateral for speculators to buy more. This
worked well as long as the market kept going up. When the prices fell
in 1929, the speculators could not cover their debts.[7] Hoover moved
immediately to stop this practice after the market collapsed.[8]

But historians agree that the original cause of the economic slump was
much more complex. In the first place, the crash was compounded by
weakened retail markets. Americans had spent lavishly in the 1920s, especially on large consumer items. This fueled expansion of retail and
industrial output drastically.[9] By the end of the decade, with personal
debt obligation increasing and excess consumption surfeited, buyers
turned more cautious. The expanded industrial and retail base was
caught short. Second, a worldwide glut in agricultural products had developed. Third, the U.S. banking system had been weakened by a lack of
controls on loans. Finally, a downswing was the natural order of a cyclical
economy. The prosperous years between 1922 and 1929 would have
been followed by a period of recession regardless of the other factors.[10]

Hoover himself claimed that as early as two years before the crash many
countries around the globe had already experienced economic down-
turns. He argued that the precipitous drop in the U.S. stock market was
the most visible example of the changing world economy, but by no
means the most telling. The European fiscal collapse in 1931, something
beyond his or any American's control, was the real cause of the Great
Depression, Hoover contended.[11]

Americans quaked over frenzied headlines on the afternoon of October
23 and the morning of October 24, after the initial market collapse. Headlines and stories encouraged fear. The lead of the top October 24 story
in *The New York Times* read:

Frightened by the decline in stock prices during the last month and a half,
thousands of stockholders dumped their shares on the market yesterday afternoon in such an avalanche of selling as to bring about one of the widest declines
in history. Even the best of seasoned, dividend-paying shares were sold, regardless
of the prices they would bring, and the result was a tremendous smash in which
stocks lost from a few points to as much as ninety-six.[12]

The lead and headline in *The Times* were mirrored in newspapers across
the country.[13] After the first day, the headlines changed quickly, though.

Stories between October 25 and October 28 emphasized a trend to recovery and a $30 million stock purchase by bankers seeking to bolster the market. On the same day that the panic headline led *The New York Times*, an inside story in the same newspaper quoted Irving Fisher, professor of economics at Yale University, as saying that the slump was just a temporary phenomenon.[14] This sentiment appeared everywhere. "Nation's Financiers Declare Security Panic Has No Economic Basis," read a *New York World* headline.[15] The *Washington Post* lead headline informed: "Bankers Act to Curb Stock Panic."[16] When the market dropped precipitously again on October 29, another round of scare headlines was followed by reassuring stories and editorials. Probably, readers tended to pay more attention to the original frenzied headlines about the sell-offs and not so much to the later stories and headlines that attempted to reassure them, however.

Hoover was in Louisville, Kentucky, helping to dedicate a new Ohio River transportation project, when the market convulsed on October 23. He returned to Washington the next day and at a regular press conference on Friday, October 25, reluctantly issued a bland statement expressing confidence in the market and optimism for the future.[17] Privately, Hoover felt contempt toward the business people, bankers, and journalists who painted rosy pictures. "I am not a pessimistic soul, but I was not impressed by any of this optimism," he wrote in his memoirs. But he also did not want to comment on the crash, feeling that it was not his place to reassure the public. "I had no business to make things worse in the middle of a crash," he wrote years later.[18] He obviously did not have a good sense of the panic that was developing.

But Hoover's contempt for newspaper and magazine reaction was justified. The uninformed optimism was a reflection of the problems of journalism at the time. Newspapers, magazines, and journalists were becoming more independent and less closely tied to political parties. But in their search for objectivity, journalists became obsessed with facts. They refused to go beyond reporting unswervingly on the passage of events and issuance of statements. Reporters were neither expected to nor inclined to interpret. They simply reported. The market dropped, and experts, businessmen, and government spokespersons all discounted its impact. What else was there to say? Certainly few journalists, even business reporters, had the expertise or education to explain how the market operated and what the record plunge in stock values meant or could mean. Few even bothered to sit down at length with expert economists and have them review what the future might hold. Instead, they simply obtained canned quotes from appropriate sources and proceeded to the next story.

Even if reporters did possess the backgrounds to analyze the crash and had been inclined to do so, they still could not have foreseen what was to occur in the months and years to come. The experts, who brushed off the market plunge as a minor adjustment in the nation's economic structure, could not have predicted that government would react badly, that a weakened U.S. banking system would fuel public fears, that the agricultural market would dip even more severely, and that all the other unfortunate events that ensued would push the United States further and further into the depths of depression. And probably many editors and publishers simply did not want to contribute to public panic any more after their morning-after headlines screamed that the market had crashed. Their caution could have been fueled as much by a sense of public responsibility as self-preservation. In fairness, only hindsight makes the universal optimism tossed around after the crash seem blind and foolish. Yet, certainly the continued unchecked aplomb in the weeks and months that followed was unjustified and the result of much journalistic ignorance.

If newspaper and magazine reporters were unprepared and disinclined to interpret the complexities of the U.S. economy, some editorial writers were not. These opinion makers were just as uninformed, but also, even more damaging to their credibility, they were closely tied to business interests and mixed their evaluations with establishment bias. Even financial magazines applied only superficial logic to the crash. "The President has continued his laudable efforts to minimize the effects of the collapse of values on the Stock Exchange," observed the *Commercial & Financial Chronicle*. Though business had slowed by the end of November, the magazine noted that the slowdown after an inflated market period was probably good in the long run.[19] *Literary Digest* suggested that the government would "turn its powerful hand" toward preventing any panic.[20] At the *San Francisco Chronicle*, writers explained that stocks were just as valuable as they had always been, but speculators who had pyramided their purchases were panicking and others followed out of fear and ignorance. Big money interests will buy the stocks when they go low enough, the *Chronicle* predicted, "and then the market [will] snap back, maybe higher than ever before." The editorial added: "But the real values have not changed a pennysworth [sic]. What stocks were worth a week ago they are worth today."[21] The last observation was correct, but only if there remained markets for the goods these companies were trying to sell.

In a ludicrous bit of regionally oriented commentary, the *Atlanta Constitution* pointed out that Atlantans did not need to be concerned about the crash because "financial experts" had determined that there were few market speculators in Atlanta. The problems in New York were far away and would have negligible impact upon Atlanta, the newspaper surmised. "A million people in and around Atlanta are still wanting three meals a day, still wanting a supply of fall and winter clothing, still needing shelter and domestic necessities, and still determined to enjoy their customary services and luxuries," the newspaper concluded.[22] After the Black Tuesday crash on October 29, the *Washington Post* was a little more cautious predicting that a long slump could have a severe effect on business, but a rebound in the market on October 30 suggested that such a long-term slump would not occur.[23]

The Pulitzers may have bitterly opposed Hoover, but they did not take the opportunity to blame the president after the market crashed. Instead, a newspaper editorial writer, presumably editor Walter Lippmann, waxed philosophical, saying that the unbounded optimism of the 1920s may not have been good anyway, and the crash may have simply pulled some back to reality. Still, the United States had the largest financial reserves in the history of mankind, the editorial continued. "If men will only keep their heads on their shoulders and their shirts on their backs, the real business of America will go forward without serious hesitation," the *World* concluded. In a second editorial on the same day, the newspaper noted that the real estate and building industries had been hurt, but basically the market crash was a normal adjustment that was needed for prosperity to continue.[24] This view was repeated several times in *World* editorials over the next few days, and the newspaper's editorial writers even expressed concern that speculators might begin buying in such large amounts that there could be too strong a boom on Wall Street, fueling inflation.[25] The *Chicago Daily News* editorialized that the only real loss from the drop in stock prices would be to the federal government, because many speculators would be able to write off their losses against income tax obligations the next year.[26]

The New York Times featured several editorials over the two weeks before, during, and after the market convulsions. A little more informed on the economics of the country, the editorials were cautious but optimistic. Speculators had caused the crash, but the nation was financially sound, *The Times* editorials argued. The editorial writers cited the "absence of a money-market crisis" as evidence that investor confidence still ran high and business was sound. One of the few newspapers to even mention Hoover in connection with its stock market editorials, *The Times* criticized unnamed second-guessers who argued that the Hoover Administration was responsible. The crash had nothing to do with politics, *The Times* argued. In an ominous afterthought, *The Times* assured readers that nothing major was afoot, but the crash just illustrated that the old superstition about Republican rule always bringing prosperity was nonsense.[27]

Throughout November, as the situation worsened, Hoover met with leaders of business from all over the country. After his meetings he issued reassuring statements. Hoover encouraged local and state governments to step up spending on public projects, and many pledged to do so.[28]

This met with approval from journals of all political persuasions, including the *New York World*, which praised the "fine display of executive efficiency which the President is making." The independent *New York Post* added: "No man could better be entrusted with the particular job that now faces the President of the United States."[29] Even liberal magazines such as *New Republic* and *Nation* felt that Hoover's cautious optimism was warranted.[30] In January 1930 Hoover confidant Julius H. Barnes, the chairman of the board of the U.S. Chamber of Commerce, told readers in the *American Review of Reviews* that the market crash was good for the country, because it helped to define more clearly the role of business. If errors had been made, they were not made by business, but by those in the general public who overestimated the impact of the stock market collapse, Barnes added.[31] A survey of the nation's newspapers the same month by the *Literary Digest* indicated that most editors looked for a prosperous year in 1930.[32]

But the hopeful attitudes and friendly support disappeared quickly. As historian Ellis Hawley observed: "Hoover it seemed had overestimated both the cohesiveness of 'business' and the structural soundness of the economy and before long numerous critics were pointing out his errors and calling for new lines of action."[33] Still, buoyed by the initial public optimism, most Americans went about their daily affairs, letting wiser and more influential people worry about stocks, bonds, commodities, futures, building contracts, government spending, inflation, deflation, and business orders. The sun came out. The sun set. It rained. The weather became chilly. The grass turned brown. Thanksgiving and then Christmas came and went. Americans spent about the same amount of money on Christmas gifts as they had in 1928.[34] The year 1929 ended with uneasiness and apprehension everywhere, but outwardly nothing appeared to have changed.

Unlike the market crash, the depression was not a visible phenomenon that could be duly recorded and digested in a few editorials over a week's time. Its monoxides crept in under the doors, through the knotholes in the walls, and between the slits in the window sills. Gradually, Americans breathed and choked on the unrelenting fumes, unable to escape the paralyzing but invisible poison.

First, the building trades industry slowed as worried business executives put off planned construction and homeowners delayed breaking ground for new houses. Credit tightened, and banks foreclosed on shaky loans. Customers withdrew their money, and a few banks closed their doors. Depositors, who in those days were uninsured, lost their savings. Word spread and other depositors at other banks ran to withdraw their money and those banks closed. And so on. Between 1921 and 1929, 4,000 banks failed. In the five years after the crash more than 10,000 closed their doors.[35] Factories and businesses, both large and small, began to lay off workers. By mid-1930 the unemployment rolls nationwide had increased nearly 50 percent from 2.7 million to 4 million.[36] When primary industries slowed down, secondary suppliers and service industries also experienced cash-flow problems.

At first, the unemployed, accustomed to the plentiful job supply of the 1920s, merely eliminated luxury spending and maintained their usual lifestyles. As the weeks and months rolled by and no jobs were forthcoming, families cut back on food consumption, turned down the heat, parked the car and walked, eliminated all vacations, and spent little money on entertainment. But still jobs could not be found. They dipped into their savings and when the savings were either lost in a bank closing or spent, they pawned their jewelry and personal items. Then they sold the furniture and whatever else brought money. And, finally, when everything was gone and the bank foreclosed on the mortgage, they either moved in with relatives or lived on the streets seeking solace in soup kitchens or in shantytowns they named "Hoovervilles" after the unlucky person who was asked to shut off the unrelenting monoxide. Hoover was wrong about the soundness of American business and the economic system. But his real task was to stop the monoxide that was seeping into every crevice and corner of the nation. Part of the cause of the depression, after all, was fear and panic and the perception that nothing could be done about the impending disaster. Hoover recognized this and asked reporters at a press conference in late 1929 not to write negatively about the crash or "we may create a sense that the situation is worse than it really is."[37]

But he was not a public relations man and could not impress the public with the need for calm. What Hoover needed to combat those fumes were a strong public presence, a positive image, and well-chosen, well-delivered words of solace and confidence. The shy Quaker orphan from Iowa did not hold the tools he would need to stem the tide of fear. All his positive, workmanlike accomplishments achieved in 16 years of public life would come crashing about him just as the prices of stocks had tumbled on Wall Street.

THE PRESS AND THE DEPRESSION

In general, newspapers and magazine management did not level with the American public during the early depression or did not fathom well what was happening. There were selfish reasons for publishers to continue to reassure nervous readers. Newspaper owners knew that their industry would not be immune to the ravages of an economic downturn. Readers in the 1930s were certainly more attached to newspapers and serious magazines than Americans were a generation later during the television age, but given a choice between eating and reading, most Americans chose the former rather than the latter.

Consequently, despite the increasingly gloomy prospects for the 1930s, publishers spouted optimism. During the annual dinner for the staff of the *Chicago American* in January, owner William Randolph Hearst cabled his employees with a message that 1930 would be a good year because "money that has gone into speculation will now go into creative enterprises."[38] *Editor & Publisher* magazine gleefully noted that readers, curious about the crash, had purchased newspapers in record numbers in late October 1929, while reporters and editors worked feverishly to gather and publish the breaking news, suggesting that the crash had actually been good for newspapers.[39]

New York Post financial editor Ralph West Robey denounced his fellow journalists in the fall of 1931 for painting a false, positive picture of economic conditions. Robey told an interviewer:

People read the bad news with trepidation, but in the end they are much better informed of the true conditions, and are more ready and able to face the depressing condition. Think of what a factory employe, for instance, must think when, after getting the impression from his newspaper that better times are just around the corner, he is suddenly faced with a layoff or a drastic cut in wages. If, on the other hand, he knows what is actually going on, or, not knowing that, is not being buoyed up by false hopes, he is more able to take a wage cut with equanimity or even a layoff more philosophically.

The pessimism that true fact presentation must engender in these times is intelligent pessimism at any rate.[40]

The *New Yorker* observed in September 1930 that the Treasury Department flip-flopped weekly on the condition of the nation's cash reserves, and the nation's newspapers dutifully reported the changing predictions without comment or protest.[41]

Most newspapers and magazines did not reflect Robey's honesty. Advertisers were particularly concerned that public spending continue unabated. Agency leaders collectively issued positive messages days after the crash, and even automotive magnate Henry Ford took out full-page ads in newspapers nationwide to assure shaken readers that all was well.[42] During most of the first years of the post-crash period, advertisers continued to pretend that nothing had changed. Ads featured happy, satisfied middle-class families enjoying all that a wonderfully successful modern society had to offer.

News stories focused on political and governmental reaction to the depression, infrequently reporting on the misery and hopelessness that swept the country. *Editor & Publisher* marveled at their ingenuity when reporters for the *Albany Evening News* actually pretended to join the ranks of the unemployed to report firsthand on joblessness.[43] Print media owners, far removed from the panic and chaos in the streets below them, devoted their editorial commentary and debate to what policies and courses of action might be most expeditious in bringing back a healthy business climate.

Even in mid-1930 when the effects of the crash were apparent, *Editor & Publisher* chided writers who had expressed alarm, noting that "distress on current business conditions seems no more warranted by the facts today than was the unbridled optimism which came to a reluctant end after, not before, the stock market caved in last October." The magazine predicted that the pessimism would all be forgotten in six months to a year.[44]

The optimism translated to continued early support for the president. Newspapers and magazines in March of 1930 reflected upon Hoover's first year in office and generally praised his work, noting that he had handled a difficult economic situation well or that no one could have been expected to continue the unabated prosperity of the Coolidge years.[45]

But there were also alarming signs for those who supported the president. Some newspapers and magazines had noticeably abandoned Hoover and were highly critical of his financial policies. Paul Y. Anderson, who only nine months before had smoothed the way for press secretary George Akerson to join a Washington-area country club, was now berating Hoover in no uncertain terms. Writing for *Nation* magazine, Anderson blamed the depressed economy on Coolidge but wrote that Hoover was in serious trouble because of many weaknesses in his character. Among those that Anderson listed were a lack of candor and a Hoover propensity to disavow ideas when they did not pan out well.[46] Elliott Thurston, of the *New York World*, found that Hoover had accomplished nothing in his first year.[47] In May, the *Nation* editorialized that the Hoover Administration was "bankrupt—intellectually, morally, and politically."[48] Writing for *Harper's* magazine, *World* editor Walter Lippmann described Hoover as weak and indecisive in his first year and reminded readers that he had ascended to the presidency through a public relations blitz. Public relations would not get the nation through hard economic times, Lippmann asserted.[49] Added Father John A. Ryan in *Commonweal*: "The things that he has done and things that he has left undone since last November have shown that Mr. Hoover does not possess the superior qualities which were attributed to him during the presidential campaign and for some years previously."[50]

All this criticism came from liberal publications, which one would expect would be vocal in their opposition to the president. Yet, the tone and harshness of the criticism was unusual, considering the short time Hoover had been in office and the positive comments publications such as *Nation* had been offering only months before. Middle-of-the-road newspapers and magazines would soon follow their leads as the depression deepened.

The persons who could serve the most important roles in passing along Herbert Hoover's message of encouragement and reassurance to the American people were the White House correspondents. While the names changed from day to day and month to month, depending upon the demands of the day and the employment situation, the White House regulars included Richard Oulahan, the dean of the press corps and chief correspondent of *The New York Times* and fellow staffer Turner Catledge; J. Fred Essary, of the *Baltimore Sun*; Henry Suydam, of the *Brooklyn Eagle*; Arthur Sears Henning, of the *Chicago Tribune*; Lawrence Sullivan, of the United Press; Paul Anderson and Charles G. Ross, of the *St.Louis Post-Dispatch*; Theodore Wallen, of the *New York Herald Tribune*; and Byron Price, of the Associated Press. Others who covered the White House in 1930, according to a press pass list drawn up during a Hoover trip to Virginia in May 1930 included: James P. Selvage, Associated Press; H. O. Thompson, United Press; William P. Flythe, Universal Service; George E. Durno, International News Service; Russell Young, of the *Washington Star*; Lewis Wood of *The New York Times*; Thomas F. Healey, of the *Philadelphia Public Ledger*; Guy McKinney, of the *Chicago Tribune*; W. A. MacDonald, of the *Boston Transcript*; Ralph A. Collins, of the *New York Sun*; Harry Stringer, of the *Washington Herald*; John T. Whitaker, of the *New York Herald Tribune*; William Woodford, of the *New York World*; K. Foster Murray, of the *Norfolk (Va.) Pilot*; several foreign reporters; and 21 newsreel cameramen and photographers including Stephen Early, of Paramount News, who would later become Franklin D. Roosevelt's press secretary.[51]

All the print journalists were men and all had worked their way up to the White House through local newspapers. Except for the Chicago and St. Louis newspapermen, all were representatives of wire services, newsreel organizations, or East Coast newspapers. This press corps was composed largely of people whose job it was to gather news and report it. They were much more interested in getting copy to their newspapers than ignoring the bad news in an attempt to boost circulation. Except for a few, their main objectives were not to denigrate Hoover. They could have been invaluable to Hoover. Yet, the president failed miserably in his relations with the Washington press corps and could not use reporters to get a reassuring message to the American public.

On Black Tuesday, when the market crashed for a second time in a week, Hoover met with reporters and told them he really had nothing to say on any topic. The few written questions that he had received from the correspondents had not been researched well enough for him to answer them, he said. "You seem to be able to find a supply of news elsewhere," he added snootily.[52]

At a press conference a week later Hoover provided background information to reporters on his views of the economy, and he compared the crash with other routine economic misfortunes in the nation's history. He concluded by saying that the downturn was limited to the stock market and would not affect either "production activities of the country or the financial fabric of the country." He refused to allow correspondents to report any of the conversation, however, insisting that it remain on background.[53] He explained frequently that the less said at press conferences, the better. "My own experience, however, has been that words are of no very great importance in times of economic disturbance. It is action that counts," Hoover told reporters in mid-November 1929.[54]

Despite the crash and a crisis atmosphere, Hoover refused to change his attitude toward reporters and news flow. Photographers and their cameras, newsreel teams and their equipment, radio reporters and their microphones and recording devices were all banned from regular press conferences. Hoover almost always read a brief statement from a typed sheet of paper and handed copies to the reporters. They would ask a few innocuous questions about his upcoming travel plans or meetings, and he would respond to those inquiries with one- or two-word answers, but Hoover almost never answered questions on substantive matters extemporaneously. Usually, he started the press conference by telling reporters that he really had nothing to say. After the hefty turnout of 200 or so correspondents at his first few press meetings, the numbers dwindled gradually until only about a dozen reporters attended the regular meetings. Most simply picked up Hoover's written statement later in the day at their leisure, skipping the press conference, because he never went beyond the written comments anyway. Hoover ignored the protests around him. After several long conversations with the president, friend and financial advisor Edgar Rickard recorded in his diary in early 1930 that Hoover was "complacent and criticism does not seem to disturb him as much as of yore."[55]

At the same time, Hoover shared his confidences with favored journalists such as Leroy Vernon, David Lawrence, Roy Roberts, Mark Sullivan, Will Irwin, and William Hard. He invited Sullivan and Irwin to fish with him at Rapidan, while other reporters were banned from even following Hoover's automobile as he was driven from Washington to his fishing retreat. The two reporters dined frequently in the White House. One evening in January of 1930 Hoover spent much of the dinner criticizing an article by Lawrence in the *Saturday Evening Post*, though Lawrence was one of his favorites. Irwin was one of the guests that evening. Hoover panned Lawrence because he wrote that Hoover was using his former Food Administration aide and friend Julius Barnes as an informal secretary of state just as President Woodrow Wilson had used Colonel Edward House. During the same dinner, Hoover offered to Irwin many anecdotes and observations about Secretary of the Treasury Andrew Mellon, whose background Irwin was researching for a separate *Saturday Evening Post* story.[56]

The worst of the White House excesses, however, was setting reporters up with trial balloons. Charles Michelson, *New York World* correspondent and later Democratic Party publicity director, said that secretaries Lawrence Richie or Walter Newton often passed out written press releases to reporters, only to have Akerson or someone else in the White House recant the information when adverse reaction resulted. "Consequently, the news gatherers got reputations for inaccuracy in their own offices," Michelson recalled. "The President's peculiarities of this sort were appreciated only by the correspondent corps."[57]

Disgruntled reporters and editors struck back in 1930. *American Mercury*, with H. L. Mencken leading the way, launched a series of attacks on Hoover and his staff, beginning with an acerbic piece in the December 1929 edition. The unsigned 1929 article derided Hoover's use of former private investigator Lawrence Richey as a personal secretary, suggesting that Richey was there only to spy on political opponents. The editorial writer reported that the "sagacious Mr. Akerson" was better than anyone else in Washington at "breaking or taking the edge off a story" and that he met twice a day with reporters only to plant stories and keep correspondents busy with minutiae while important stories went unwritten. French Strother was described as a pleasant but overpaid speechwriter. Walter Newton, a former U.S. representative from Minnesota and another Hoover aide, was labeled a purveyor of patronage and a presidential snoop into congressional affairs. Akerson and Richey did not get along well, the magazine reported, predicting that Akerson would not last in the White House. Hoover always needed a snoop like Richey, but everyone else was expendable, the editorial concluded. Interestingly, while excoriating the entire White House staff, the magazine kept the code of the times and did not discuss personal problems such as Akerson's drinking.[58] The *Mercury* and Mencken regularly criticized White House press relations throughout the Hoover Administration.[59]

In an article in *Outlook and Independent* magazine (formerly *Outlook*) in September 1930, Washington correspondent Harold Brayman wrote that, besides the visitors to Rapidan, Hoover had a second level of favored reporters or "assistant favorites," who received inside information from Akerson. "Occasionally," Brayman added sarcastically, "they obtain a brief confidential conversation with the President during a free moment, after which they explain obscure morsels of inner secrecy that demonstrate what base individuals the President's critics are."[60]

The president continued to court high-level magazine and newspaper editors and publishers, thus once again attempting to bypass White House correspondents. He wrote frequently to friendly editors and publishers. Mr. and Mrs. Arthur Ochs spent a weekend in August with the Hoovers at Rapidan. Ochs, publisher of *The New York Times*, wrote to Hoover a few days later thanking him for his hospitality and for the "frank expression of your views on so many important national and international questions, from which I gained much information and inspiration."[61] Months later, Ochs responded with a ringing personal endorsement of Hoover during a speech in Cincinnati.[62] Frank Gannett, owner of a chain of newspapers in upstate New York, and his wife dined with the Hoovers in the White House in November, during which time Gannett learned exclusively that Hoover had no plans to compromise on Prohibition.[63] Marie Brown Meloney, who had served on a women's campaign committee for Hoover during the 1928 election, and Hard were appointed to a voluntary unemployment-aid committee in late 1930. Both wrote publicity for the aid committee, the President's Emergency Committee for Employment (PECE), though Meloney continued in her position as editor of the *New York Herald Tribune* Sunday magazine at the same time.[64] Meloney even filed frequent memos with Hoover and called the White House often with gossip, with suggestions on books that Hoover should read, with advice on what newspaper publishers Hoover should host at the White House, and with warnings to Hoover about impending negative articles soon to be published in New York magazines or newspapers.[65]

Roy Howard, chairman of the board of Scripps-Howard newspapers, sent Akerson a telegram in June 1930 asking if Hoover actually saw all the correspondence that voters sent to him. Akerson responded that the president did see each letter. In a separate, private telegram the same day Howard informed Akerson that the original telegram was a result of a concern from his editorial board and that he had worded his cable so that Akerson could offer the most advantageous response. "If you have any idea of a different wording which you would prefer to reply to, redraft the inquiry [Howard's] and I'll re-file it," Howard added.[66]

Warren C. Fairbanks, owner of the *Indianapolis News*, had heard that Hoover had made derogatory remarks about him in late 1930. Learning of Fairbanks' concerns, Hoover sought to smooth relations and invited Fairbanks to the White House. After a warm reception, Fairbanks was so pleased that he "went about saying that President Hoover is the greatest man in the world," Hoover confidant Mark Sullivan noted later.[67] According to Sullivan, Fairbanks ordered Washington correspondent Jim Hornaday to write a "long article which should summarize President Hoover's achievements."[68] Hornaday wrote the article and sent a copy to Hoover,[69] but Hoover never responded. Puzzled by Hoover's lack of acknowledgment, Sullivan sent a memo to the president describing the *In-*

dianapolis News as "decidedly the most important one in Indiana" and told Hoover that Fairbanks "wants to be a Hoover man." He suggested that a letter of acknowledgment about the article be sent immediately.[70] Presumably, then, such a letter was sent.

Hoover even invited unfriendly newspaper managers to visit him in the White House, including *New York World* editor Walter Lippmann.[71] But he would not share any of his confidences with most White House reporters, who daily churned out copy that affected Americans much more than the opinions of the few editors and publishers with whom he favored his confidence and insights. Brayman in his September 1930 article in the *Outlook and Independent* remarked about Hoover's frequent visits with editors and publishers. "Mr. Hoover's intentions are no doubt entirely proper but his cordiality, coupled with the social prestige of the White House, sometimes works profound witchery not only upon Washington correspondents but also editorial writers," Brayman concluded. He claimed that editors whom Hoover had entertained later watered down stories and editorials about the London Naval Conference. Many other stories on other national topics had been killed by coopted publishers and editors, he added.[72]

During a March 7, 1930, press conference Hoover acknowledged to reporters that some of his press conference guidelines had not been working as well as he had hoped. He invited the correspondents' committee to meet again and to offer suggestions, but nothing came of the gesture.[73] The reporters obviously felt that if Hoover wanted better press conferences, he need only have been more forthcoming in his discussions with them. The next month, Hoover four times had the opportunity to talk openly about White House press problems with large numbers of news people. He addressed the American Society of Newspaper Editors in Washington on April 19. Many of the nation's most influential editors were at the dinner, but he only talked about the London Naval Conference while philosophizing about the press's role in world peace.[74] Similarly, he made fatuous remarks about press reporting in written messages he sent on April 21 to the Associated Press and the United Press Association annual conventions held in New York at separate locations on the same day.[75] Again on the 26th, he was the guest speaker at the annual Gridiron Dinner, but offered only a long, rambling speech on topics ranging from electricity to unemployment insurance to foreign relations.[76]

PRESS RELATIONS WORSEN

Many print editors who admired Hoover began to worry about the obviously strained relations with the press corps and the president's resulting negative publicity. Neither Hoover nor his supporters had come to expect this. Hoover was the master of public relations and had always found ways to control reporters and ensure that what they wrote reflected only his best side.

In May 1930, Verne Marshall, an editor with the *Cedar Rapids (Iowa) Gazette*, wrote a three-page confidential letter to Hoover. Marshall had only recently visited the White House and then returned home to attend an annual convention of Iowa newspaper editors. There, Marshall, an avid Hoover advocate, took it upon himself to explain at length to about 40 publishers his version of the details of Hoover's policies and programs and why newspapers should support them. Marshall wrote to Hoover that the crowd reacted well and, in fact, some suggested similar discussions on Hoover's behalf with groups of other newspaper executives in other states might be helpful. "All the press needs to know is what is going on," Marshall wrote. Later he added: "I almost weep when I think of the possibilities for constructive publicity that are being passed up. . . . if we can get even a slight start in the right direction we can be most happy . . . the setup never will be as good for the attempt as it is right now."[77] Hoover did not take Marshall up on his offer.

Hoover did address press relations once in the spring of 1930, but naturally he chose the forum and dictated how his message would be delivered. He allowed Frank Parker Stockbridge, a writer for the newspaper trade magazine *The American Press*, to interview him in March 1930 for an article that appeared in April. Hoover permitted no direct quotes as was his policy on personal interviews, and he required that he review the story before it was printed. Stockbridge noted that Hoover had actually been a newspaper man in 1919 when he had obtained part ownership in the *Washington Herald*. Stockbridge apparently assumed that buying a small share of a newspaper made Hoover a journalist. Hoover's guideline banning the use of all but prepared quotes actually worked to the reporters' advantage, Stockbridge wrote. That way no reporter was given an unfair advantage with special direct quotes in a private interview.[78]

The article went on to outline Hoover's general philosophy of news dissemination. Hoover gave every reporter an even chance and actually liberalized quote policies by permitting direct, prepared quotes and doing away with Coolidge's "a White House spokesman said." Hoover believed fervently in a free press, he met twice a week alternately in the morning and afternoon to give each newspaper cycle a fair chance at breaking news, and he generally considered the newspaper men his friends, Stockbridge wrote.[79]

The article contained a complete description of the president's newspaper monitoring habits. Hoover read more newspapers and paid for more clipping services than any other president before him, the article claimed. Not only did Hoover read seven newspapers a day—three from New York, three from Washington, and one from Baltimore[80]—but his aides closely watched all references to Hoover in publications and responded to those that they felt were unfair, the article revealed.[81] Stockbridge claimed correctly that "no more careful scrutiny of the daily dispatches of Washington correspondents was ever made by any President."[82]

The Stockbridge article, then, was not so much an explanation as a justification. It was not an olive branch to White House correspondents as much as a way of illustrating to the rest of the newspaper industry that the Washington reporters were really criticizing him unjustly. Many of his arguments were spurious. If Hoover considered the White House press corps his friends, he did not show it by allowing them any access to his inner sanctum, nor had his tone and manner at weekly press conferences illustrated anything but cold contempt for the reporters. His argument that he was "fair" was undercut by the way he treated his favorites such as Irwin and Sullivan. Certainly, his concept of a free press was tainted by his insistence that any journalist who published even the slightest negative comment about him had to be considered not only an enemy, but someone who could no longer write the truth.

Throughout 1930, friendly newspaper people approached the president about his press relations and public image. Henry L. Stoddard, the former editor and owner of the *New York Mail*, wrote to Sullivan in June:

I don't believe an Administration should be content with calm, factual statements when the obvious need of the hour is for somebody to say something that has an heroic ring to it—a battle-cry rousing the spirits of the people.

A dazed, bewildered country is for the moment under the spell of these conspirators [Wall Street] . . . We need, we badly need, someone to do it; not next month, or next week, or never. . . . The people are like one crying in the wilderness; they need a voice and a way out. Silence is no guide, and calm statement, however sound, has no inspiration.[83]

Alfred H. Kirchhofer, who had served as a publicity advisor in the 1928 campaign, visited the White House in June and then wrote a nine-page letter to Hoover on July 15, 1930. Still managing editor of the *Buffalo Evening News*, Kirchhofer believed unwaveringly in Hoover, but he was plainly worried. "If you were running in New York today, I am sure that under present conditions you could not carry the election," Kirchhofer advised. "The public, generally speaking and without regard to party, thinks the administration to date has been a failure." Kirchhofer then acknowledged that many of Hoover's problems were not of his doing, but that he needed to appear more forceful in dealing with Congress and be more open and informative with reporters.[84] Only 17 months into office and after a landslide victory at the polls, Hoover must have been jarred by Kirchhofer's suggestion that political trouble was brewing. The president, however, politely acknowledged Kirchhofer's letter and ignored it.[85]

Mutual friends attempted to persuade ad executive Bruce Barton, who had helped guide Hoover's publicity strategy during the 1928 election, to talk to Hoover about his image with the public. Barton eventually agreed to see Hoover, but he wanted Hoover to know that he would speak plainly. Hoover had bungled the handling of his public image, Barton confided, and some of his problems could have been avoided. Hoover and Coolidge were invited to speak at an American Legion meeting in Boston, but Hoover canceled and Coolidge was left to enjoy a big ovation all to himself, he recalled. Coolidge could be a problem in 1932, Barton was suggesting. Barton continued by saying that all who called upon Hoover were carrying away the impression that Hoover was harassed, unhappy, and disillusioned. The public was beginning to perceive this. Hoover needed to delegate more authority to his Cabinet officers and spend more time looking and being presidential, Barton told a mutual friend.[86] Apparently, Barton never met with Hoover.

Instead, Hoover responded by forming a quasi-governmental newspaper, *Washington: A Journal of Information and Opinion Concerning the Operation of Our National Government*, under the direction of White House aide David Hinshaw. Not surprisingly, the lead article in the first edition was written by Will Irwin. It was an interview with Ray Lyman Wilbur, secretary of the interior, in which Wilbur touted the Hoover Administration's scientific approach toward government.[87] The paper was founded to convince Republican precinct workers of the effectiveness of the Hoover Administration, but it was an obvious propaganda vehicle and its publishers met with labor problems. The newspaper folded after three issues.[88]

In October 1930, the *New York World* carried a series of 14 articles written by Ralph S. Kelley, a former Land Office employee in the Department of the Interior. Kelley charged that Hoover Administration officials had permitted oil barons to reap billions of dollars in profits from U.S.–owned oil reserves, hinting at another Teapot Dome scandal. The articles dominated the front pages of the *World* every day from October 6 to October 19, just weeks before the 1930 congressional elections.[89] Hoover claimed later that the *World* had paid Kelley $12,000 for the articles, two years' salary for a well-paid journalist in those days.[90] Ten days after the completion of the newspaper series, Hoover told White House reporters that the attorney general's office had investigated the charges and they were baseless.[91] "As a piece of journalism it may well be that the newspaper involved was misled. It certainly does not represent the practice of better American journalism," Hoover told reporters.[92]

The Senate's Public Lands Committee held preliminary hearings and decided not to pursue the allegations.[93]

The *World's* series of articles, a particularly unfair and untrue set of
wild allegations, miffed and wounded the beleaguered president. If the
paranoid and suspicious Hoover ever needed evidence that he could not
trust the villainous press, it was provided by the phony oil shale series.
That the *World* had been a Hoover nemesis since the Pulitzers and Hoover parted ways in the early 1920s and that the *World* had always been
highly politicized and biased did not impress Hoover. He eagerly gener-
alized about all newspapers from that experience. "I received a modicum
of satisfaction because the exposure so discredited *The World* that it died
soon after," Hoover wrote in his memoirs about the newspaper's ceasing
publication in 1931.[94] In fact, the *World* died from a combination of the
economic downturn and ineffective management by Joseph Pulitzer's
three sons, but, of course, Hoover saw things only from his narrow perspective.

The crucial blow to Hoover's image among news people was Brayman's
scathing article in September 1930 in the *Outlook and Independent*. Not
only highly critical of Hoover, Brayman's arguments were quite focused,
well documented, and specific about incidents and events. Hoover's press
relations were the worst since the last two years of Wilson's Administration, when Wilson was confined to his bedroom by a paralyzing stroke,
Brayman wrote. Coolidge, while he refused to be quoted on anything by
name, at least responded to reporters' questions. Hoover hardly answered even written questions, Brayman concluded. "Most of the correspondents no longer take the trouble to write them [questions] out."[95]
He also claimed that Hoover controlled about half the correspondents
with his favors and constantly met secretly with congressmen and important officials at Rapidan or elsewhere, away from the prying eyes of
reporters. After one meeting at Rapidan, reporters speculated in print on
the substance and nature of the discussions, and Hoover aide Lawrence
Richey notified the correspondents that such speculation must stop. "It
was a bland intimation that unless stories were written that did not dis-
please the president the correspondents would be left high and dry for
information over the week-ends," Brayman wrote. He charged also that
Hoover's attitude was seeping into every federal department in Washington, where reporters had to work through press officials and often were
blocked from doing interviews. Reporters had turned to relying on senators for information, Brayman told his readers.[96]

Compounding his problems, Hoover was forced to leave most daily
activities to inept and sometimes inebriated press secretary George Akerson. Akerson met with reporters twice a day. Newsmen liked Akerson,
but he was no more helpful in providing them with stories than Hoover.

As he became more of an embarrassment to Hoover, the president realized a change was needed.

Hoover was loyal to the people who served with him. Just as it was not in his nature to forgive those who opposed him, it was not easy for him to abandon those who had worked hard to support him. Akerson had served Hoover faithfully for four years. Akerson's son George, Jr., told an interviewer years later that Akerson actually left on good terms with Hoover and that the departure was due to a difference of opinion between Richey and Akerson, just as the *American Mercury* had predicted in early 1930.[97]

Rickard noted in his diary that as early as mid-November Hoover confidants talked among themselves about a replacement for Akerson.[98] To make matters worse, word leaked in early December that White House correspondents had decided to ask Hoover to remove Akerson.[99] Whatever the justification, the president reached a painful decision about Akerson in late December of 1930, and it was agreed that Akerson would leave. He took a job as a publicity agent for Paramount Pictures and ironically was hired by Stephen Early, who later become Franklin D. Roosevelt's press secretary. Akerson stayed on into February until a new secretary was appointed. "[This is] good news to a great many who feel he has alienated many from H.H., but hard to find a successor as H.H. demands that the man must have political background," Rickard wrote in his diary.[100]

Hoover waited until after New Year's Day to announce Akerson's departure. Newspapers had greeted Akerson's appointment two years earlier with jovial enthusiasm. They accepted his departure with muted good wishes, emphasizing that he was leaving the $10,000-a-year job for more money with Paramount. Reporters did not delve into personal problems of political and public figures in those days, and mention of Akerson's drinking problems never reached print.[101] Hoover formally accepted Akerson's resignation on February 8, 1931. Under the salutation "My dear George," Hoover wrote:

This is an occasion when I can repeat only part of what I have said and thought as to the debt I owe you for so many years of loyal and unremitting service. It has been an association of fine friendship, but I realize that the time has come when you must make provision for your family beyond that which is possible in the employ of the Government. Were it not for this consideration I would have pressed you to remain.[102]

Akerson died seven years later at age 48 in New York from the effects of a heart attack and kidney problems.[103] For most of his life, Akerson had had only one kidney, as a result of contracting diphtheria as a child.[104]

Hoover considered a number of persons inside his administration as candidates to succeed Akerson and even considered advertising executive Bruce Barton, but dismissed him as "too emotional."[105] After two months of indecision Hoover settled on Theodore Joslin, the reporter for the *Boston Transcript*, who had, among other things, covered Al Smith's anti-whispering campaign speech in Oklahoma City during the 1928 election. He took Akerson's place in March 1931. A year earlier, Joslin had written a lengthy analysis of the first year of the Hoover Administration for *World's Work*, telling readers that not only had Hoover accomplished much but he had shown his fellow Americans that he truly cared about their well being.[106] Apparently, Joslin's praise had impressed Hoover.

French Strother, Hoover's literary and research secretary, left in May 1931 and was replaced by a professional press agent, George Aubrey Hastings. Neither Joslin nor Hastings made much impact on Hoover's interaction with reporters or the public. "The Administration failed to get its viewpoint across to the people," David Lawrence of the *New York Post* recalled years later. "This could hardly have been done by subordinates. It had to be done by the President himself. Mr. Hoover was not a dramatic figure, nor did he relish the idea of getting on a platform and exhorting the people."[107] It was Hoover who had to set the course for a change in press relations, and he was incapable of making such a move.

Could press policies have been changed easily? In truth, Hoover was following the same guidelines that had been established by every president since Theodore Roosevelt, when reporters first were granted regular press-president relations. Theodore Roosevelt had cultivated a positive image in newspapers and magazines by controlling reporters and banishing those who dared to criticize him. Every president after Roosevelt and before Hoover had a rocky relationship with the White House press corps, including former newspaper publisher Warren G. Harding. In 1967 David Lawrence remembered a conversation with Melville Stone, general manager of the Associated Press, whose staff reported on President William Howard Taft. Taft told Stone that reporters played up Theodore Roosevelt's criticism of his administration in 1912 more than his own comments. According to Lawrence, Stone told Taft, "That's your fault. You don't make enough news on your side."[108]

Hoover historian Craig Lloyd points out that failed public relations policies and Hoover's arrogance accounted for the decline in Hoover's image.[109] To an extent, he is correct. But the Hoover press debacle is much more complex. Even with his personality, another man might have mended the severed press-presidential relationship that existed in 1930. But Hoover was a nineteenth-century man with a nineteenth-century concept of newspapers and magazines. Many early newspapers were published to support a political party or an ideology. A print medium was either for or against a politician in every way. What would be the sense of trying to mediate with such journalists? Unless they were Hoover admirers, they, in the end, would only try to undermine him and his policies anyway, Hoover reasoned. This was how Hoover had approached media relations since the beginning of his public life. He had been successful without parallel in every public capacity to which he had agreed to serve, and he had been adored by the U.S. news media. This convinced him that he needed total control of reporters. Those who would not be controlled simply could not be trusted anyway. As Hoover told *Chicago Daily News* publisher Walter Strong in late 1928, he would choose his friends. He did not understand the world of journalism had changed. Many reporters had news and news gathering on their minds, not the furtherance of one party or another. The same rise in objectivity that had made Hoover the nonpolitician so popular in 1920 was discounted by Hoover the president, thus ransacking his standing among the Washington press. He was not only thin-skinned and high-handed but also badly out of touch with how valuable a commodity pure news was in Washington in 1930.

Still, the general public did not scrutinize the U.S. news media in the same way it would years later after Richard Nixon and the Watergate scandal of 1973 and 1974. In 1930, only occasionally did magazine and newspaper readers think about who was writing the copy they were reading. They were much more attentive to the political leanings of some of their reading material and the influence of powerful publishers like William Randolph Hearst, Robert R. McCormick, and Adolph S. Ochs. Reporters were nameless, faceless individuals, whose stories did not even carry bylines. Formal press criticism was limited. Most of the attacks on the press came not from public ad hoc groups, but from rival newspapers and magazines.

In the final analysis, had times been as good as they were during the Coolidge Administration, the public generally would not have even worried about what was happening in Washington. Strained press relations in 1929 and 1930 were crucial because the nation itself was sinking into an economic quagmire, and voters focused their attention increasingly on Washington's daily affairs. In 1934 Harry Hopkins, director of Franklin D. Roosevelt's Federal Emergency Relief Administration, enlisted veteran reporters and novelists to fan out across the country and report on the human side of the depression. At Roosevelt's urging, Hopkins helped to bring the story of the depression home to American readers.[110] But Hoover did not recognize the value of reporters. Americans demanded to know what their government was going to do about their increasingly desperate plight, and Hoover could not get along with White House correspondents well enough to even begin to adequately tell them.

DEEPENING DEPRESSION

Hoover did not accept the strictly laissez-faire approach to the oncoming depression that Treasury Secretary Andrew Mellon advocated, but even so he refused to make major governmental adjustments. As historian Albert U. Romasco argues, business was expected to take a leadership role in those days, not the president[111]; and it was expected that the recession would not last long.[112] In fact, by the end of 1929 the stock market had advanced enough to wipe out a considerable portion of the losses in October, though unemployment continued to climb.[113] By the spring of 1930 breadlines appeared in major cities and communists organized demonstrations in New York, where scuffles with police broke out, and also in Washington, where demonstrations were more peaceful.[114] Spending on public capital projects throughout 1930 increased at Hoover's instigation. Early in 1930 he formed the National Building Survey Conference, a coalition of representatives from the buildings trade industries chaired by Fenton B. Turck, Jr., vice president of the American Radiator Company of New York.

In October 1930, the President's Emergency Committee for Employment was organized with former New York Police Commissioner Arthur Woods as director. As mentioned earlier, Marie Brown Meloney, of the *New York Herald Tribune*, and Hoover journalist-protege Will Irwin served as publicity writers for the agency. Days later, the president named Commerce Secretary Robert Lamont as chairman of still another voluntary committee, the Cabinet Committee on Unemployment. These panels represented informal, quasi-governmental, voluntary approaches to unemployment, and all were expected to make recommendations to Hoover on what steps needed to be taken. By the time these committees had been organized, however, official unemployment figures had more than doubled. In all likelihood, the situation was probably worse than that. Many persons counted as employed had only part-time jobs and still others, lost through erratic government statistics, were out of work but not listed in the official statistical counts.

Plagued by emboldened Democrats and regular Old Guard Republicans in Congress, Hoover also sustained major legislative setbacks throughout 1930. In the spring he nominated Republican John J. Parker, of North Carolina, for the Supreme Court. Parker, a noted antilabor and segregationist judge, was strongly opposed by blacks and organized labor. Hoover ignored warnings of impending disaster and refused to withdraw the nomination. In one of the strongest showings of black political power since Reconstruction, the NAACP was able to muster enough votes in the Senate to defeat Parker's nomination in May, 1930. Appointments to the high court were rarely turned down in those days and Hoover was acutely embarrassed.[115] In his memoirs Hoover dismissed objections by blacks, saying that allegedly racist statements attributed to Parker were fabricated. He conceded, however, that the defeat of the Parker nomination "greatly lowered the prestige of my administration."[116]

Worried that foreign products would flood the U.S. market and further aggravate the unemployment problem, Congress pushed through the Smoot-Hawley Tariff bill in the spring of 1930. Hoover, who was philosophically opposed to protective tariff legislation, reluctantly signed the ill-advised bill in June, partially accepting the arguments of the protectionists. Many other countries had already enacted tariffs, Hoover reasoned, and he wanted to get on to other legislative matters. A survey of newspaper editors in June 1930 showed that the nation's opinion-makers were overwhelmingly opposed to the tariff bill. The *North American Review* found that of the 345 newspapers surveyed more than 75 percent were opposed to the tariff,[117] but as the general public wanted protection from an influx of foreign goods, the measure became law. The Smoot-Hawley tariff slowed international trade to a crawl and further aggravated the U.S. business climate. The panic that began to seize the country, the high tariff wall that Congress erected with Hoover's consenting signature, and a drought in the Western states all combined to enhance the scope of the economic disaster that had befallen the country.

The drought also eroded Hoover's political base. Crops in the West in 1930 were all but lost, and tight money added to the farmers' misery. Unlike most Americans, farmers had not fared well in the 1920s, suffering from glutted markets and overextended credit after the booming war years. The drought of 1930 was a dire warning of what was to come in the next decade for the nation's beleaguered agricultural community.

But as Hoover historian Martin Fausold points out, the Administration's antidepression efforts made little news during the first half of 1930. The London Naval Conference drew far more attention.[118] The depression still had not caught on as a major news story. It just continued to seep quietly in through the windows and under the doors. Agriculture Secretary Arthur M. Hyde told an Indianapolis audience in mid-1930 that in avoiding a panic Hoover had "scored the greatest victory ever in peace time."[119]

What did draw media attention was the elections in the fall of 1930. Parties in power normally lose a modest number of seats in Congress during off years. Despite Republican successes at the polls just two years before, rising unemployment appeared to ensure that 1930 would bring more than a minor shift to the Democrats. Republican congressman Henry P. Fletcher wrote to Kansas editor William Allen White that "the Republican party is going to get the damndest licking it has had for a long time. . . . "[120] But the 1930 results were not a total disaster for Hoover. Republicans still won 54 percent of the ballots cast and maintained a scant majority, 48-47, in the Senate. Democrats and Republicans each occupied 217 seats in the House, with one lone Farmer-Labor Party member holding the balance of power.

The only particularly alarming trend was in the Midwest, where Democrats made serious inroads into Republican strength, especially in Indiana and Illinois. In Illinois Ruth McCormick lost badly to Democrat James Hamilton Lewis in her bid for the U.S. Senate seat. It was the first time in nearly two decades of direct election of U.S. senators that a Republican had not won a senatorial contest in Illinois. Ruth McCormick was the widow of former *Tribune* publisher and U.S. Senator Medill McCormick, the sister-in-law of *Chicago Tribune* editor and publisher Robert R. McCormick, and the daughter of Cleveland industrialist and Harding protegé Mark Hanna, who had owned the *Cleveland Leader*. Mrs. McCormick herself was a newspaper publisher, having acquired control of all the newspapers in Rockford, Illinois, in the summer of 1930, while consolidating them into one afternoon and one morning newspaper.[121] Not only did Mrs. McCormick have extensive newspaper influence, but she was an old-line Republican of the type that had been dominating American politics for nearly 35 years. She had been expected to run a strong race in Illinois. Hers was a classic example of the decline of Republican influence among voters.

Many defeated Republicans blamed their losses on Hoover, and many newspapers and magazines described the Democratic resurgence as a "Democratic landslide."[122] Anti-Hoover and pro-Hoover newspapers and magazines translated the results as either a sweeping indictment of the president or an expected switch to the party out of power in an off-year election. Mark Sullivan, writing for the *New York Herald Tribune*, took great pains to illustrate that Democratic inroads did not really constitute a landslide, that New York Gov. Franklin D. Roosevelt's overwhelming reelection victory was a "freak accident," and that the 1930 results did not necessarily portend anything for 1932.[123] The heretofore friendly *Washington News* asked rhetorically if Hoover were through. No, he was not, answered the editorial writers, citing the economic situation as the cause of the turnaround and suggesting that Hoover could reverse the trend simply by abandoning his support of Prohibition.[124]

The election was not a landslide, then, in a traditional sense because Republicans still polled more than half the votes cast and the Democrats gained control of neither House. Yet, the 1930 election was a stunning comedown for the Republicans who had rolled up such large majorities in the previous four congressional elections that some political observers had wondered if the Democratic Party had lost its power as a major political institution. Suddenly, the Democrats were even with their previously dominant counterparts, and Hoover would need a miracle to get his programs through Congress. The Democratic Party would be rekindled by a dynamo who would burst on the political scene. A small, one-column, postelection headline in November 1930 on the front page of *The New York Times* read: "Roosevelt Denies Seeking Presidency." The first speculative story on the 1932 presidential election quoted James Farley, New York Democratic Party chairman, as saying that Roosevelt's nomination for president was inevitable.[125]

With unemployment spiraling and emboldened Democrats and Old Guard Republicans opposing him, Hoover faced a most difficult task at the midpoint of his presidency. He was still as dedicated as ever, but it would take a confident, outspoken man to retain the presidency. Hoover was a quiet, behind-the-scenes engineer who put his trust in hard work and common sense. But if he thought that some unseen hand might intervene to help Americans see his virtues, he was greatly mistaken. The final two years of his presidency would prove to be as trying as any faced by a U.S. president. The years 1931 and 1932 would bring the country to the depths of depression and accelerate the voting trend that began in the fall of 1930. The nation would forget about the man who had introduced institutional humanitarianism to the twentieth century. In 1932 voters would turn overwhelmingly to someone who would promise more than Hoover could deliver. By then, Herbert Hoover would be awash in bylines in despair.

NOTES

1. This according to Byron Price, Associated Press Washington Bureau Chief during the Hoover administration. Price Oral History Interview in Washington, D.C., March 21, 1969, Washington, D.C., p. 2, Oral History Files, HHPL.

2. Herbert Hoover, *The Memoirs of Herbert Hoover: The Great Depression 1929–1941* [hereafter referred to as Hoover Memoirs, vol. 3] pp. 5–6; David Burner, *Herbert Hoover: A Public Life* (New York: Knopf, 1979), p. 246.

3. Hoover memoirs, vol. 3, p. 17; Burner, *Herbert Hoover*, p. 247.

4. Walter Trohan interview with author, Sept. 19, 1989. Also see Hoover Memoirs, vol. 3, pp. 16–19, for details on some of these meetings.

5. Burner, *Herbert Hoover*, p. 247.

6. Hoover memoirs, vol. 3, p. 30.

7. Robert Sobel, *The Great Bull Market: Wall Street in the 1920s* (New York: W. W. Norton and Co., 1968), pp. 74–76.

8. Hoover memoirs, vol. 3, p. 41.

9. For a discussion of 1920s economic speculation, see Edgar Eugene Robinson and Vaughn Davis Bornet, *Herbert Hoover: President of the United States* (Stanford: Hoover Institution Press, 1975), pp. 241–45.

10. For a discussion of the history of cyclical economic factors see Albert U. Romasco, *The Poverty of Abundance: Hoover, the Nation, the Depression* (New York: Oxford University Press, 1965), pp. 31–35.

11. Hoover memoirs, vol. 3, pp. 2–4.

12. "Prices of Stocks Crash in Heavy Liquidation, Total Drop of Billions," *The New York Times*, Oct. 24, 1929, p. 1.

13. See, for instance, "Billions Lost in Wild Stock Market Crash," *Chicago Tribune*, Oct. 24, 1929, p. 1; "Huge Selling Wave Creates Near-Panic As Stocks Collapse," *Washington Post*, Oct. 24, 1929, p. 1; "Brokers Toil All Night in Record Stock Market Crash," *San Francisco Chronicle*, Oct. 24, 1929, p. 1; "Millions Fade in Bears' Raid at Market's End," *Chicago Daily News*, Oct. 23, 1929, p. 1; "Stocks Off 5 billion, Crash Is the Worst in Wall St. History," *New York World*, Oct. 24, 1929, p. 1.

14. "Says Stock Slump Is Only Temporary," *The New York Times*, Oct. 24, 1929, p. 2; Hoover memoirs, vol. 3, p. 19.

15. "Nation's Financiers Declare Security Panic Has No Economic Basis," *New York World*, Oct. 25, 1929, p. 1.

16. "Bankers Act to Curb Stock Panic," *Washington Post*, Oct. 25, 1929, p. 1. See also "Worst Stock Crash Stemmed by Banks; 12,894,650-Share Day Swamps Market; Leaders Confer, Find Conditions Sound," *The New York Times*, Oct. 25, 1929, p. 1; "Stocks Gain As Market Is Steadied, Bankers Pledge Continued Support; Hoover Says Business Basis Is Sound," *The New York Times*, Oct. 26, 1929, p. 1; "Banks Restore Stability to Raging Stocks," *Chicago Tribune*, Oct. 26, 1929, p. 1; "Business Prosperity Unaffected By Stock Slump, Say Leaders As Paper Values Drop $3,000,000,000," *Atlanta Constitution*, Oct. 24, 1929, p. 1.

17. "President's News Conference of Oct. 25, 1929," *Public Papers of the Presidents, 1929*, pp. 354–55; Hoover memoirs, vol. 3, p. 19; "U.S. Business on Prosperous Basis, Says Hoover," *San Francisco Chronicle*, Oct. 26, 1929, p. 1; "President Hoover Issues a Statement of Reassurance on Continued Prosperity of Fundamental Business," *The New York Times*, Oct. 26, 1929, p. 1.

18. Hoover memoirs, vol. 3, p. 19.

19. "The Financial Situation," *Commercial & Financial Chronicle*, 129 (Nov. 30, 1929), pp. 3361–63.

20. "The Hoover Panic Cure," *Literary Digest*, 103, no. 9 (Nov. 30, 1929), pp. 3–4.

21. "Actual Stock Values Remain Same Whatever Price Is Paid," *San Francisco Chronicle* editorial, Oct. 26, 1929.

22. "All's Well Here at Home," *Atlanta Constitution* editorial, Oct. 31, 1929.

23. "The Market Steadies," *Washington Post* editorial, Oct. 31, 1929.

24. "All Is Not Lost By Any Means" and "The Stock Market and General Business," *New York World* editorials, Oct. 30, 1929.

25. See, for instance, "Order Restored in Wall Street," *New York World* editorial, Oct. 31, 1929; and "Do We Want Another Boom?" *New York World* editorial, Nov. 1, 1929.

26. "Business Rises While Stocks Fall," *Chicago Daily News* editorial, Oct. 25, 1929.

27. "After the Fall in Stocks," Oct. 26, 1929; "The Stock Market," Oct. 30, 1929; "A Political, Superstition," Oct. 31, 1929; "The Speculative Reckoning," Nov. 3, 1929; *The New York Times* editorials.

28. "8 Billion Pledged for Hoover Boom," *The New York Post*, Nov. 30, 1929, section 3, p. 1; "Hoover's Formulas for Our Prosperity," *The New York Times*, Nov. 24, 1929, section 11, p. 1.

29. For these and a roundup of other newspaper editorial commentaries, see "The Hoover Panic Cure," *Literary Digest*, 103, no. 9 (Nov. 30, 1929), pp. 3–4.

30. Ellis W. Hawley in J. Joseph Huthmacher and Warren I. Sussman, eds., *Herbert Hoover and the Crisis of American Capitalism* (Cambridge, Mass.: Schenkman Publishing, 1973), p. 21.

31. Julius H. Barnes, "Business in the New Year," *Review of Reviews*, January 1930, pp. 48–49.

32. "The Outlook for Prosperity in 1930," *Literary Digest*, 104, no. 3 (Jan. 18, 1930), p. 5.

33. Ibid., p. 22.

34. According to Hoover himself, who told reporters this at his regular press conference of Dec. 13 and 27, 1929. See "The President's Conference of Dec. 13 and 27, 1929," *Public Papers of the President 1929*, pp. 467–68 and p. 484.

35. Hoover memoirs, vol. 3, p. 21.

36. Burner, *Herbert Hoover*, p. 249. Estimates vary depending upon the author. Hoover himself set the actual figure much lower. Hoover memoirs, vol. 3, p. 49.

37. "The President's Press Conference of Nov. 29, 1929," in *Public Papers of the President, 1929*, p. 401.

38. "Hearst Views 1930 As Good Business Year," *Editor & Publisher*, 62, no. 34 (Jan. 11, 1930), p. 26.

39. John F. Roche, "Stock Crash Made Circulations Soar," *Editor & Publisher*, 62, no. 24 (Nov. 2, 1929), pp. 7, 58.

40. John W. Perry, "Reporting Depression a Delicate Job," *Editor & Publisher*, 64, no. 18 (Sept. 12, 1931), p. 37.

41. "The Wayward Press," *New Yorker*, Sept. 6, 1930, pp. 50–54.

42. Robert S. Mann, "Business Not Hurt by Market Depression, Advertising Leaders Declare," *Editor & Publisher*, 62, no. 25 (Nov. 9, 1929), pp. 9, 57; James T. Sullivan, "Automobile Industry Has Confidence," *Editor & Publisher*, 62, no. 28 (Nov. 30, 1929), p. 6.

43. "Reporters Joined Ranks of Jobless to Write of Unemployment," *Editor & Publisher*, 63, no. 12 (Aug. 9, 1930), p. 38.

44. "What's the Matter?" *Editor & Publisher* editorial, 63, no. 5 (June 21, 1930), p. 32.

45. See, for instance, "Mr. Hoover's Popularity," *The New York Times* editorial, Feb. 23, 1930; Garet Garrett, "The First Hoover Year," *Saturday Evening Post*, 202, no. 33 (March 1, 1930), pp. 3–4, 121; Wilbur Forrest, "Achievements of President's First Year in Office Reviewed," *New York Herald Tribune*, Feb. 23, 1930, special features section, p. 1; Clinton W. Gilbert, "Worst Over, Hoover Starts Second Year," *New York Post*, March 8, 1930; Mark Sullivan, "Hoover's First Year," *New York Herald Tribune* Sunday magazine, March 2, 1930, pp. 1–3; "Mr. Hoover Today," *Commonweal*, March 12, 1930, pp. 521–22; "Born to Trouble," *Collier's*, April 5, 1930, p. 74; "Fair Play for Mr. Hoover," *Outlook and Independent*, Oct. 22, 1930, pp. 290–91; Ashmun Brown, *Forum*, November 1930, pp. 289–90.

46. Paul Y. Anderson, "The Hoover Hippodrome," 130, no. 3375 (March 12, 1930), pp. 293–94.

47. Elliott Thurston, "Hoover Finishes Difficult First Year," *New York World*, March 2, 1930, editorial section, p. 1.

48. "Ballyhooer," *Nation*, 130, no. 3384 (May 14, 1930), p. 560.

49. Walter Lippmann, "The Peculiar Weakness of Mr. Hoover," *Harper's*, 161 (June 1930), pp. 1–7.

50. John A. Ryan, "Mr. Hoover and the Depression," *Commonweal*, Sept. 3, 1930, pp. 435–38.

51. Reporter-photographer credentials list for trip to Old Point Comfort, Va., May 19–20, 1930, George Akerson Papers, Box 17, HHPL.

52. "The President's News Conference of Oct. 29, 1929," *Public Papers of the President, 1929*, p. 359.

53. "The President's News Conference of Nov. 5, 1929," in ibid., pp. 366–68.

54. "The President's News Conference of Nov. 15, 1929," in ibid., p. 383.

55. Edgar Rickard diary entry of Jan. 19, 1930, Rickard Papers, HHPL.

56. Ibid.

57. Charles Michelson, *The Ghost Talks* (New York: G. P. Putnam's Sons, 1944), pp. 18–19.

58. "The Secretariat," *American Mercury*, 18, no. 71 (December 1929), pp. 385–95.

59. For another example of Mencken's criticism see "The Presidency," *Baltimore Sun*, Sept. 1, 1930.

60. "Hooverizing the Press," *Outlook and Independent*, Sept. 24, 1930, pp. 123–25, 155–56.

61. AO letter to AH, Aug. 19, 1930, PPF, Newspapers, New York Times, Box 277, HHPL.

62. Untitled April 1, 1931, article from the *Cincinnati Times*, PPF, Newspapers, New York Times, Box 277, HHPL.

63. Rickard diary entry, Nov. 9, 1930.

64. Craig Lloyd, *Aggressive Introvert* (Columbus: Ohio State University Press, 1972), p. 159.

65. Mrs. William B. Meloney correspondence, PPF, Box 172, HHPL.

66. RH to GA telegrams, June 10, 1930; GA to RH response, June 12, 1930, PPF, Newspapers, Scripps-Howard, Box 277, HHPL.

67. MS to HH letter, December 1930, PPF, Mark Sullivan File, Box 210.

68. Ibid.

69. "Hoover Viewed as One Who Achieves," *Indianapolis News*, Dec. 10, 1930. pp. 1, 12.

70. MS to HH, December 1930, Sullivan File.

71. Rickard Diary entry of Feb. 20, 1930. *New York Post* editor Julian Mason attended the same dinner. Both editors expressed displeasure to Hoover about the way Henry Stimson, secretary of state, was treating reporters.

72. Harold Brayman, "Hooverizing the Press," *Outlook and Independent*, Sept. 24, 1930, pp. 125, 155.

73. "The President's News Conference of March 4, 1930," *Public Papers of the President 1930*, p. 73.

74. "Remarks to the American Society of Newspaper Editors," April 19, 1930, pp. 140–44 in ibid.

75. "Message to the Annual Convention of the Associated Press," and "Mes-

sage to the Annual Convention of the United Press Association," both April 21, 1930, in ibid., pp. 147–48.

76. "Address to the Gridiron Club," April 26, 1930, in ibid., pp. 157–63.

77. VM to HH letter, May 4, 1930, pp. 1–3, PPF, Verne Marshall, Box 171, HHPL.

78. Frank Parker Stockbridge, "President Hoover Describes His Contacts with the Press," *The American Press*, 48, no. 7 (April 1930), pp. 1, 7.

79. Ibid.

80. Hazarding a guess based on Hoover's other correspondence and on his clippings collections, the author would surmise that these newspapers are the *New York World*, the *New York Herald Tribune*, *The New York Times*, the *Washington Post*, the *Washington Herald*, the *Washington News*, and the *Baltimore Sun*.

81. Ibid., p. 7. Interestingly, the misrepresentation files and the smear files that Hoover Administration staff kept are now housed in the Herbert Hoover Presidential Library in West Branch, Iowa. Those files and the 37,000 clippings that the White House compiled are the sources for some of the research in this study.

82. Harold Brayman, "Hooverizing the Press," *Outlook and Independent*, Sept. 24, 1930, p. 155.

83. HLS to MS, June 23, 1930, pp. 1–3, Sullivan File.

84. AH to HH, July 15, 1927, pp. 3–8, PPF, Newspapers, The Buffalo Evening News, HHPL.

85. HH to AH, July 18, 1930, in ibid.

86. Rickard diary entry, Nov. 25, 1930.

87. Will Irwin, "Government Is Science on Basis of Sentiment, Wilbur Tells Will Irwin," *Washington: The Journal of Information and Opinion*, Oct. 18, 1930, p. 1.

88. Lloyd, *Aggressive Introvert*, pp. 172–73.

89. Beginning with "Kelley's Own Story Quotes Wilbur's Files Showing How Favorites Got Oil Billions," *New York World*, Oct. 6, 1930, p. 1.

90. Hoover memoirs, vol. 3, pp. 223–24.

91. "The President's News Conference of Oct. 28, 1930," *Public Papers of the President 1930*, pp. 451–53. See also "Statement about the Charges of Misfeasance in the Handling of Oil Shale Lands by the Department of the Interior," in ibid., pp. 454–56.

92. Ibid., p. 455.

93. Ibid., p. 456.

94. Hoover memoirs, vol. 3, p. 223.

95. Harold Brayman, "Hooverizing the Press," *Outlook and Independent*, p. 124.

96. Ibid., pp. 155–56.

97. George Akerson, Jr., oral history interview with Charles Morrissey, Herbert Hoover Oral History Project interviewer, in Boston, Mass., March 11, 1969, p. 6, oral history files, HHPL.

98. Conversation with Walter Hope, Rickard Diary entry, Nov. 20, 1930.

99. Rickard diary entry of Dec. 5, 1930.

100. Rickard diary entry, Dec. 18, 1930.

101. See, for instance, "Akerson Quits President's Staff to Be Executive of Film Company," *New York World*, Jan. 2, 1931, p. 1; "Akerson Takes Movie Post/Resigns As Aid to Hoover for Higher Salary," *Minneapolis Tribune*, Jan. 3, 1931, p. 1.

102. HH to GA, Feb. 8, 1931, Akerson Papers, HHPL.

103. "G. E. Akerson Funeral Today at Bronxville," *New York Herald Tribune* obituary, Dec. 23, 1937.

104. George Akerson, Jr., oral history interview, p. 12.

105. See Rickard diary, Jan. 15, 1931, entry.

106. Theodore G. Joslin, "Hoover's First Year," *World's Work*, pp. 61–65.

107. David Lawrence oral history interview with Raymond Henle, director of the Herbert Hoover History Project, Sarasota, Fla., Feb. 14, 1967, p. 22, oral history files, HHPL.

108. Ibid.

109. Lloyd, *Aggressive Introvert*, pp. 168, 175.

110. John F. Bauman and Thomas H. Coode, *In the Eye of the Great Depression* (DeKalb: Northern Illinois University Press, 1988), p. 15.

111. Romasco, *Poverty of Abundance*, p. 39.

112. Burner, *Herbert Hoover*, p. 248.

113. Ibid.

114. Arthur Schlesinger, *The Age of Roosevelt: The Crisis of the Old Order, 1919–1933* (Boston: Houghton-Mifflin, 1957), p. 166.

115. Jordan A. Schwarz, *The Interregnum of Despair: Hoover, Congress, and the Depression* (Urbana: University of Illinois Press, 1970), pp. 9–10; Robinson and Bornet, *President*, pp. 144–47; Martin Fausold, *The Presidency of Herbert C. Hoover* (Lawrence: University of Kansas Press, 1985), pp. 89–93.

116. Hoover memoirs, vol. 2, pp. 268–69.

117. "Poll Shows Press Opposed to Tariff," *The New York Times*, June 2, 1930.

118. Fausold, *Presidency*, p. 92.

119. "Says Hoover Saved Nation from Panic," *The New York Times*, June 6, 1930.

120. Fletcher to White letter, Oct. 29, 1930, as quoted in Schwarz, p. 17.

121. "Merger of Rockford (Ill.) Dailies Effected by Mrs. McCormick," *Editor & Publisher*, 63, no. 19 (Sept. 27, 1930), p. 12.

122. See "Topics of the Day/The Democratic Landslide," *Literary Digest*, Nov. 15, 1930, pp. 7–8; "1928 and 1930," *New York World* editorial, Nov. 3, 1930; "Democratic Landslide Sweeps Country; Republicans May Lose Congress Control," *The New York Times*, Nov. 5, 1930, p. 1; "The Republican Debacle," *The New York Times* editorial, Nov. 5, 1930; "The House/Hoover's Next-to-Worst," *Time*, Nov. 10, 1930. For a discussion of reaction by disgruntled Republicans, see Harris Gaylord Warren, *Herbert Hoover and the Great Depression* (New York: Oxford, 1959), p. 127.

123. Mark Sullivan, "Election Result No Landslide, Analysis Shows," *New York Herald Tribune*, Nov. 8, 1930, p. 1.

124. "Is Hoover Thru?" *Washington News* editorial, Nov. 14, 1930.

125. "Roosevelt Denies Seeking Presidency," *The New York Times*, Nov. 8, 1930, p. 1.

The 1894 Stanford University football squad. Student manager and team treasurer Herbert Hoover is pictured in the back row, third from the right. Courtesy of the Herbert Hoover Presidential Library, West Branch, Iowa.

A home is washed away by raging waters along the Mississippi in 1927. Hoover gained the respect of journalists and the public during his stewardship as flood relief director in the summer of 1927, setting the stage for his 1928 run for the presidency. Courtesy of the Herbert Hoover Presidential Library, West Branch, Iowa.

Hoover meets with reporters on the campaign trail in 1928. Courtesy of the Herbert Hoover Presidential Library, West Branch, Iowa.

Hoover and his predecessor Calvin Coolidge ride to Hoover's inaugural, March 4, 1929. Courtesy of the Herbert Hoover Presidential Library, West Branch, Iowa.

Hoover personal secretary Lawrence Richey (right) and press secretary George Akerson at the 1929 inaugural. Courtesy of the Herbert Hoover Presidential Library, West Branch, Iowa.

Hoover poses with British Foreign Minister Ramsay MacDonald on the steps
of the White House on Oct. 4, 1929 after a Washington meeting in preparation
for the 1930 London Naval Conference. Reporter Edward Price Bell, of the
Chicago Daily News, acted as a Hoover courier to London before the session
with MacDonald. Courtesy of the Herbert Hoover Presidential Library, West
Branch, Iowa.

Herbert and Lou Henry Hoover pause on a shaded bridge during a walk at their White House retreat, Rapidan, during a weekend in 1930. Except for a favored few, reporters were barred from Rapidan. Courtesy of the Herbert Hoover Presidential Library, West Branch, Iowa.

The burned out ruins of the Bonus Marchers' camp along the Anacostia River in Washington, D.C., after the marchers were routed by regular Army legions under the direction of Chief of Staff Douglas MacArthur in July 1932. Courtesy of the Herbert Hoover Presidential Library, West Branch, Iowa.

Hoover and Franklin Delano Roosevelt en route to Roosevelt's inauguration, March 4, 1932. Courtesy of the Herbert Hoover Presidential Library, West Branch, Iowa.

6

Radio, Newsreels, Newspapers, and the Presidency

Unable to reconcile his differences with hostile White House correspondents, President Hoover faced a serious communications problem in 1931. As the months passed, Hoover was swept further away from the voters and into a public relations disaster. He needed to change his communications tactics, but he was too stubborn and self-righteous, and his presidency lost its momentum. What he failed to recognize was that new opportunities for communication were emerging all around him. These new media might give him a better opportunity to recapture the admiration that the public had always lavished upon him.

The most obvious new ways to reach the voters in the second half of the Hoover presidency were radio and sound newsreels. These two media were employed effectively from 1933 to 1945 by Franklin D. Roosevelt, who also wanted to circumvent caustic editors and publishers. In 1931 with a reelection campaign drawing near and the need for positive imagery obvious, why did Hoover not pursue the same course? The answer lies not only in his inflexibility but also in the development of both radio and newsreel technology.

Radio had cultivated a vast audience by 1931, but mostly the airwaves were filled with advertising and entertainment. News programming was crude and largely confined to local spot stories, live transmission of speeches, and rewritten newspaper articles. Two networks, the National Broadcasting Company and the Columbia Broadcasting System, were founded in 1926 and 1927 and had developed national news centers by the late 1920s. William Paley, an advocate of better news programming, was appointed CBS president in 1928.[1] David Sarnoff was named president of the Radio Corporation of America, NBC's parent company, and he also strengthened NBC's news-gathering capabilities.[2] Still, neither network had developed an extensive system of news bureaus by 1931, one that could begin to cover the White House adequately or seriously challenge newspapers for enterprise stories.

As has been noted, new stations began operations all over the nation after the first commercial broadcast, KDKA's coverage of the 1920 presidential election results. Only eight years later, more than 1,000 stations aired the Smith-Hoover vote counts. Still, network relations with stations were casual and limited. In 1931, CBS claimed only 79 affiliates and NBC just 61, mostly in larger cities, and comprising together less than 15 percent of the stations in the country. These affiliates were provided with news bulletins and occasional short news programs. The Mutual Broadcasting System did not begin operations until 1934.

Radio's role then was quite different from what it would be during the New Deal years. Attempts to satisfy public service news obligations resulted largely in 1931 in broadcasts of speeches or in the transmissions of live, staged news events such as awards presentations or studio interviews. NBC aired 24 of Hoover's public speeches and appearances in 1931 and CBS 19.[3] But both networks also carried hundreds of addresses by cabinet members, senators, and U.S. representatives. These years were marked by a weak emphasis upon news gathering, and only a mild focus upon the presidency. "Radio had already arrived but its usefulness to a president had not yet been recognized," recalled journalist and Hoover enthusiast David Lawrence.[4]

To a large extent, national radio news coverage provided a convenient forum for politicians or public figures who were crafty and articulate enough to usurp the airwaves. By the time Hoover took office, Detroit's Father Charles Coughlin, the famous radio priest of the New Deal era, had already begun to regularly deliver his anti-Semitic, incendiary, populist message to listeners over CBS. In January 1931 the network tried to discontinue Coughlin's program because he was constantly attacking Hoover and big business with wild, unsubstantiated charges. Network executives were forced to back down when Coughlin appealed to listeners who, in turn, flooded CBS with angry letters. When Coughlin's contract expired in April 1931, CBS did not renew it, but Coughlin's popularity was not to be denied. He simply formed his own syndicated network and continued his radio oratory for years to come.[5]

Many radio stations in the early 1920s were started by newspapers, but newspaper ownership had dwindled from 80 to 40 stations by 1930.[6] Newspaper publishing was a cousin to radio, but a distant cousin. Radio programming required fresh insights and skills, not necessarily indigenous to newspapers, and many frustrated publishers soon sold their radio holdings. Most publishers saw radio only as a competitor, whose proprietors openly pirated information from daily papers. The newspaper people plotted to prevent wire services from signing contracts with radio stations and tried to convince advertisers that radio had no impact on audiences.[7]

Newspaper management even blocked early television broadcast experiments by CBS in 1930. The network wanted to transmit wire service pictures simultaneously with radio broadcasts to a few television receivers in New York, but newspaper publishers persuaded the wire services to deny use of the pictures to CBS. "The newspapers are scared to death of television," Jesse Butcher, publicity director for CBS, declared at the time.[8]

In an interview published in early 1931, radio commentator H. V. Kaltenborn publicly decried any spread of radio's influence. He told *Editor & Publisher* that radio undercut newspapers with its frequent bulletins, while, at the same time, broadcasters ignored informational and educational responsibilities by featuring mostly advertising and lowbrow entertainment.[9] One of the earliest radio figures, he began his 30-year tradition of nightly news and commentary first with New York radio station WEAF in 1922 and then WOR a year later, before joining CBS part-time in 1929. He was still associate managing editor of the *Brooklyn Eagle*, but when Frank Gannett sold the *Eagle* a year later, Kaltenborn left newspapers and worked at CBS full-time. Ten years later, Kaltenborn moved to NBC, where he remained until his retirement in 1953.[10] But in early 1931, his national broadcasting career was barely more than a year old. He had been a reporter and editor for more than two decades, and his comments for *Editor & Publisher* probably reflected a newspaperman's judgment more than a critique from a radio industry insider. Still, critical comments about radio by one of its pioneers stung and encouraged those who wanted to see that radio would never challenge newspapers.

But radio was the future, and newspapers slowed radio news development only slightly. A survey of advertising sales at the end of 1930 showed that newspaper receipts had declined by 10 to 15 percent since 1929, while revenue for radio had risen 40 percent.[11] Americans listened to radio. During the Hoover years, they heard major news events live far more often than during Harding's or Coolidge's presidency. For many, listening to radio had become part of their daily routines for the first time.

Like Kaltenborn, early news broadcasters were often moonlighting newspaper columnists and reporters. For instance, syndicated newspaper columnist Frederic W. Wile was also a CBS political analyst. In June of 1930 he accompanied Hoover on a trip through the western states, gathering insight for his radio show, "The Political Situation in Washington Tonight."[12] The trip allowed Wile personal access to the president. He liked Hoover and frequently praised the president during the remainder of Hoover's term. The president reciprocated by allowing Wile to enter his personal circle of favored journalists. After Hoover's election defeat, Wile wrote to him: "No one will be sadder at the thought [Hoover's impending departure from Washington] than myself, who has so often been the recipient of important and generous consideration at your hands."[13]

In the spring of 1930 columnist William Hard, Hoover's close friend, and Wile both covered the London Naval Conference for radio; Wile on CBS and Hard on NBC. This was radio's first on-the-air presence at an international conference.[14] When King George V welcomed delegates during the opening ceremonies, early-morning listeners in the United States heard his words instantaneously. At that time, the complex logistical wireless hookup that provided access to the speech thousands of miles away was considered to be the greatest radio broadcasting feat in history.[15] It offered hope that the type of clandestine agreements that led to the Great War might never be negotiated in secret by the world's great powers again. Back at the White House, Hoover himself sat tuned to the radio listening to the conference's opening speeches simultaneously with millions of other Americans.[16] With Wile and Hard handling the commentary, Hoover naturally enjoyed the broadcasts. This was the kind of revolution that radio had wrought. In another unique radio event a year later, both Calvin Coolidge and Al Smith participated in an unusual bipartisan radio appeal over NBC to raise money for the Red Cross to aid drought-stricken farmers in the West.[17]

So while radio news could not compete with newspapers in 1931 and 1932, world leaders, including Hoover, realized that they could still employ the airwaves for their own purposes. The United States did not have a well-developed, national radio news system, but Hoover did have the option throughout his years in office of simply using the air waves to talk directly and live to Americans in all parts of the country. Radio chats were just as possible in 1931 as in 1933, when Franklin D. Roosevelt began his famous fireside talks.

No world head of state was more informed about radio's potential value than Hoover. As Secretary of Commerce, he had for seven years watched radio grow while he mediated among warring factions seeking to dominate the air waves. Also, Herbert Jr. had become a radio aeronautics expert in the 1920s, working as radio director for Western Air

Express. He wrote articles in 1931 and delivered speeches about the future of air flight and how radio technology might influence it.[18]

The problem was that President Hoover just was not a radio pontificator or someone who could unbend long enough to sit before a microphone for an interview with a radio journalist. He hated chitchat, He was not a dynamic speaker, and he made no distinction between annoying radio journalists and pesky print reporters. In his own mind, he had been elected to look after the nation's affairs, not to jabber into a microphone or inflate the egos of men who prattled into round metal speaker disks every night. "[I] urged him to get on the radio and talk to the nation, and I could tell by the expression on his face that it was not the kind of role he liked to play," remembered journalist David Lawrence.[19]

About once a month in 1929, 1930, and 1932 and twice a month in 1931, Hoover allowed radio to broadcast one of his prepared speeches. Usually, this simply meant that microphones were permitted nearby while he delivered a talk on important issues of the day in a hurried monotone to a civic or business group. To Hoover, the millions who listened over the radio were just eavesdroppers. He directed his words to the live audience in front of him, and he did not always give radio's needs much consideration.

Paley wrote to Hoover in May of 1931 to complain diplomatically about White House handling of a botched radio broadcast. Hoover was supposed to address a Washington conference of the International Chamber of Commerce at 11:45 A.M. The chamber program was ahead of schedule because a musical score had been canceled, so Hoover rose to speak a minute and a half early. To him, it was no major change but to CBS, tied to a rigid programming schedule, it meant that listeners would have to try to pick up the thread of the speech 90 seconds after it had begun. Programmers decided this would not do. They scratched the broadcast entirely rather than confuse listeners. While camouflaging his letter as an apology, Paley obviously wanted to make certain the incident would not be repeated. He reminded the president of the needs of radio and how valuable a commodity network time was for a president. Paley concluded, "We are exceedingly glad to use our entire facilities to carry your words to the American people just as often as possible . . . it just was not possible in this particular instance. I hope that we may have many future opportunities to make amends."[20] But to Hoover, radio was more of an intrusion than a tool to reach millions of voters' ears, and Paley's polite letter probably had little impact.

Hoover did not particularly care if a long period of time passed between radio addresses or if the airwaves were being used to his best advantage. Once a month was only an average. In 1932, from September 29 to November 7, with his own reelection at stake, Hoover did use network radio 12 times, sometimes speaking only to the radio audience.

But this was a desperate last-minute gesture. Radio carried only three other addresses the whole year. During the first 15 weeks of 1931, he spoke live on radio only twice.[21]

Most speeches were a waste of air time. In November 1930 network microphones captured Hoover's remarks as he delivered the medal of honor to World War I flying ace Eddie Rickenbacker, congratulated the H. J. Heinz Co. on its 61st anniversary, spoke to the World Alliance for International Friendship through the Churches, appeared before the White House conference on child health and protection, and addressed the annual convention of the Association of National Advertisers.[22] All told, radio carried an estimated 70 to 80 Hoover speeches in four years.[23] His words were heard infrequently and were hardly designed to galvanize a depression-ravaged public.

In one instance, though, a national police story and the anguish of a famous family prodded the president to eagerly seek the air. In March of 1932, the infant son of aviator-hero Charles Lindbergh was kidnapped. The Lindberghs asked Hoover himself to address the nation and seek public assistance in finding the child. Hoover was about to comply, but the Lindberghs changed their minds.[24] The baby was found dead days later. The same month, when speeches by congressional Democrats angered him, Hoover responded on radio.[25] These instances, even during an election year, were not common occurrences, though.

Just as Hoover employed "minute men" in the 1928 election, he usually preferred to let party officials or members of the Administration speak for him. Press Secretary George Akerson, for instance, was a guest on the "Collier's Radio Hour" on NBC in June 1930. He told Americans that Hoover was doing everything he could to improve economic conditions, and he described in detail a typical harried day in the White House.[26] The discussion helped humanize the president, but Akerson's honey-coated radio talk earned him the scorn of disgruntled White House reporters.

The few radio commentators and reporters who did have some contact with Hoover were usually friends, but all were still required to abide by Hoover's stringent restrictions on information. In a brief conversation with Kaltenborn at the White House in May of 1932 Hoover told the radio commentator that he did not care whether he was renominated or not. After Kaltenborn left, Hoover told Joslin about the conversation, and Joslin asked the president if Kaltenborn knew that such conversations had to be off the record. Neither Hoover nor Joslin was certain, so Joslin tracked Kaltenborn down and reminded him.[27] No one, not even radio commentators, could be exempted from Hoover's rules. He may have been aware of radio's potential, but it was not a medium Hoover used well. Hoover's personality allowed him to derive only minimal political benefit from what limited potential the airwaves did offer at that time.

If radio made Hoover uneasy, newsreels were doubly problematic. As has been noted, sound newsreels captured the 1929 inauguration in great detail, but the film that moviegoers saw in theaters was both uninteresting and primitive. Sound newsreel technical quality and directing did not progress much past that stage during Hoover's presidency. Silent newsreels were still used extensively as late as the beginnings of the Hoover presidency.

It was quite an accomplishment for the sound newsreel cameramen, when on May 1, 1930, Hoover allowed them into the south grounds of the White House to film the presentation of the proposed London Naval Treaty agreement. Secretary of State Henry Stimson handed the document to Hoover, and both men made a few perfunctory remarks. Print reporters, photographers, and silent newsreel cameramen were kept 75 feet away, while the sound cameras recorded 15 minutes of film. George H. Manning, *Editor & Publisher*'s Washington correspondent, angrily informed his readers that the occasion marked a new era for important news events. Hoover had apparently established a policy of "staging" important public occurrences while barring legitimate print reporters, Manning complained.[28]

Of course, nothing was further from the truth. Hoover detested sound newsreel film opportunities. Most newsreel footage of him featured a wooden man awkwardly shaking hands and speaking in a monotone to the camera or delivering an uninspired address to a crowd. Rare newsreel camera footage at Rapidan revealed an obviously uncomfortable president awkwardly casting his line into the water and mumbling some rehearsed words.[29] Sound newsreel cameras and lights were extremely bulky and heavy and required literally hours of setup for a few minutes of film footage. Cameraman Robert H. Denton recalled that huge power lines had to be installed and indoor film required bright lights that elevated the room's temperature to over 100 degrees.[30]

As the Naval Treaty press conference indicates, Hoover did recognize the value of newsreels, but it was a real struggle for him to pose. Just as the 1932 election campaign was getting underway, he complained to Joslin that "Movietone" newsreel footage of Roosevelt made the soon-to-be Democratic nominee look younger than his years, while Hoover looked 82 years old on camera. "That's the end of [the] Movietones," Hoover told Joslin. "Mrs. Hoover was so disturbed that she broke down and cried."[31]

Most world leaders felt uncomfortable about appearing in sound newsreels in the early 1930s. Sydney Hollinger MacKean, writing for the *New York Herald Tribune* in late 1930, interviewed newsreel directors. They told him they were experiencing great difficulties in getting any public figures to pose on camera, even those leaders who did not object to radio interviews or silent newsreel appearances. Reasons varied, and most potential interviewees just gave vague explanations. Newsreel directors had "advanced every conceivable argument [to get public figures before the cameras] without success," MacKean wrote. Fascist Italian leader Benito Mussolini was one exception. The egocentric dictator always wanted to be heard and photographed.[32] Perhaps it was a distrust of the new medium and how the film and the sound track might be edited or, as in Hoover's case, a fear of looking older than his years while on camera. Unfamiliar to the president and bearing that mysterious, heavy equipment, the cameramen struggled to be taken seriously. Denton observed, "[We were] trying to make a name for ourselves and to obtain face [in the early 1930s], but we did not have the closeness to the president . . . that his favorite [newspaper]men had. We had to fight for everything we could get."[33]

It was not just Hoover's physical appearance on film. He was shy and impatient. He mourned the time lost while posing for cameras, and he hated the attention. "As a matter of fact, he reversed when he got in front of the camera—he stiffened up," Denton recalled. "If he would have softened up the way he did with some of his favorite newspapermen when he was alone with them, he would have been tremendous on the screen. He just did not do that."[34] One magazine writer in 1930 found that even Coolidge was less squeamish about appearing before cameras than was Hoover.[35]

Hoover saw himself as a practical, no-nonsense leader. He despised showmanship. So, though he could not get along with most White House correspondents, for him the burgeoning radio and sound newsreel industries were just not suitable surrogates for reaching the American public.

DEPRESSION NEWSPAPERS

Newspaper and magazine writers did not need to struggle for acceptance, but the Hoover years did bring many changes for them. Important newspapers were bought, sold, or merged in 1931 and 1932 or switched political allegiance away from Hoover. Ownership changes resulted largely from natural turnover, but some from the depressed economy. Dwindling support for the president, however, was more often a by-product of his poor press relations or the impressions among many editors and publishers that he was a loser who would drag the country into ruin.

One of the most dramatic events in the history of the newspaper industry came early in 1931, when the famed *New York World* essentially closed its doors. Joseph Pulitzer acquired the failing *World* in 1883. He transformed an unpopular and uninfluential paper into one of the most powerful and revolutionary journals in the history of the nation. He used innovative writing and layout techniques, a sympathy for the working classes, forceful but sometimes scurrilous attacks upon the Republicans, and sensational, exaggerated stories to build the *World* into the most powerful force in American journalism.[36] But in the paper's final two decades, Pulitzer's heirs had allowed the *World* to decline until an increasingly complicated financial world forced them to cease publication.[37] The Scripps-Howard chain acquired the newspaper for $5 million and so technically it still existed through a merger with the *Telegram*, but, for all intents, the *World* was no longer part of the New York newspaper market. Hundreds of stunned workers were left jobless. *Editor & Publisher* devoted six full pages of its next edition to stories about the *World*'s demise.[38] Naturally, in the White House there was no mourning. Hoover no longer had to deal with his most powerful and vociferous antagonist.

World editor Walter Lippmann joined the staff of the *New York Herald Tribune* in September 1931 and remained there as the nation's most influential columnist of all time until he left the newspaper for *Newsweek* magazine in 1962.[39] Still, despite Lippmann's move to the friendly *Herald Tribune*, Hoover remained suspicious and aloof from him. Not even a personal plea from Marie Meloney, *Herald Tribune* Sunday magazine editor and long-time friend of the Hoovers, could convince the president to grant Lippmann a personal interview.[40]

The death of the *World* was only one of many changes in the Hoover years. In August 1931, Robert McLean succeeded his father William L. McLean, as president of the *Philadelphia Bulletin* after the elder McLean died at age 80, ending decades of his leadership at the *Bulletin*. A month earlier the *Washington Post* nearly folded. After much wrangling in court about who had been promised the sale of the newspaper, owner Edward B. McLean decided to spurn an offer from the Hearst Corporation for $3 million and to lead a much weakened *Post* through the depression years. It is likely that Hearst would have merged the *Post* out of existence. The other bidder had been Hoover supporter David Lawrence, who a few years later began publication of the magazine, *U.S. News*. Lawrence probably would have provided a strong base for published pro-Hoover sentiment in Washington.[41]

In Chicago, *Daily News* owner Walter Strong, one of the most ardent Hoover enthusiasts among newspaper moguls, died in the spring of 1931. This could have been a blow to Hoover's influence among Midwest readers, but the newspaper was purchased six months later by Frank Knox, a former high-level Hearst executive, and by Theodore T. Ellis, a blanket-company executive.[42] Knox assumed the duties of publisher of the *Daily News* and immediately wired to Hoover that he would appreciate a message of congratulations from the president that could be published in the newspaper.[43] Hoover complied,[44] and Knox and Hoover became mutual admirers. In early 1932 Knox was named by the president as chair of a citizen's group against hoarding.[45] Hoover even considered asking Knox to be chairman of the Republican National Committee in 1932.[46] In 1932, the *Chicago Post* merged with the *Daily News* leaving that city with one less newspaper. Through the next nine years, the *Tribune* dominated the morning market in Chicago, until the creation of the *Chicago Sun* in 1941.[47]

Hoover and his financial advisor Edgar Rickard passed on an opportunity to directly influence New York newspaper readers. Frank Gannett, who had called on Hoover at Rapidan, and Stanley High, the editor of the *Christian Herald*, visited Rickard in January 1931. Both Gannett and High wanted Rickard's financial support for a new pro-Hoover newspaper in New York. Rickard told them he was in a delicate position, because he was in charge of Hoover's personal finances and could not appear to be funding a newspaper. In late 1931 and early 1932 Gannett pressed Rickard during a series of five visits, but again Rickard declined.[48] Gannett's former newspaper, the troubled *Brooklyn Eagle*, folded in 1932. In the White House and in his dealings with publishers and editors nationwide, Hoover saw new faces and unfamiliar personalities.

Lippmann's departure for the *New York Herald Tribune* also signaled two new trends in serious newspaper coverage. His column marked the first time that a major newspaper opened its news pages to regular commentary of a different political point of view and the first time one invested heavily in a signed column of political commentary. Lippmann, a liberal, was hired by conservative publisher Ogden Reid, because Reid realized that Lippmann could draw new *Herald Tribune* readers. For six months, Reid advertised Lippmann's impending arrival and created an air of expectation. Allan Nevins, a noted biographer, sketched a laudatory piece on Lippmann that appeared in the *Herald Tribune* just two days after Lippmann's first column was published.[49] Reid's experiment worked perfectly. Despite his left-of-center philosophy, Lippmann was an immediate success and became one of the first powerful American columnists. He eventually claimed a readership independent of the flagship newspaper, reaching syndication among 600 newspapers. Many popular and successful columnists would grace the pages of American newspapers in the ensuing decade, including some who would begin their commentary during the Hoover Administration. They would bring new editorial voices to the political scene, expanding greatly the number of political observers writing about Washington. But, of course, none would ever be as popular as Lippmann.[50]

At the same time, there was a growing insistence among newspaper editors that news pages operate independently from the ideology and philosophy of the editorial page. This editorial independence was accompanied by a call for probing interpretation that went beyond the surface of the news. Lippmann himself told a Yale University audience in early 1931 that the era of the "dramatic, disorderly, episodic type" of personal journalism had ended and a new era of "objective orderly and comprehensive presentation of the news" was ascending.[51] Marie Meloney, the editor of the *New York Herald Tribune* magazine, said in an interview a few months earlier that journalists had to begin to look at complex world affairs more expansively and stop reporting surface details. "I have always thought there was a place in newspapers for an interpretation of the daily trend of news," she added.[52] Unfortunately, in retrospect, Mrs. Meloney's words seem unconvincing. She was the same editor who worked industriously behind the scenes for Hoover's causes, even tattling to the White House about those who might criticize the president.

Still, many Washington journalists in 1931 considered themselves independent of ideology. Within the industry, discussion of this concept drew more attention. Certainly, for years to come many newspapers such as the *Chicago Tribune* and the *Baltimore Sun* would remain heavily biased even in their news coverage, but hard times and an increasingly despondent readership had caused newspapers to rethink how they ought to interact with government and the people. One of the largest universities in the country, the University of Illinois (11,000 students), even went so far as to require its few journalism students to take a two-day battery of exams to earn certification as journalists.[53] The highly subjective exams smacked of government interference with free expression and were soon dropped, but the experiment at the University of Illinois demonstrated that many in the profession were trying to establish journalistic standards.

But for Hoover, the greatest change was not in newspaper leadership or in the rise of objectivity, but in how leading publishers perceived his qualifications. Many publishers had climbed aboard the Hoover bandwagon in 1928 because of their dislike for Al Smith or because they saw in Hoover a nonpolitician who would lead the country away from politics as usual. Democrats such as William Randolph Hearst were among the first to abandon Hoover after the Wall Street crash. Roy Howard, Scripps-Howard chairman of the board, had found Hoover unreceptive to his suggestions for better press relations, and his newspapers reflected an increasingly anti-Hoover attitude. "Well, it will be some consolation if the depression would only break Roy Howard and Hearst," Hoover told Joslin in April 1932. Joslin noted in his diary: "He actually hates both of them and for good and sufficient reasons."[54] When intermediaries tried to arrange a reconciliation between Howard and Hoover a few weeks later, Hoover angrily responded: "I won't ask that crook Howard to come here. If that swine wants to come here he will have to come without an invitation."[55] Hoover relented, but when the meeting took place, it did not go well. "On the contrary," Joslin wrote in his diary that night, "the president bawled him out on half a dozen different issues. It wasn't the right tactics for Howard is thoroughly frightened by conditions and is ready to come to a truce."[56]

Some Southern Democratic publishers, whose dislike for Smith in 1928 goaded them into supporting Hoover, quickly abandoned the president after the Wall Street crash. The *Washington Post* retreated from its pro-Hoover position, and while Adolph S. Ochs continued to visit with Hoover frequently and cultivate his friendship, even *The New York Times* cooled.

The smell of failure drove some newspaper editorial writers and newspaper owners away from the president, but many sincerely felt that Hoover had not turned out to be the leader they had hoped for. He seemed to them to be mired in indecision and personal animosity toward those who would criticize his administration. John Cowles, owner of the *Des Moines Register*, told Mark Sullivan in mid-1932 that newspaper publishers were waiting anxiously for Hoover to promote some government program to combat the economic downturn, any program. "He thinks this is true almost regardless of the nature of the program or the details of it," Sullivan wrote to Hoover.[57] The overwhelming newspaper support that Hoover had enjoyed in 1928 and throughout his public career had quickly fallen away. Joslin noted in his diary in August 1931: "The press is giving the president grave concern. Many of the men are hostile, not only the Democratic but the Republican writers." He incorrectly blamed the hostility on an increasingly "wet" and "pink" philosophy among newspapers.[58] Hoover still supported Prohibition, but the country was turning away from the unsuccessful social experiment, and Hoover could not muster editorial support for the cause. "One significant turn is the President's refusal to talk with any of the newspapermen about prohibition," Joslin noted in early 1932.[59]

Hoover maintained a thin majority of support from American newspapers through 1932, but even among many Hoover loyalists, the ardor had abated. Only a few large dailies remained dedicated supporters. Among those were Harry Chandler's *Los Angeles Times*, the *Boston Globe*, the *Boston Transcript*, the *New York Herald Tribune*, the *Chicago Daily News*, the *Kansas City Star*, the *Oakland Tribune*, the *Des Moines Register*, the *Kansas City Times*, the *Christian Science Monitor*, and the *Buffalo News*.

Magazines, less influential in American politics than were newspapers, sustained heavy economic losses during the early years of the depression from both decreased advertising and declining circulation. Most of the nation's most popular magazines continued to publish, but with fewer readers. Among the political or public affairs magazines, only one actually increased its circulation substantially during the Hoover years: *Time*. Founder Henry Luce had cultivated a successful formula of condensed weekly news coverage that appealed to busy readers. Luce, a committed Republican, assumed sole ownership of *Time* just as Hoover reached the White House, and the famed magazine entrepreneur continued to expand *Time*'s influence and readership throughout the early 1930s. Luce even expanded his publishing interests in 1930 by establishing *Fortune* magazine while other publishers cut back.[60]

But Hoover did not fare well among even sympathetic magazine publishers during the latter half of his presidency. As with the newspaper people, the publishers were becoming either restless or downright hostile. As the election campaign got into full swing in March of 1932, Joslin approached Hoover about setting up a special interview with the *Saturday Evening Post*. "Forget it," Hoover responded irritably. Joslin reminded the president that the *Post* had been loyal to him and deserved better. "Get over worrying about the Saturday Post," Hoover snapped back. "That's a Republican publication. It will come around all right in June [GOP convention]. It has nowhere to go." Joslin dropped the subject, noting in his diary that night that it was no use trying to reason with Hoover when he was in that frame of mind.[61] Among newspaper and magazine people, Hoover's enemy list was growing, but he showed no inclination to soothe the supporters he still had and he failed to use any media route open to him to improve his image and reassure the uneasy electorate.

THE WHITE HOUSE PRESS CORPS

The greatest deficiency in Hoover's media strategy, however, continued to be the deteriorating relationship with White House reporters. Though there were brief occasions when relations thawed, Hoover's running battle with correspondents became so stormy that by the time the reelection campaign was underway, both the president and the reporters were looking for reasons to criticize each other. Hoover held 61 press conferences in 1931 and 1932 and only a few times did he comment much beyond the material contained in written handouts.[62] Meanwhile, his favorite journalists enjoyed his confidence and personal attention. Hoover's daily appointment record shows that Hoover continued to visit over breakfast with Mark Sullivan three and sometimes four times a week, for instance.[63]

Resentment built into an insolent silence on both sides. Major media throughout 1931 carried hardly any articles devoted to White House press relations. Nothing much was left to say. In April 1931 Frederick Landis, a columnist with the Scripps-Howard *Indianapolis Times* (circ. 74,000), did address the topic, telling his readers that White House reporters had found Hoover less communicative then even Coolidge. "This is a risky experiment, since the newspaper men can do as much to make as unmake the chief executive," Landis wrote.[64]

Hoover's close advisors—including Sullivan, Rickard, Joslin, and Akerson—also greatly resented the White House press corps and usually supported Hoover's stubborn denunciations. The misrepresentations file that had grown fat during the Secretary of Commerce years was used during the presidency, too. But so much was written about Hoover during his White House years that aides could focus only on what they considered to be the most grievous misstatements. They responded to major accusations such as the *New York World* series on the supposed oil scandal or to major magazine articles or books. To the misrepresentations file was added the "smear" file for those particularly odious affronts.[65] But when the market crashed and the voters began to turn on Hoover, the responses to the misrepresentations and smears drew little public sympathy. Collecting copies of the offending articles or books and responding to them without receiving the heretofore expected public outrage merely served to add to the gloom and suspicions in the White House.

Still fulfilling Hoover's personal financial needs, Rickard offered advice and counsel to the president but looked on helplessly and with increasing anger as Hoover's image faded. "Fully 50 percent of the Washington correspondents are radical, or representing papers inimical to HH, such as Hearst or Scripps chain and independent *Baltimore Sun* and *Chicago Tribune*," Rickard noted in his diary in mid-1931. "This group have regular meeting [*sic*] to find ways and means of discrediting HH." Rickard predicted correctly that *The New York Times* would support Hoover between elections and revert to favoring the Democrats during the 1932 campaign. He reflected that newspapers were experiencing financial difficulties and that it would be prudent to suggest to sympathetic businesses that they could help Hoover and squeeze some newspapers by withdrawing all advertising from the offending papers.[66]

Replacing Akerson with veteran reporter Theodore Joslin certainly did not alleviate press antagonism either. Joslin's perspective shifted when he assumed his duties as press secretary. Hardly able to contain his disdain and contempt for his former colleagues, Joslin filled his diary with disparaging remarks about the White House correspondents and scorn for their reporting techniques. In mid-1931, Hoover, in the presence of many reporters, was suddenly called away from a political gathering to a secret meeting with Secretary of State Stimson. The sudden departure went unreported. Joslin sneered that reporters were "awfully dumb" not to catch on.[67] Two months later he recorded:

As a newspaperman, it is amazing to me that the press does not watch the White House itself more closely in such a time as this. Hardly a night passes but the President has some outstanding person to the House for a conference—Gifford of the telephone company a few days ago, for example, and Henry Ford some weeks ago. Yet they come, confer and go without the press ever getting wise, even coming at five in the afternoon. The fellows are asleep at the switch. Not the kind of work us men did during the World War. The present day correspondents seem to think all the news should be given to them without any effort on their part and are continuously crabbing because they don't get more. If they were active at all, they would be worked ragged. If they were awake, the President's task would be that much harder and goodness knows it is hard enough now.[68]

When several large industries threatened to cut employee wages in September 1931, Hoover issued a public statement condemning the decision. Joslin described press handling of the statement as "not entirely satisfactory" but "adequate." He wrote in his diary that a "policy of silence" by Hoover would have been best, suggesting that reporters did not handle such policy statements well and it would be more politic not to tell them anything.[69] Like Hoover, Joslin neither respected nor commiserated with White House reporters. Joslin thought that the new generation of correspondents in the White House was unredeemable. If Hoover and his supporters had hoped Joslin might be able to better interact with White House reporters than Akerson, they were badly disappointed.

Personal conversations and comments by Hoover during this period reveal a schizophrenic president, angry and combative toward reporters one day and remorseful and forgiving the next. The pressure of a deepening depression and a stubborn Congress had taken its toll on the president. In June 1931 Byron Price, Associated Press chief White House correspondent, received a surprise request from Joslin. The press secretary pleaded with Price to visit with the president, who, in Joslin's words, was "in a state." Joslin added: "Maybe a talk with you will do him good." When Price entered the Oval Office, he was stunned. "He didn't look to me like the Hoover I had been seeing. His hair was rumpled. He was almost crouching behind his desk, and he burst out at me with a volley of angry words—not against me or against the press, but against the politicians and foreign governments." Price met privately with the president several times after that, not to obtain comments for an interview but to soothe the distraught president, who, during each of those sessions, would complain that the public and politicians had let him down.[70] It is interesting that he unburdened his troubles onto a member of the press corps with which he ostensibly was feuding.

In January 1932 Hoover and Joslin ventured over to the Washington Press Club to attend a Gridiron Dinner, as was the custom for presidents in those days. They had agreed that they would stay only for about 15 minutes, but "the club gave them a good hand," Joslin wrote in his diary that night, and so the two stayed for several hours until the room had to be cleared of tables to provide extra space for dancing. Even then, Hoover, enjoying himself immensely while mixing with the journalists, left only reluctantly.[71] A few weeks earlier, both the journalists and the president's staff came together in a reverent tribute to pay their respects to Richard Oulahan, *The New York Times* Washington bureau chief, who died on December 30, 1931.[72] "It can well be said of him that he collected his news as a gentleman and wrote his articles as a scholar," Joslin noted in his diary.[73]

As all these incidents suggest, Hoover and Joslin knew that reporters were human, just like everyone else. Some were honorable; some were not. But Hoover just could not get over his fear that reporters would misquote him or otherwise intentionally distort his ideas, and he really felt ill at ease around them. In October 1932, a month before the fateful presidential election, Hoover was scheduled to speak at the annual meeting of the American Bar Association and he was squirming at the thought of addressing a large gathering of lawyers. "There are two classes of people who always make me nervous," Hoover told Joslin. "One is your profession and the other is lawyers. Whenever I appear before newspapermen or lawyers I feel like a microbe on a needle under a microscope."[74] In January 1932, Herbert Corey of the *Saturday Evening Post* came to Hoover's defense, telling readers that the president had been mistreated by reporters. Hoover was not responsible for his bad press, Corey wrote. All presidents struggled to deal with demanding reporters, and Hoover was no exception, Corey added.[75]

On those days of uneasiness, Hoover took umbrage with everything reporters wrote or did. In a July 1931 article in *The New York Times* Turner Catledge described to his readers how Hoover's motorcade had driven quickly back to Washington from Rapidan when a conference on a moratorium on German reparations was suddenly convened. The reference to the speeding motorcade was innocuous enough, but Hoover disliked the suggestion that his entourage was endangering lives and warned Catledge about such comments.[76] Correspondents asked to be allowed to follow the president to Rapidan during the same month, and a nettled Hoover told Joslin: "If they stop within five miles of my camp, I'll have them arrested." Joslin noted in his diary, "There is almost as much love lost between the president and the press as between God Almighty and the devil himself."[77] Two weeks later, Joslin urged Hoover to host a reception for reporters. It would have been good public relations especially just before the general election campaign. Hoover said, no. He added:

Don't mention it again. That is one thing I won't do. They have no respect for the office I hold. . . . Once I am re-elected I am going to clean that bunch out whatever the consequences may be. I have stood for all from them that I can. I don't understand how you can defend them. They have not treated you with even common decency. I have enough on fifty of them to hang them. Let any of them make one move after November and I'll go for them.[78]

Joslin wrote that night: "How the president hates the press!"[79]

Disgusted reporters remained quiet through most of 1931, except for a volley of articles and editorials in *Editor & Publisher* magazine, the newspaper trade journal.[80] But eventually the reporters openly criticized the president. J. Frederick Essary, *Baltimore Sun* White House correspondent, wrote a commentary for *American Mercury* outlining how every single department in Washington had a press agent who tried to block legitimate stories or put a positive spin on them. He called the federal government the "greatest propaganda establishment in the world."[81]

Two months later, Paul Anderson, correspondent for the Pulitzer-owned *St. Louis Post-Dispatch*, wrote a lengthy article for the *Nation*, castigating the White House for its surly attitude toward reporters. Of Hoover he wrote: "His incredible sensitiveness to unfavorable publicity arises from a peculiar but not illogical cause. Knowing that the newspapers made him, he assumes they can with equal ease destroy him. In this he is mistaken."[82] Anderson reviewed the previous three years of press-presidential interaction and claimed that Hoover had forced the relationship to a low point, because of his dislike for reporters. Anderson told his readers that Hoover had even pressured publishers to fire two reporters who had written articles unfavorable toward the Administration, recalling, without mentioning any names, incidents involving Drew Pearson, *Baltimore Sun* correspondent, and Robert S. Allen, of the *Christian Science Monitor*, in August of 1931.[83] Anderson described Catledge's article about the speeding Hoover caravan as a "wholly sympathetic story" and exclaimed that Hoover was angered by the story "for God knows what reason." He concluded: "The Washington correspondents are being requested—and, as many of them believe, under duress—to swallow and act upon the theory that devotion to a rotten and inept political administration is synonymous with patriotism."[84] The criticism might have been better accepted if it had not come from correspondents working for strongly Democratic journals. Nevertheless, it was clear that press relations had deteriorated badly even from the tenuous days early in the presidency and that both Hoover and his staff had turned to plotting against reporters rather than working out their differences.

DEEPENING NATIONAL CRISIS

The great tragedy of the Hoover Administration's failed press relations was, of course, his resulting inability to calm the public's uneasiness over business and bank failures and farm foreclosures. The panic mounted and perpetuated itself. Many in the Hoover Administration and in the Republican Party had anticipated a natural upward swing in business after the initial shock of the Wall Street crash had died away. But conditions only worsened in 1931 and 1932 and, in the absence of a daily message of reassurance from the White House to the news media and finally to the public, whispers began that Hoover was incompetent and a do-nothing. The whispers soon turned to shouts. By mid-1931, few spoke with much enthusiasm about an impending recovery, and discussion of better days ahead nearly ceased.

On January 3, 1931, a group of 300 farmers and their wives entered the town of England, Arkansas, armed with shotguns. Drought had wiped out the 1930 crop, and they had no sustenance to carry them through the winter. Many had families who had not eaten in three days. The Red Cross had exhausted its food supplies, so the farmers approached local merchants and told them their families must have food. After a brief exchange, the farmers were given what they needed and they left. Exaggerated accounts of the incident spread and in some quarters the farmers were described as an unruly mob, though most major newspapers only recounted what had happened and made note that state authorities had to be summoned. Congress took note of the pathetic plight of the Arkansas farmers and the incident served as a catalyst for drought aid to farmers in the West. A bill for $45 million in aid moved quickly through Congress in the next two weeks.[85] In his memoirs Hoover denounced the reporting of the incident as a plot by newspapers and political adversaries to make him look unkind. In fact, much of the exaggeration in print was probably just confusion and sloppy reporting. Hoover himself incorrectly listed in his memoirs the month that the Arkansas incident occurred.[86] But the confrontation illustrated the extent of the hopelessness and despair that dominated the country and started 1931 ominously.

The farmers' desperate actions and the response by Congress helps also to underline the dilemma that the Administration faced in 1931. Help was needed everywhere. Where to start and how much to spend? Both Congress and Hoover, clinging to nineteenth-century public policies, were reluctant either to unbalance the budget or to raise taxes, but everyone in Washington knew something needed to be done. "The presidency at this time is primarily an employment agency to find jobs for some 120,000,000 people," Joslin noted in August 1931.[87] The United States Employment Service expanded its activities in 1931 with an extra $500,000 appropriation.[88] The fiscal budget for 1931 included a 5 percent increase, and most of the extra money was used for more spending on construction, rivers and harbors, public works, and veterans relief.[89] But by early 1931 six million were unemployed, business was down 28 percent from the previous year, and there had been 1,345 bank failures in the previous 12 months.[90] The public demanded more, but Hoover hesitated. He could not advocate direct governmental loans to businesses or, even worse, public assistance to individuals. The "dole" had come to Great Britain, and U.S. conservatives, including Hoover, recoiled from such tactics.

The collapse of the European economy in 1931 destroyed any hope of recovery in the United States, and conditions worsened. Britain left the gold standard in September, and twenty-five other countries followed suit. World trade slackened even more.[91] The same month, Japan invaded Manchuria. Militarists had gained the upper hand in the Japanese government. Cramped for living space in the islands off the Asian continent, the Japanese coveted Manchuria and all of Asia as their sphere of influence, a large land mass where the Japanese could spread out and prosper. Hoover and Stimson squabbled over imposing sanctions against Japan. The more isolationist Hoover saw sanctions as a way of provoking war, as indeed they finally did in 1941 when Roosevelt banned the sale of U.S. scrap iron and oil to Japan.[92] In truth, Hoover worried about Manchuria, but domestic problems had so overwhelmed his presidency that he did not have the time or the support for dealing vigorously with the Japanese invasion. The League of Nations did eventually impose sanctions on Japan, but the Japanese simply withdrew from the League and ignored the condemnation.

In August 1931 the committee that drew up Hoover's voluntary plan of action to combat unemployment, PECE, was renamed the President's Organization on Unemployment Relief (POUR) under Walter S. Gifford, the president of the American Telephone and Telegraph Company and continued the fight for voluntary aid to fight unemployment.[93] The president tried to encourage spending in the private sector by expanding credit to banks, industry, and individuals.[94] But voluntary relief efforts were hardly sufficient. Unemployment climbed to 13 percent, and Gifford's efforts seemed pitifully inadequate.[95] In October Hoover met with the nation's leading bankers in hopes of devising a more liberal credit system and to save failing banks, but even his own Secretary of the Treasury Andrew Mellon refused to contribute money to a sinking bank in Mellon's hometown of Pittsburgh, and the attempt at voluntary cooperation failed miserably.[96]

Now the president would be facing voters in little more than a year and, instead of the economy rebounding just before the election as had been predicted since the Wall Street crash in 1929, it appeared that the depression would continue. Hoover would be forced to tell voters that they would have to accept his judgment that better times were just ahead. Reluctantly, he realized that volunteerism was not working. During his state of the union address on December 8, 1931, he proposed to Congress the creation of the Reconstruction Finance Corporation (RFC) to provide direct federal aid to business and local governments. The RFC came into being in January 1932 with a $1.5 billion budget and by March had loaned hundreds of millions of dollars to ailing banks, insurance companies, and other institutions. Bank failures slowed from 346 in January to 46 in April.[97]

Enraged conservatives felt Hoover had abandoned his ideals. Many less conservative congressmen, who were being bombarded with pleas for help from their home districts, felt that only direct relief to individuals would provide adequate relief and reassure the public. Hoover could not go that far. It was his feeling that aid to businesses would prime the pump and would provide enough additional funding to revive the economy, while putting people back to work. But basically recipients of the government loans paid off their debts and refused to spend more or to hire more. The RFC, the most extraordinarily populist step in Hoover's career, had little or no impact. Public unrest grew daily.

By the spring of 1932, the situation had grown desperate, and special interest groups clamored for the president's and Congress's attention. Many middle-class and poor people had reached the end of their resources. They were destitute, hungry, and desperate. They had somehow expected someone somewhere to save them, and in three years no one had stepped forward. What they read in their newspapers and magazines, and what they heard and saw on radio and in newsreels did not reassure them. They complained that the president had failed them, and they began to associate the Great Humanitarian with the inhumanity of hunger and homelessness. One such group decided in early spring 1932 to take matters into their own hands, and so would begin a series of events that would tarnish the president's name forever.

NOTES

1. Erik Barnouw, *A Tower in Babel: A History of Broadcasting in the United States*, vol. 1 (New York: Oxford, 1966), pp. 223–24.

2. Ibid., pp. 193, 251.

3. Ibid., pp. 250–51. See also "Appendix F—Radio Addresses by the President," *Public Papers of the Presidents: Herbert Hoover 1932–1933*, pp. 1277–88.

4. David Lawrence oral history interview with Raymond Henle, director of the Herbert Hoover oral history project, Sarasota, Fla., Feb. 14, 1967, p. 23, Oral History Files, HHPL.

5. "Radio Firm Denies Barring Priest, Critic of Hoover: He Quits Talks," *New York Herald Tribune*, Jan. 5, 1931. See also Alan Brinkley, *Voices of Protest: Huey Long, Father Coughlin, and the Great Depression* (New York: Knopf, 1982), p. 100.

6. John F. Roche, "Kaltenborn Views Radio As Menace," *Editor & Publisher*, 62, no. 38 (Feb. 8, 1930), p. 9.

7. "Bickel on Radio," *Editor & Publisher*, 63, no. 24 (Nov. 1, 1930), p. 34;

"Radio 'Circulation,' " *Editor & Publisher* editorial, 64, no. 8 (July 11, 1931), p. 26; "Radio Owners' Habits Shown by Survey," *Editor & Publisher*, 64, no. 8 (July 11, 1931), p. 9.

8. "Radio Chain Refused News Pictures for Television Transmission," *Editor & Publisher* 64, no. 9 (July 18, 1930), p. 16.

9. John F. Roche, "Kaltenborn Views Radio As Menace," *Editor & Publisher*, 62, no. 38 (Feb. 8, 1930), p. 9.

10. H. V. Kaltenborn, *Fifty Fabulous Years 1900–1950* (New York: G. P. Putnam's Sons, 1950), pp. 111, 168.

11. "Radio Competition," *Editor & Publisher*, 63, no. 35 (Jan. 17, 1931), p. 26.

12. "Wile Accompanies Mr. Hoover on Proposed Mid-Western Trip," *New York Herald Tribune*, June 1, 1930.

13. Frederic Wile, President's Personal File, Columbia Broadcasting System, Box 216, HHPL.

14. Barnouw, *Tower in Babel*, p. 247.

15. Lloyd Jacquet, "Greatest Broadcasting Feat to Be Attempted This Week," *New York Herald Tribune*, Jan. 19, 1930, entertainment section, pp. 1–2.

16. Harold Brayman, "Hoover Listens In on Naval Parley," *New York Post*, Jan. 21, 1930, p. 1.

17. "Radio to Carry Red Cross Plea by Mr. Coolidge," *New York Herald Tribune*, Jan. 20, 1931, pp. 1–2.

18. See cover and cover story, "Aeronautical Radio Inc.," *Time*, 16:2 (July 14, 1930), p. 32; Herbert Hoover, Jr., "Radio Speeds the Airplane," *Speed* magazine, June 1930, p. 5; "Hoover, Jr., Talks before Radio Group," *Los Angeles Times* undated 1931 article from clipping file, 1931, HHPL.

19. David Lawrence oral history interview with Raymond Henle, director of the Herbert Hoover Oral History project, Sarasota, Fla., Feb. 14, 1966, p. 22, oral history files, HHPL.

20. WSP to HH, May 5, 1931, pp. 1–2, President's Personal File, Columbia Broadcasting System, Box 216, HHPL.

21. "Appendix F—Radio Speeches of the President," *Public Papers of the President: Herbert Hoover 1932–1933*, pp. 1276–78.

22. "President Plans to Make 5 Speeches in November," *New York Herald Tribune*, Nov. 4, 1930.

23. "Appendix F"—*Public Papers of the President 1932–1933*, pp. 1275–79. These estimates are based largely on this citation, which shows a total of 71 speeches and addresses; but as newspaper articles during the Hoover presidency sometimes discussed radio addresses that did not appear in Appendix F, it is assumed that a few of Hoover's speeches somehow were not included in the official presidential papers. Probably, there were more nearly 80 speeches overall.

24. Theodore Joslin diary entry, March 6, 1932, Joslin Papers, Box 10, HHPL.

25. Joslin diary entry, March 27, 1932.

26. "Pictures a Day in President's Life," *The New York Times*, June 9, 1930, p. 1; "President Called Most Devoted to Duty in History," *New York Herald Tribune*, June 9, 1930, p. 1.

27. Joslin diary entry, May 14, 1932.

28. George H. Manning, "Talkies Get Breaks in Treaty News," *Editor & Publisher*, 62, no. 50 (May 3, 1930).

29. See Paramount and Pathé news footage, Hoover audio-visual archives, HHPL.

30. Robert H. Denton oral history interview with Stephen V. Feeley, Hoover oral history project interviewer, p. 9, Aug. 5, 1971, Rockville, Md.

31. Joslin diary entry, April 30, 1932.

32. Sydney Hollinger MacKean, "The 'Mike' and the Mighty," *New York Herald Tribune*, Nov. 23, 1930, pp. 12–13.

33. Denton oral history interview, p. 19.

34. Ibid., p. 17.

35. Richard Carroll, "The President and the Photographers," *Liberty*, July 19, 1930, pp. 42–46.

36. See George Juergens, *Joseph Pulitzer and the New York World* (Princeton: Princeton University Press, 1966).

37. Daniel Pfaff, *Joseph Pulitzer II and the Post-Dispatch: A Newspaperman's Life* (University Park: Pennsylvania State University, 1991), pp. 168–94.

38. "Scripps-Howard Buys the 'World,' " *Editor & Publisher*, 63, no. 41 (Feb. 28, 1931), pp. 5–10. See also Ronald Steel, *Walter Lippmann and the American Century* (Boston: Little, Brown, 1980), pp. 272–73.

39. Ibid., pp. 539–40.

40. Edgar Rickard diary entry, Jan. 23, 1932, Rickard Papers, HHPL.

41. "Washington Post Sale Called Off When Publisher Changes Mind," *Editor & Publisher*, 64, no. 7 (July 4, 1931), p. 12.

42. "Knox and Ellis Buy Chicago Daily News Control from W. A. Strong Estate," *Editor & Publisher*, 64, no. 13 (Aug. 15, 1931), p. 5.

43. FK telegram to HH, Aug. 11, 1931, Presidential Personal Files, Newspapers, Chicago Daily News, Box 180, HHPL.

44. HH to FK letter, Aug. 12, 1931, in ibid.

45. Richard Norton Smith, *An Uncommon Man: The Triumph of Herbert Hoover* (New York: Simon and Schuster, 1984), p. 134.

46. Joslin diary entry, April 10, 1932.

47. "Chicago News Buys and Merges Post; Sells AP to Hearst," *Editor & Publisher*, 65, no. 25 (Nov. 5, 1932), p. 6; and "Chicago Post's Passing," *Editor & Publisher* editorial, 65, no. 25 (Nov. 5, 1932), p. 18.

48. Rickard diary entries of Jan. 14, 1931; Dec. 10, 1931; Dec. 22, 1931; and Jan. 5, 1932.

49. Allan Nevins, "Walter Lippmann," *New York Herald Tribune*, Sept. 11, 1931, pp. 8–11.

50. Steel, pp. 269–82.

51. "Lippmann Sees Passing of Popular Press," *Editor & Publisher*, 63, no. 35 (Jan. 17, 1931), p. 10.

52. John F. Roche, "Sunday Stories Should Interpret News," *Editor & Publisher*, 63, no. 16 (Sept. 6, 1930), p. 9.

53. Lawrence W. Murphy, "Students Take Newspaper Examination," *Editor & Publisher*, 63, no. 1 (May 24, 1930), p. 15.

54. Joslin diary entry, April 27, 1932.

55. Joslin diary entry, May 5, 1932.

56. Ibid.

57. MS memo to HH, May 26, 1932, President's Personal Papers, Individuals, Mark Sullivan, HHPL.

58. Joslin diary entry, Aug. 25, 1931.

59. Joslin diary entry, March 14, 1932.

60. James L. Baughman, *Henry R. Luce and the Rise of the American News Media* (Boston: Twayne, 1987), pp. 62–81; W. A. Swanberg, *Luce and His Empire* (New York: Charles Scribner's Sons, 1972), pp. 66–92; Robert T. Elson, *Time Inc.: The Intimate History of a Publishing Enterprise 1923–1941* (New York: Atheneum, 1968), pp. 123–52.

61. Joslin diary entry, March 9, 1932.

62. See texts of press conferences in *Public Papers of the Presidents of the United States: Herbert Hoover 1931* (Washington: U.S. Government Printing Office, 1976).

63. "Appendix E—The President's Calendar," *Public Papers of the Presidents: Herbert Hoover 1931, 1932, and 1933*, pp. 808–26 (1931), pp. 1141–1247 (1932 and 1933).

64. Frederick Landis column, *Indianapolis Times*, April 18, 1931.

65. For a discussion of "smear books," see *The Memoirs of Herbert Hoover: The Great Depression 1929–1941* (New York: Macmillan, 1953), pp. 224–25 [hereafter referred to as Hoover memoirs, vol. 3].

66. Rickard diary entry, July 29, 1931.

67. Joslin diary entry, June 16, 1931.

68. Joslin diary entry, Aug. 7, 1931. For other Joslin comments about reporters' lack of initiative, see entries of April 25, 1932; April 28, 1932; and May 1, 1932.

69. Joslin diary entry, Sept. 24, 1931.

70. Byron Price oral history interview with Raymond Henle, director of the Herbert Hoover oral history project, March 21, 1969, Chesterton, N.Y., pp. 5–6.

71. Joslin diary entry, Jan. 23, 1932.

72. "Richard Victor Oulahan," *Editor & Publisher* editorial, 64, no. 33 (Jan. 2, 1932), p. 22.

73. Joslin diary entry, Jan. 2, 1932.

74. Joslin diary entry, Oct. 12, 1932.

75. Herbert Corey, "Presidents and the Press," *Saturday Evening Post*, 203, no. 2 (Jan. 9, 1932), pp. 25, 96.

76. Joslin diary entry, July 6, 1931.

77. Joslin diary entry, July 23, 1932.

78. Joslin diary entry, Aug. 8, 1932.

79. Ibid.

80. See "White House Censorship," *Editor & Publisher* editorial, 64, no. 9 (July 18, 1931), p. 40; "Subtle Censorship of Government News is Arising Steadily on Washington," *Editor & Publisher* 64, no. 16 (Sept. 5, 1931), p. 5; "White House News Ban on Bank Parley Upset by Correspondents," *Editor & Publisher*, 64, no. 21 (Oct. 10, 1931), p. 5.

81. J. Frederick Essary, "Uncle Sam's Ballyhoo Men," *American Mercury*, August 1931, pp. 419–22.

82. Paul Y. Anderson, "Hoover and the Press," *Nation*, 133, no. 3458 (Oct. 14, 1931), pp. 382–84.

83. "More Merry-Go-Round," *Time*, Sept. 19, 1932.

84. Ibid.

85. See "Arkansas to Urge More Aid in Drought" and "Farmers Quit at England," *The New York Times*, Jan. 5, 1931, p. 1; "Says Red Cross Can Meet Drought Need," *The New York Times*, Jan. 7, 1931, p. 1; "Red Cross Urges 10 Million Fund for Drought Aid," *New York Herald Tribune*, Jan. 11, 1931; "Red Cross Opens Drought Aid Drive," *The New York Times*, Jan. 13, 1931, p. 1; "More for the Red Cross," *The New York Times* editorial, Jan. 13, 1931; Harold Brayman, "Hoover Victory on Drought Fund Is Due in House," *New York Post*, Jan. 13, 1931, p. 1; "President Issues Red Cross Appeal; House Drops Dole," *New York Herald Tribune*, Jan. 14, 1931, p. 1; "Nation Responding to Red Cross Plea," *The New York Times*, Jan. 15, 1931, p. 1; "Drought Relief Signed; Dole Move Persists," *New York Herald Tribune*, Jan. 16, 1931, p. 1.

86. Hoover memoirs, vol. 3, pp. 55, 224.

87. Joslin diary entry, Aug. 21, 1931.

88. David Burner, *Herbert Hoover: A Public Life* (New York: Knopf, 1979), p. 262.

89. Edgar Eugene Robinson and Vaughn Davis Bornet, *Herbert Hoover: President of the United States* (Stanford: Hoover Institution Press, 1975), p. 154.

90. Ibid., p. 170.

91. Robinson and Bornet, *Herbert Hoover*, p. 184.

92. Hoover memoirs, vol. 2, p. 366; Fausold, *Presidency*, pp. 177—81; Robinson and Bornet, *Herbert Hoover*, pp. 196–200.

93. Fausold, *Presidency*, p. 149; Smith, *Uncommon Man*, p. 126.

94. Fausold, *Presidency*, p. 151.

95. Ibid., p. 150; Albert U. Romasco, *The Poverty of Abundance: Hoover, the Nation, the Depression* (New York: Oxford, 1965), pp. 165–66.

96. Jordan A. Schwarz, *The Interregnum of Despair* (Urbana: University of Illinois Press, 1970), pp. 88–89.

97. Smith, *Uncommon Man*, pp. 133–34.

7

The Bonus March

In the spring and summer of 1932 President Hoover and Congress became embroiled in a controversy that would end in tragedy and national disgrace. A bonus payment had been promised to World War I veterans in 1924 and, figuring the nation owed them money for their loyal and brave service during the European conflict, they wanted to be paid when they most needed it. In April 1932 a group of Portland, Oregon, veterans decided to take matters into their own hands and travel to Washington to lobby for a bonus payment owed to them for their military service. Historians generally agree that the eventual clash over payment of the bonus was a virtual public relations disaster for the president, but, as will be seen, most media publicly acclaimed the president when the sorry confrontation ended, and the impact upon the Hoover presidency is questionable.

The controversy began in 1924 when Congress voted to issue service certificates as part of the World War Omnibus Bill. These promissory notes were intended to provide four million war veterans with a modest retirement lump sum payment of about $1,000 each in 1945, or about half a year's wages. Veterans of the Civil War and the Spanish-American War had retirement benefits, and World War veterans hoped for more than the $60 they had received when they returned to civilian life in 1919.

Congressmen assumed that the prosperity of 1924 would continue indefinitely and the money would be provided from interest and increased government revenues during the 21 years from passage to payment. The Omnibus Bill, as it emerged, was a compromise. The American Legion had pushed hard for an immediate bonus, but settled for a payout in 1945 because fiscal conservatives did not want to burden the country with an immediate cash obligation. President Calvin Coolidge, himself a staunch conservative, vetoed the bill; but the measure enjoyed widespread support from the public and Congress overrode Coolidge's opposition.[1] The memory of the veterans' sacrifices was fresh, and the payment would be due in the distant future.

When the market crashed, many veterans were thrown out of work and clamored for their money immediately. Congress responded with a partial measure in 1931 that would allow ex-soldiers to borrow half the money at 4.5 percent interest. This was passed over Hoover's veto.[2] But this did not seem enough for many who had been out of work for two years and who had no means to pay back the loan or the interest. The unemployed veterans wanted payment in full immediately. Yet, they met stiff opposition. In September 1931 at an annual convention even the leaders of the American Legion, with Hoover's urging, voted against endorsing the immediate payment.[3]

In January 1932 Texas Rep. Wright Patman, prime sponsor of several bonus bills, introduced a measure that called for such an immediate payment. It would have cost the government $2.4 billion at a time when the entire national budget totaled about $3.7 billion. The money would have been paid by printing currency not backed by gold reserves and so would have caused inflation and weakened the dollar. The bill came before the House Ways and Means Committee in April. There, members voted 15 to 10 against bringing it to the House floor. By mid-May the bill appeared to be permanently thwarted.[4]

Three thousand miles away in Portland, Oregon, a group of bedraggled veterans read about the stalled measure and reacted with disappointment and concern. They decided to take their case to Washington. As in other American cities, the unemployment rate in Portland was climbing. Many original bonus marchers had held decent jobs and were used to a middle-class lifestyle.[5] They saw themselves as war heroes down on their luck.[6]

Their leader was Walter W. Waters, 34, a former assistant supervisor of a cannery in Portland. By 1932, he and his family had spent all their savings. Waters, a former Army sergeant, had nowhere to turn. Waters had charisma and leadership qualities. During the ordeal in Washington, the marchers followed many paths, and sometimes Waters came under fire from his own men. But in the end, they came back to him because his powerful personality held them together.[7]

The veterans had risked their lives for their country. Some had been wounded, had suffered the horrible pains of mustard gas attacks or had endured cold, disease, privation, and hunger. They felt the nation owed something in return. Calling themselves the Bonus Expeditionary Force, or B.E.F., 300 ex-soldiers left Portand for Washington in mid-May. They rode in empty railroad boxcars or occasionally traveled on foot.[8]

The cross-country journey was essentially a spontaneous gesture. Bonus historian Roger Daniels notes that the first report anywhere of the march came on April 29 in the *Portland Oregonian* in a brief story on page 17. In that story a meeting to discuss a planned march to Washington was announced.[9] This modest article reflected the veterans' lack of knowledge of public relations. Rather than doing something spectacular to attract national attention, they went about their protest isolated from other veterans, proceeding almost as if they were announcing formation of a staid, would-be tourist club.

The marchers gained their first national publicity from an incident in St. Louis on May 20, and it was hardly favorable. When officials of the Baltimore & Ohio Railroad prevented them from boarding the boxcars in St. Louis, the men marched across a bridge over the Mississippi River and into the railyards at East St. Louis, Illinois. There, an impasse developed. When the engines were first brought out, the veterans scrambled aboard the waiting boxcars. Railroad officials responded by returning the engines to the roundhouses. This scene repeated itself several times. On May 24, Illinois Gov. Louis L. Emmerson sent the National Guard to East St. Louis, and the Guard transported the men to the Indiana state line. In turn, the governors of Indiana, Ohio, Pennsylvania, and Maryland arranged for truck transportation through their states. No politician wanted the marchers tarrying in his jurisdiction.[10] The marchers hardly were in control of their public image.

The East St. Louis standoff had two other important side effects. The marchers entered the national limelight, and thereafter their activities were reported by the nation's major newspapers and wire services. Meanwhile, other veterans from around the country took note of the marchers' determination. Separate, independent groups of veterans set out for Washington. What had been a spontaneous gesture by a few hundred desperate men turned into a national march of several thousand veterans.

Such abrupt national attention created a public relations problem, which the Portland group did not fully recognize. The first facts that many Americans read about these men were that they had illegally boarded trains and refused to disembark. It was reported that they blocked the trains from leaving while, at one point, soaping the rail tracks. Then, stories were written about their transportation across much of the country at taxpayer expense by the National Guard. No matter how miserable these men were and no matter how noble their past service, this first impression hurt their cause.

Conservative journals jumped on them, labeling them rabble-rousers and troublemakers. Moderate and liberal publications clucked unsympathetically or remained silent. An organized lobbying campaign may not have been a logical step for such a group of unemployed. But attention to press relations and public imagery could have convinced more reporters and editors that the marchers, at least, had the same aims and goals to which all American citizens were entitled in seeking redress of their grievances.

News reports and editorials reflected generally unfavorable reaction. A negative May 24 article in the conservative *Chicago Tribune*, for example, described a "rising temper on the part of the veterans." The next day, an editorial, "If This Is a Lark What's a Riot?" characterized the veterans as a "nucleus of a destructive mob." The editorial said, "They will be a disturbance wherever they go, if not a potential danger."[11]

The liberal *St. Louis Post-Dispatch* withheld editorial comment, but local staff news stories reported that the veterans had "descended on Caseyville, Illinois," and "took charge of trains in East St. Louis" while the railroad refused to "haul them the rest of the way east as nonpaying passengers."[12] A front page Associated Press story in *The New York Times* gave a detailed report of the confrontation saying the marchers had "seized" a train and quoting Illinois state officials who described the situation as "very serious."[13] The *San Francisco Examiner*, the flagship newspaper of the William Randolph Hearst chain, carried almost no coverage of the East St. Louis confrontation, just a two-paragraph front-page article and a four-paragraph article inside.[14] These news reports and editorials were typical and were mirrored on the pages of the other newspapers sampled. Editorial and news reaction reflected little support for the marchers, among liberal, moderate, and conservative newspapers. The incidents in St. Louis gave the ex-soldiers attention, but not the sympathy and public support they needed to convert Congress to their cause.

When the veterans arrived in Washington, most of them settled in an area of mud flats along the Anacostia River near the Capitol, though smaller camps sprouted in several other places. In their early weeks in Washington, the veterans sought food from residents and charitable organizations and tried to establish contact with congressmen. Marchers from other parts of the country joined the Portland group, and by the middle of June more than 20,000 were in Washington.

Hoover at first decided to leave supervision and control of the Bonus Marchers to Pelham D. Glassford, D.C. superintendent of police and a former Army general. Glassford, a veteran, was sympathetic to the men and soon became their benefactor rather than antagonist.[15]

The president understood the plight of the veterans but feared they would turn into a mob. Press Secretary Theodore Joslin advised Hoover to turn the marchers away at the D.C. boundary lines before they entered

Washington in late May. Hoover rejected the idea noting that it would "almost inevitably result in bloodshed." He added, "Trouble most be avoided at all costs."[16] Bonus March historian Donald Lisio points out that, despite these fears, Hoover quietly ordered that the veterans be provided with hundreds of tents, cots, bedsacks, field kitchens, Army rations, and clothing by the federal government while they were camped in Washington. He was, after all, the same man who had provided humanitarian aid to Europeans before, during, and after World War I and who had engineered widespread relief to victims of the nation's worst flood in history in 1927. But Hoover failed to publicize his help to the veterans, and the public was left to believe that the aid was Glassford's idea. Later, when disease broke out among the veterans in their filthy encampment, Hoover ordered that a makeshift hospital be built but did not publicize his order and, again, it was generally reported that the hospital was Glassford's idea.[17]

Whatever his motives in these gestures, the president convinced himself that many elements of the B.E.F. were dangerous. After the marchers had been camped in Washington for two weeks, for example, Hoover told Joslin that he would not go out in public because "too many assassins [are] around."[18] Hoover also told Joslin that he would meet with the veterans (though he never did), but not with any who were communists. He suggested that all the marchers should be fingerprinted to prove they were veterans and to ensure they were not criminals or subversives.[19] Hoover consistently contended that many of the marchers were not legitimate veterans or war heroes. He argued in his memoirs 20 years later, "The march was in considerable part organized and promoted by the Communists and included a large number of hoodlums and ex-convicts determined to raise a public disturbance."[20]

News coverage changed once the marchers reached Washington. Instead of a curious traveling show, the ex-soldiers had become a political and social force with which Congress and the president had to contend. News organizations turned their attention to both the human and the political sides of the confrontation. The veterans were variously portrayed as tragic victims of the Depression, brave and daring representatives of the downtrodden, misguided war heroes, unrealistic political neophytes, unruly social outcasts, or dangerous communists.

But they had two main problems, neither of which they overcame. First, they did not realize that congressmen would not yield unless the public was demonstrably supportive of the marchers and their cause. In his 1933 published description of the march, Waters said the men were desperate and he saw no reason why they should not make this known to congressmen. "Other lobbies had moved to Washington, supported by money. We had no money, but perhaps a group, whose only support was in its numbers, might go to Congress and make some impression."[21]

Apparently, they thought they would merely influence legislators by personal contact and reasoned arguments. Second, they had an extremely weak financial argument. It was highly unlikely that the public or Congress would agree to allot money totaling more than half the annual federal budget so that 4 percent of the population could temporarily solve their desperate personal needs. Many in the country were out of work. Everyone needed money, and giving the veterans $2.4 billion would not even begin to address a nationwide problem. Writing in the liberal Catholic magazine *American*, Richard W. O'Neill, himself a veteran, observed, "American citizens and taxpayers already are spending, this fiscal year, more than *one billion dollars* for relief of ex-soldiers. This is the largest single item in the whole federal budget."[22] Even organized veterans groups, the Veterans of Foreign Wars and the American Legion, opposed an immediate bonus payment. The legion vote in September 1931 was a major blow to the Patman Bill.[23]

Still, thousands of men representing middle-class, blue-collar America were camped in the nation's capital with hundreds of reporters on hand. Even the extravagant expectations of the veterans could not be ignored by either Congress or the news media. Congressmen were uncertain as to what kind of power base the veterans represented, and many hedged their positions. Walter Davenport wrote in *Collier's* magazine: "However, a change of spirit is noticeable on Capitol Hill. . . . Unhappily, the party leaders have now reached a point where they haven't the money to pay for what they are afraid to refuse."[24] The marchers believed they could win the day, and congressmen were afraid to tell them they could not.

Meanwhile, the Administration was not the only group anxious to emphasize the B.E.F.'s alleged communist influence. So did American communist leaders, who saw an opportunity to exaggerate their power and influence. Emmanuel Levine, former state chief of the California Communist party, held a news conference on June 1 and boldly proclaimed that it was the communists who had organized the march, not Waters or his cohorts.[25] John T. Pace, the communists' field commander in Detroit, later arrived in Washington and with pamphlets and speeches tried to stir the veterans to more violent action.[26] The preponderance of veterans were virulently anti-communist. Communist agitators met with harsh treatment at the hands of the ex-soldiers, who were eager to demonstrate their disdain for the radicals. Waters recalled:

Yet my chief problems with the Communists was to prevent the men of the B.E.F., literally, from almost killing any Communist they found among them. Had the men of the B.E.F. had their way they would have refused the Communists any food and have run the entire outfit out of Washington. As it was, men of the B.E.F. spent many days in June taking "Reds' out to the district line and pointing them north. Finally, at the end of June, General Glassford was forced to say:

"Some of the men of the B.E.F. are going too far in their brutality to eliminate the 'Reds.' " And the District Attorney pointed out that I would be held personally responsible for the rights and life of any 'Red' who fell into our hands.[27]

Still, Hoover Administration officials, Republican congressmen, and even many American Legion and VFW leaders, darkly warned of communist subversion. So did newspapers and magazines. The *Washington Post* in an editorial said veterans were being duped by communist agitators and "federal authorities have conclusive evidence that the reds are largely responsible for the bonus march."[28] The "federal authorities" reference indicates from what source such innuendos emanated. Two days later, however, the *Post* backed off. In a front-page news article, it reported that in a "kangaroo court martial" Emmanuel Levine and another communist leader had been ordered out of town by the B.E.F. leaders. A second article reported that communists were being thrown out of camp daily.[29] *The New York Times* carried an Associated Press wire article that reported that the government had "turned an inquiring eye on Communist activities," suggesting that communists have "seized upon the [B.E.F.] movement to promote their doctrine." Another article quoted a speech by an American Legion commander in New York. He disavowed the bonus marchers and said the B.E.F. was concocted by communists.[30] The Hearst *San Francisco Examiner*, though sympathetic to the marchers, dutifully reported that the national commander of the Veterans of Foreign Wars told an audience in Sacramento the marchers were Reds. Even Waters' hometown newspaper flatly reported that communists had infiltrated the Anacostia River camp.[31]

But many other newspapers and magazines questioned these charges. Reporters who visited the Anacostia encampment agreed that Waters and his men detested the communists. For instance, *Time* magazine reported in early June "the Red(s) . . . were scrupulously shunned by the non-radical element."[32] The Scripps-Howard *Washington News* noted that the bonus marchers had lashed two communists with a strap and thrown them out of the Anacostia River camp.[33] "They are misled not by agents of Moscow," wrote columnist Walter Lippmann, of the *New York Herald Tribune*, "but by duly elected representatives and Senators at the Capitol."[34] The communist bugaboo stayed with the marchers during the encampment and for many years, but the acceptance of this accusation by newspapers and magazines was sporadic.

Aside from the issue of possible communist influence, news reports in early June generally were two types: sympathetic human interest pieces filled with descriptions of the marchers and the miserable conditions at the Anacostia River encampment, and political stories focusing upon the Patman bill. Floyd Gibbons, a writer for Hearst's Universal Service, captured the mood of the B.E.F. most poignantly as he compared the ex-soldiers to ghosts. Gibbons wrote:

Tonight they marched in the dark like ghosts out of the forgotten past. Four abreast they marched—five thousand strong. Few uniforms tonight, and those ragged and wear-worn. The grease stained overalls of jobless factory workers. The frayed straw hats of unemployed farm hands. The shoddy elbow-patched garments of idle clerks. All were down at the heel. All were slim and gaunt and their eyes had a light in them. There were empty sleeves and limping men with canes.[35]

This type of first-person piece touched both reader and veteran and placed the entire confrontation into another perspective.[36] Gibbons and other writers generated sympathy and reader empathy for the downtrodden veterans. If the editors and publishers did not agree with the B.E.F.'s goals, they at least sympathized with the plight into which the men had fallen. The only public relations tools the men had available were the personal stories they had to tell to news reporters. Such reporting generated the veterans' only positive press in their fight for the bonus. How this positive stacked up against the other negatives is difficult to judge, but certainly Americans who read Gibbons' words could see the marchers as more than just a mob. Even the most conservative newspapers carried some personal pieces on the veterans.

Most of the reporting, though, was not personal but political. It focused upon the jockeying in Congress as Patman attempted to maneuver passage of the bonus bill. The bill reached the House floor and passed by 35 votes on June 15. Two days later the Senate soundly defeated the measure. The government funding story was more familiar to the Washington press corps and offered an opportunity for reporters and for editorial writers to review the merits of the marchers' arguments. The sympathy engendered by the human interest pieces was countermanded by the basic fiscal opposition to the bonus payment.

The amount of money asked was just too much for many papers. The same fiscal opposition that existed in 1924 resurfaced. Opinion makers who had seen a patriotic motive in supporting a long-range bonus payout were convinced that the treasury could not meet the cost of an immediate payment. *The New York Times* carried a full-page discussion of the bonus proposal in a Sunday newspaper spread. Articles and charts showed how more money was being spent on veterans' relief than on national defense and public works combined. It illustrated how these payments accounted for four times the percentage of the federal budget spent in Great Britain and half again as much as in France. The United States' two key allies in the war, whose soldiers had fought much longer and who collectively suffered many more injuries, were spending proportionately a great deal less for veterans' aid.[37]

Opinion makers' fiscal opposition was deep and wide. A private, confidential poll of newspaper editorial opinion conducted by Hoover research assistants showed a consistent editorial support for Hoover's position. A sampling of 205 newspapers in early 1931 showed that 85 newspapers with 4.4 million total circulation favored payment of the bonus and 120 with 7 million circulation opposed it. After the marchers arrived in Washington, newspaper editorial support for the bonus payment dropped to nearly zero. The House vote in favor of the bonus drew the support of one 10,300 circulation newspaper in Indiana, Pennsylvania. The other 70 newspapers sampled, with a total circulation of 4.9 million, opposed the House vote.[38] The *Literary Digest* summarized:

Surprizing [*sic*] to the United States Senate, accustomed to getting editorial brick-bats, must be the sudden transformation of a majority of the press to the role of bouquet-tossers.

For, in all parts of the country editors are praising the Senate for its decisive defeat of the bonus bill, 62–18.[39]

Particularly telling in this study's print-media sampling was the commentary from publications whose political leanings would normally have dictated support for the marchers. They opposed the high cost of the bonus measure. Left-wing periodicals proclaimed that any aid to the marchers would be unfair and create economic chaos. *The Nation*, a liberal magazine that sympathized with the veterans' personal plights and that was resentful of Hoover's handling of economic matters,[40] still noted that "we are as much opposed to the bonus as ever."[41] The *St. Louis Post-Dispatch*, the long-time champion of the poor and working class, commented: "We do not believe that Congress is so foolish as to be stampeded by any such demonstration as that being made."[42] This stance was so surprising to one letter writer that he demanded to know: "Why is it that a normally liberal newspaper like the Post-Dispatch becomes so bitterly conservative on the subject of the veterans' bonus? Your editorial, 'The Bonus Marchers,' could easily have graced the editorial pages of the Chicago Tribune."[43] The *Baltimore Sun* observed that the Patman Bill was "founded on favoritism to a small but highly organized minority."[44] The liberal Catholic magazine *The Commonweal* praised the veterans' courage both in their march and in their past service to the country. Then the magazine writers added, "So much having been said, it remains to add that Congress has never been more emphatically obligated to ignore pleas of this character than it is now."[45] Lippmann, the liberal *New York Herald Tribune* columnist, summarized, "When the answer has been given explaining why the Government owes these veterans no money at this time, it should be followed immediately by a decisive announcement that no money will be paid."[46] After this column in early June, Lippmann wrote nothing about the veterans for the rest of the summer. The Scripps-Howard *Pittsburgh Press* expressed sympathy for the bonus marchers and called upon Congress to pay more attention to widespread hunger in the country, but added that the Senate had "wisely disposed" of the bonus bill.[47]

Unlike mainstream newspapers, labor and socialist newspapers saw the marchers as naive or as dupes of either the communists or capitalists, but again they did not offer editorial support. The Socialist newspaper, *The Milwaukee Leader*, described the soldiers' efforts as politically ineffective. The real answer, the newspaper concluded, was not to trek to Washington, but to march to the ballot box and "elect socialists from top to bottom."[48] The *Industrial Worker*, the journal of the Industrial Workers of the World, editorialized:

Even though they should force payment of their bonus, that small sum which they may receive will supply them with the necessities of life for but a very short period. . . . The Shorter Working Day is the "bonus" the entire working class has earned in the advancement of machine production. Widespread agitation will hasten its demand by workers everywhere from the individual bosses for whom they toil.[49]

Another I.W.W. editorial asserted, "They are asking little enough and they know it. But their faith in capitalism is somewhat naive."[50] The *United Mine Workers Journal* said "communists and revolutionists" had "wormed their way" into the B.E.F., which caused the marchers to remain in Washington.[51] *Labor*, a Washington union publication, never did editorially address the march. Reporter Budd L. McKillips covered the unfolding events from the time the ex-soldiers entered Washington and frequently editorialized sympathetically about the marchers' plight. Still, he did not defend their economic demands and often referred to them as threats to the safety of the residents of Washington.[52] The moderate and conservative press were far more intense and unequivocal than the liberal papers in the denunciation of the marchers.[53]

Clearly, the veterans had not captured the sympathy of any segment of the nation's opinion makers. Whether the man on the street felt the same way is a matter of some conjecture. However, the lack of support from established veterans groups, the general silence from the public, and the wide variety of printed opinion sampled here suggests the expressed opposition to the veterans reflected public sentiment. Hoover's office had no flood of letters.[54] Only a scattered few letters appeared on the pages of the nation's newspapers. There were no mass demonstrations around the nation in support of the veterans. The marchers seemed to have lost their case both in the Senate and in the public arena.

President Hoover eventually would be the person to whom the marchers and the press would turn for a decision on what should be done about the marchers' presence in Washington. But in early June, Hoover had yet to become a major figure in this confrontation. He had clashed with Glassford over how the marchers should be handled, and he had passed on some opportunities to promote his own benevolence. Sometimes, reporters would publicize the poor sanitary and dietary conditions at their camp and tie Hoover into the picture. Robert Considine, later to become a renowned broadcast and print journalist, was a young reporter for the *Washington Post* at the time. Considine recalled 36 years later that one enterprising reporter obtained a copy of the weekly bill for milk delivered to the White House and compared it with the food spent on the marchers. "I'm sure that Mr. Hoover didn't drink all that milk, but suddenly he became the image of government possessiveness and niggardliness, and many people resented him," Considine recalled.[55] Such stories about the B.E.F. were infrequent in June, however.

Until the Senate rejected the bonus bill, the attention of the public had been upon both legislators and the veterans, not Hoover. Both Congress and the marchers came in for editorial criticism; the marchers for their insistence upon financial aid and their menacing presence in Washington and Congress for fomenting such demonstrations by enacting the 1931 Bonus package and waffling over the ex-soldiers' demands in 1932.

Hoover, himself, was preoccupied with his limited economic package for the entire country—the Reconstruction Finance Corporation (RFC)—and with the Republican National Convention, which took place in June. Theodore Joslin, Hoover's press secretary wrote about the marchers in his diary only about a half-dozen times. Hoover was much more concerned about the convention and whether the northern Republicans would force an anti-Prohibition plank on the party, according to Joslin's diary.[56]

Other public and private documents point to Hoover's preoccupation with other issues. Hoover devoted only about seven pages of his memoirs to the Bonus March, dismissing the B.E.F. contingent as "thugs, hoodlums, and communists."[57] Edgar Rickard, Hoover's personal confidant and financial advisor, mentions the Bonus March in his diary only once during the entire summer of 1932, denouncing the marchers.[58] Hoover held four press conferences between May 27 and July 1 and never referred to the marchers once. He did not talk about the B.E.F. in any other public appearances, nor did he issue any statements about the ex-soldiers during that period. Mostly, he talked about the RFC.[59] Bonus historian Donald Lisio also points out that Hoover was preoccupied with details of the Geneva Disarmament Conference in Europe and Japanese aggression in Manchuria.[60] Walter Trohan, a *Chicago Tribune* Washington bureau reporter during the Roosevelt era and a close companion of Hoover's in later years, recalled: "I don't think Hoover considered it [the march] a turning point in his career. As a matter of fact, I'm sure he didn't. He didn't talk about it [later]. I guess it did him harm, but to my knowledge, I don't think it concerned him that much."[61] Hoover watched and worried, but from a distance.

By late June, Congress had left the problem of the marchers to administrative officials in Washington. Legislators turned to other matters. Of the 23,000 protesters who had arrived in Washington by mid-June, more than half continued into July to brave the steamy summer heat along the increasingly polluted banks of the Anacostia River. They waited for a miracle and swore not to leave, even if they had to stay until 1945. Food ran short, tempers flared, Waters became ill, and still the summer dragged on. Reporters and editors lost interest in the story. For weeks, only occasional brief articles appeared in newspapers about the B.E.F. The veterans were temporarily forgotten but also hungry, haggard, and restless.

In mid-July, authorities in Washington were becoming alarmed. Some marchers had moved into abandoned buildings nearer to the Capitol. Glassford told the editor of the *Baltimore Sun* that he feared the communists would take advantage of the situation.[62] The *Washington Post* observed: "Even if the bonus army evacuates the building sites along Pennsylvania Avenue, serious problems as to their status here will remain unsolved. So long as the bonus seekers stay here they will be a menace to peace and order."[63] This was a desperate band of ragtag ex-soldiers, and every day their presence in Washington frightened the residents more. By early July, Waters realized that the men left in Washington could no longer achieve their goals, but he feared a revolt if he ordered everyone to return to his home state. Yet, privately and without fanfare he did urge those who still had homes to return to them. Waters himself was uncertain that he could keep the veterans in line.[64] Bonus historian Lisio put blame for the fear on Waters. He noted that by early July Waters was ordering his camp security officers to rough up marchers who did not agree with his policies and that even Patman and Hearst, two of the B.E.F.'s strongest supporters, feared violence and asked the men to go home.[65] Historian Roger Daniels wrote: "While the lawmakers were throwing their departing sops to the bonus army, the veterans, or some of them, were abandoning their passive policy and pursuing a course of limited activism."[66]

One change that led to more activism was the arrival on July 9 of a contingent of marchers from California under the leadership of Roy W. Robertson. Days later, the Californians marched to the capitol under parade permit, read a petition, and then refused to leave, insisting they would sleep on newspapers around the Capitol lawn.[67] Then Robertson and his followers tried a new tactic. They began marching around the Capitol on the sidewalks. They continued their "Death March" in shifts for three days. The scene became more volatile when Waters and part of his followers occupied the Capitol steps against Glassford's orders before eventually disbanding. Then, on July 28, when Glassford and his men attempted to evict about 50 veterans from some abandoned buildings, six officers were injured in a brick-throwing melee. A second scuffle ended when D.C. police fatally shot two veterans, William Huska and Eric Carlson. The D.C. commissioners asked Hoover to send in troops to remove the marchers from the occupied buildings.[68]

Hours later, Hoover ordered cavalry troops to proceed to Washington from nearby Fort Myers.[69] At 4:45 P.M. tanks were in place near the Capitol. At 5:20, troops successfully cleared the area around Third and Pennsylvania Avenues, and that night the cavalry routed the veterans from their main encampment near the Anacostia River. The military rammed tanks through the makeshift homes, fired tear gas at the bewildered ex-soldiers, and rode at the marchers on horseback, scattering them in every direction. Infantrymen followed with fixed bayonets to prod those who dallied. By midnight, the marchers had been driven from Washington. Most scattered to rural areas in the Maryland countryside and eventually stumbled their way on foot 200 miles to Johnstown, Pennsylvania.[70] No one was killed during the actual rout of the marchers and not one shot was fired, but many of the ex-soldiers suffered minor injuries from tear-gas fumes.

In one day, the Administration drove out the remaining remnants of the expeditionary force and quickly ended the two-month ordeal. MacArthur met with reporters at 11 P.M. the day of the rout. He set the tone for ensuing Administration explanations when he told reporters that Hoover had been patient but that "insurrectionists" had "severely threatened" the government.[71] Hoover told reporters the next day that the Department of Justice was investigating the violence by the marchers whose actions he labeled as "organized lawlessness."[72] *Editor & Publisher* observed that the War Department's cooperation with reporters was unusual, but that McArthur may have been using the openness to gain popular support among newsmen.[73]

Privately, Hoover was furious with not only the veterans but also Glassford, whom he blamed for being too lenient. Press secretary Joslin wrote in his diary two days before the rout:

The "bonus marchers" are a source of constant and growing irritation. The problem all along has been to get them out of the city without bloodshed. It has been aggravated by the impotency of General Glassford. . . . There has been too much dilly dallying already. The marchers have rapidly turned from bonus seekers to communists or bums.[74]

Three days after Joslin wrote that and as the National Guard was still mopping up in Washington, Joslin and Hoover met in the oval office to congratulate each other.

"Well, that job's done," Hoover told Joslin.

"We haven't heard the last of them," Joslin said.

"No, but they are out of the city and that is some consolation. What will the reaction of the press be [?]" Hoover asked.

"The conservative press will applaud the action. Hearst and Howard will go into eruption," Joslin said.

"I guess so. Reds and yellow press go together." Hoover responded.

Joslin handed Hoover a batch of telegrams critical of the rout. "That's all to the good," Hoover said. "Most of those are from radical organization(s). Tell the press when they come in that I have received scores of telegrams from communist organizations all over the country threatening me and the government."

Joslin noted to himself in his diary: "The telegrams certainly warranted the statement and I made it."[75]

Actually, an examination of the letters mailed to Hoover in the days after the rout showed that most of the letter writers represented themselves as concerned, ordinary citizens. How Hoover could have determined in one day that they were communists is hard to imagine. Yet, the letter file also shows that much mail supported Hoover's decision.[76]

Hoover was not exactly correct in his assessment of how newspapers and magazines would react to the veterans' forced evacuation. Hearst and Scripps-Howard did criticize him, but almost all others supported him, including, again, some of the Democratic and liberal publications. "The obvious duty of the authorities at Washington is to maintain order at whatever cost," observed the *Cleveland Plain Dealer*. "The Capitol cannot surrender to the B.E.F. or to any other group insisting on rights that do not exist."[77] Added the *San Francisco Chronicle*, "Riot is riot; whoever does it and in whatever the cause. And order must be order, if civilized life is to continue."[78] The *Philadelphia Bulletin* described the cavalry action as "acts of self defense on the part of the government."[79] The *St. Louis Post-Dispatch* editorialized, "It is impossible to judge at this distance how tactful the federal authorities were, but we cannot have government by mob and still preserve law and order."[80]

Other Democratic newspapers such as the *Miami News* came down on both sides. While agreeing with Hoover's order, the editorial writers reminded readers that the "lash of poverty" brought the marchers to Washington while demagogues "played politics with human misery."[81] Liberal columnist Walter Lippmann remained silent on the issue. The *Washington Times*, a Hearst publication, editorialized, "No group of a few thousand citizens no matter how worthy, can be allowed to defy flagrantly the rules and regulations which 120,000,000 have set up for the preservation of peace, order, and comfort." Joslin noted in his memoirs that he could not believe his eyes when he read that editorial but observed that the tone of editorials in the *Times* soon changed; he speculated that "someone higher than an editorial writer was dictating policy."[82] The *United Mine Workers Journal*, a labor newspaper sympathized with the veterans, but blamed the violence on communists.[83] The *Industrial Worker*, an I.W.W. publication, ignored Hoover and criticized the marchers for their naiveté and their past military activity. The *Worker* observed: "There is no reason here for the I.W.W. to shed thears [sic] or get excited or moralize. . . . The fact is many of these self same veterans have probably hammered I.W.W. men around plenty."[84] *Collier's* magazine decried the use of force against the B.E.F. and said Hoover was remiss in not negotiating directly with the marchers, but reminded its readers that the ex-soldiers had wrongfully tried to coerce Congress.[85]

Other Democratic publications did criticize Hoover, however. Hearst newspapers battered the president with one vitriolic editorial after another. "For sheer stupidity, President Hoover's spectacular employment of the military in evicting a mere handful of the derelicts of the World War from their wretched billets in Washington, is without parallel in American annals," a *San Francisco Examiner* editorial began.[86] Another editorial carried condemnation of Hoover as excerpted from newspapers in other countries and described Hoover and MacArthur as "cold-blooded."[87] Floyd Gibbons, whose poignant description in June had captured the despair of the veterans, wrote for Hearst's *New York Journal* and the syndicated Universal Service, "I swear I could not believe it. . . . The victims are American citizens, veteran soldiers, some of them disabled men who fought to sustain this Government."[88] *The Nation* blamed Hoover personally, while asserting that if Glassford had been left in authority, no bloodshed would have resulted. (The magazine, as with many publications, failed to note that the two deaths occurred before the National Guard had been sent into the Capitol area.) "Obviously somebody blundered and blundered badly. Given a weak and timid man in a difficulty of this kind, he is bound to be the first to turn to ruthless use of power," *The Nation* concluded. The *Baltimore Sun* said the rout resulted from "panic in high places" and said it expected that henceforth "passion will masquerade as intelligence and vehemence as conviction."[89] The *New Republic* reiterated its opposition to the payment of a bonus, but described the rout as "unforgivably stupid and cruel."[90] The *New York World-Telegram*, a Scripps-Howard newspaper, criticized Hoover and noted: "Indignant telegrams and interviews in newspapers are placing the Administration on the defensive."[91] Another Scripps-Howard paper, the *Washington News*, blamed "vote-seeking politicians."[92]

Conservative and moderate newspapers and magazines condemned the marchers and praised Hoover. In two editorials, the *Chicago Tribune* criticized Patman for creating the confrontation in Washington. The *Tribune* also commended the government for using tear gas against the marchers, saying that the gas brought the men under control immediately before serious fighting could break out and it "did the work which might otherwise have required bayonets, rifle butts or gunshots."[93] The *Los Angeles Times* blamed communists and "fake veterans" for the bonus rout and criticized Washington police for not driving the marchers from Washington much earlier. The *Times* also took the Hearst papers to task for encouraging the "ill-advised and necessarily futile march."[94] *The Boston Herald* said Hoover should have acted sooner. "Cavalry at the White House and tanks and machine guns in the streets of Washington are not pleasant spectacles, but it was evident that the riff-raff mob would not understand arguments any milder," the *Herald* concluded.

Many newspapers praised Hoover personally and vilified Congress. *The New York Times* editorial writers noted: "Congress either approves the resolute action which President Hoover finally took or is ashamed or afraid to attack it. Press opinion, accurately reflecting public opinion, has been almost unanimous in holding up the hands of Mr. Hoover."[95] The *Buffalo News* attacked Congress for pandering to the veterans in hopes of obtaining votes.[96] Added the *New York Herald Tribune*: "The country has arisen with a heartening unanimity to the support of the President in his forthright defense of law and order."[97] Use of troops was "entirely proper," wrote the *Washington Post*.[98] The *Chicago Daily News* praised Hoover and described the B.E.F. camps as "nurseries of sedition."[99] Even Waters's hometown newspaper, the *Portland Oregonian* said the rout was a proper course "when orders are held in defiance." The newspaper added, however, "There is no true heart that does not pity the veterans in Washington."[100] Henry Luce's *Time* magazine carried objective coverage of the rout with no editorial comment.[101]

At the same time, the pictures and stories that flooded the nation's newspapers and some magazines in the days after July 28 carried impact. Graphic pictures and dozens of articles dominated the front pages of newspapers and spilled onto several inside pages. Magazines that had been paying only cursory attention to the marchers combined coverage and editorial comment. All that was written about the marchers up till July 28 was perhaps equalled in the few days after the bonus rout. This certainly left an overwhelming feeling of disquiet and fear among readers, but whether the readers were angry with Hoover, with Congress, or with the marchers depended upon how the marchers were perceived. Nearly all periodicals described these ex-soldiers as misguided or, worse, unwanted agitators.

Meanwhile, 8,000 marchers found temporary quarters in an amusement park outside Johnstown, Pennsylvania. They were offered food and makeshift tents by Johnstown Mayor Eddie McCloskey. McCloskey quickly backed away from the offer when the townspeople expressed fears about the city's safety. The story stayed on front pages for about a week until many of the veterans accepted an offer from the Baltimore & Ohio Railroad (at Hoover's behest) to return to their hometowns by rail free of charge. Again, Hoover had quietly interceded to provide rail transportation, but did not publicize his role.[102]

Newspapers and magazines picked up the story off and on throughout the election campaign in the fall of 1932. A grand jury investigation in Washington resulted in no indictments. Glassford resigned as police superintendent in late October. In a *Collier's* magazine article and in a series that appeared in Hearst newspapers, he lambasted Hoover, saying that the president had plotted to force a confrontation.[103] Historian Donald Lisio's careful research showed that MacArthur had actually exceeded his orders on July 28. His men were supposed to clear the marchers from the lower Pennsylvania Avenue area only.[104] However, MacArthur's disobedience did not become apparent until years later, when historians had sifted through the evidence. Hoover, of course, suffered a landslide defeat to Democrat Franklin D. Roosevelt in November 1932 and left office in March 1933. The bonus was eventually approved by Democratic-controlled Congress during the Roosevelt Administration in 1936.

Clearly, the large sampling of periodicals here and the surveys taken by *Literary Digest, Editor & Publisher,* and aides to Hoover show that the B.E.F.'s goal of a full-paid bonus in 1932 never had the support of most of the nation's newspapers and magazines. The expectation that the federal government would commit two-thirds of its budget to the payment of a bonus to 4 percent of the population was unrealistic. Only the waffling of the U.S. House of Representatives gave the veterans even a glimmer of hope of attaining their goal. Hoover's opposition to this bonus had wide editorial support.

Despite their bedraggled condition and obvious need, the veterans could not gain the sympathy of the preponderance of the media. Reporters did interview the men and write sympathetic articles that were published in even the most conservative periodicals. But these were overwhelmed by the negative articles. The veterans were portrayed in most publications as troublemakers who prevented trains from operating, who had to be transported across states by National Guard troops, who occupied public land and public buildings creating unsanitary conditions and threats to public safety, and who caused fear among the residents of Washington, D.C.

Hoover's role was not widely discussed until late July just before the National Guard operation. Congress and B.E.F. had been the target of most of the editorial fulminations and news summaries. Hoover, himself, ordered that food and materials be provided to the marchers and eventually arranged for transportation so they could return to their hometowns. Yet, he did not publicize whatever sympathies he may have held, and readers were clearly left with the impression that he had worked to make the veterans unwanted and uncomfortable. His harangues about communists and outsiders brought inquiries and stories from newspapers, but in the end all but the most virulently conservative newspapers rejected these claims. These unfounded attacks, even after the marchers had left Washington, hurt Hoover's credibility and muddied the real issues of the march and the eventual dispersement of the ex-soldiers.

What of the rout itself? After all, periodicals could have strongly opposed the B.E.F.'s goals, could have editorialized against the veterans' presence in Washington, and still have been horrified and angered by the callous treatment meted out to marchers. They were not. Historians Sarah Miles Watts and John Tebbel argue that "editorial opinion differed politically on this episode, as they would on any other."[105] This is misleading, if not incorrect. Many liberal publications supported Hoover. Most, including labor and socialist publications, offered no sympathy for the B.E.F. If opinion was divided, it was divided quite unevenly. Bonus historian Donald J. Lisio even notes; "With the exception of the influential Hearst and Scripps-Howard chains and some independent dailies, such as the *Baltimore Sun*, most of the press offered extravagant praise."[106] The rout did not bring to the B.E.F. a wave of support in the pages of the nation's newspapers and magazines. In fact, Hoover enjoyed more editorial support than he had at any time since the Wall Street Crash in 1929.

How does this translate into actual public opinion? An extensive sampling of the nation's print media does not necessarily measure actual public sentiment. Roosevelt media historian Graham White, for instance, points out that most newspapers opposed FDR throughout his terms in office, but that at the same time Roosevelt enjoyed unparalleled popularity among voters.[107] During this period, many newspaper publishers and opinion writers had no compunction about asking Hoover for personal favors or seeking his approval on editorials. For example, Charles E. Coffin, treasurer of the *Indianapolis Star* wrote a fawning letter to Hoover two days after the Bonus rout. The letter included a copy of a *Star* editorial. "We are all for you in this affair and think you will approve the within editorial from today's *Star*," Coffin wrote.[108] Hoover thanked him for his "staunch support."[109] Even the more independent newspapers and magazines represented personalities and institutions not always reflective of public opinion. What, then, can be said of the feelings of the man on the street? Answers are not so clearcut on this question. Yet, it has been universally held that the rout stirred American passions against Hoover.

Logically, published opinion, heavily weighted in Hoover's favor, had to have had some impact. It may also be pointed out that the marchers were spurned by local townspeople wherever they went. Waters spoke glowingly of the food and support offered to the Portland group as they journeyed to Washington. Yet, the men had to be trucked by National Guard across every state after reaching Illinois, because of fear of their presence. In Washington, the marchers were cheered during a June 9 parade, but their continuing presence in Washington fanned anxieties among Washington residents. Eventually, it was the D.C. board of commissioners who asked Hoover to act. Even when the marchers scattered into Maryland after the rout and wended their way to Johnstown, Pennsylvania, they were unwelcome and forced to leave after a week. There was no overwhelming show of pity and understanding from the public. "I think most people despised the marchers," recalled *Chicago Tribune* correspondent Walter Trohan.[110]

The large numbers of Republicans turned out of office in the 1930 off-year election suggests that the shift away from Hoover was underway long before the Bonus March. Newspaper public opinion polls existed as early as 1900, but they were only straw polls and often inaccurate.[111] The *Literary Digest* conducted a poll during the weeks before the 1932 election by asking readers to voluntarily indicate their voting preference by mail. The poll closely mirrored the final vote, much to the delight of the *Digest* editors. This was neither scientific nor, as the results in 1936 showed (the *Digest* predicted a Landon victory), was the procedure foolproof. This poll also offers no insight as to the impact of the bonus march on the election. Besides, Joseph Belden, retired chairman of the board of Belden & Associates, recalled that polling, when it was instituted in the middle and late 1930s, was imprecise and frequently inaccurate anyway. "We would go out and interview 20 people, I remember. It didn't really matter where they lived as long as they fit into the right economic and age groups," Belden said.[112] There is as much or more evidence to to suggest the rout had no effect on the election as there is to assert that it did.

Still, the Bonus March is generally seen by historians as the worst blot on Hoover's public record, one that caused the public to turn on him. Historian Richard Norton Smith concluded that the incident "all but completed his [Hoover's] metamorphosis from hero to scapegoat."[113] Donald J. Lisio, who wrote an excellent book recounting the entire Bonus March ordeal, observed, "The rout violated a deep-seated sense of fair play and trust in the basic goodness and loyalty of the American people, many of whom felt betrayed and insulted."[114] Hoover biographer David Burner wrote, "In the minds of most analysts, whatever doubt had remained about the outcome of the presidential election was now gone: Hoover was going to lose. The Bonus Army was his final failure, his symbolic end."[115] Hoover historian Martin L. Fausold asserted:

The high price that Hoover finally paid for the bonus fiasco did not by itself determine the outcome of the presidential campaign, but it was an integral part of the mosaic that was crafted during the months between July and November 1932, which seemed to portray the fall of a leader more in terms of Greek tragedy than of American politics.[116]

Tebbel and Watts wrote:

While editorial opinions differed politically on this episode, as they would on any other, the bald facts as related in news columns (not to mention their sensationalizing in a few papers) did more, perhaps, to diminish Hoover's reputation and solidify his negative image than anything else while he was in office.[117]

Why have historians continually insisted that the rout of the marchers had a great impact upon Hoover and the 1932 election? First, Hoover's persistent contention, even years after the march, that communists and hoodlums were responsible for the bonus fiasco weakened the credibility of the many statements and arguments presented by the administration. Anyone who carefully checked Hoover's claims found so many holes that it was hard to acknowledge the administration's arguments at all.

Second, Hoover's dramatic turnaround at the ballot box in 1932 and the election's close proximity in time to the rout offer tempting evidence. As has been noted, it is more likely that the events of the three years preceding the Bonus March decided the 1932 campaign, but the rout came close to the election.

Thirdly, as observers look back upon the unfolding events, noting that the bonus was paid anyway in 1936, there is a tendency to forget the mood of the times. Certainly, the Bonus Rout was a tragedy and the Great Depression a calamity. Roosevelt's radical changes in public policy make Hoover seem to have been unfeeling and uncaring. But this was not necessarily the public mood toward the veterans at the time. It is not correct to identify these veterans as representing the problems of the public at large or the problems of the unemployed, in general. The veterans constituted a special interest group with whom most Americans did not identify.

Fourthly, despite the notoriety of both Hoover and the Bonus March, not a great deal of scholarship is available on the subject. Less than 20 pertinent Hoover biographies had been written by 1988.[118] Seven were written before or just after Hoover left office. The rest were written after 1948. Most early works were advocacy pieces either arguing vehemently for the marchers or, conversely, portraying the July 28 rout as a necessary action against alleged communists and subversives. Two of these pro-B.E.F. books—Waters's account of the Bonus March (1933) and Jack Douglas's book published by the Workers Library Publishers (1934)—are strong on polemics but lacking in scholarship.[119] On the other hand, works such as Eugene Lyons' biography (1948) adopt Hoover's position with little research or evidence. Lyons summarizes the march by stating, "Few minor incidents in American history have been so viciously misrepresented."[120] Dorothy Horton McGee (1959) claims that most of the men left in Washington by late July "had never served in the Army and a proportion [were] Communists as well as ex-convicts."[121] Carol Green Wilson (1968) also argues that most of the "remaining five thousand, composed principally of I.W.W.'s and communists, soon forced a crisis that reverberated across the nation."[122] As has been demonstrated here, the I.W.W. actually had no sympathy for the marchers.

Most Hoover biographies deal quickly and ineffectively with the Bonus March. Some were written before the Bonus March. Other papers and books on Hoover that are not biographies address larger questions such as Progressivism, foreign policy, overall economic policy, and Hoover's personal philosophy and his political strategy. They hardly touch on the veterans' protest. For example, William Leuchtenburg in his classic economic and political interpretation of the era of prosperity and early Depression spends only two pages on the march. He says simply that Hoover was subject to open contempt by the end of the summer of 1932.[123] Not many authors carefully examined the ex-soldiers' protest.

But soon after Hoover died, Daniels (1971) and Lisio (1974) completed their books and rebutted many of the undocumented charges and countercharges. They also took into account the role of the press in the Bonus March as they sought to reflect the published accounts of the incidents. But both authors concentrated on setting the record straight and presenting detailed accounts of the events, while eliminating the myths. In researching the march, both relied heavily upon Washington and New York newspapers and Hearst and Scripps-Howard accounts. This was an easy route. The New York and Washington papers provided the most complete news accounts. The Hearst and Scripps-Howard newspapers offered the largest chunk of editorial opinion, because they were the largest chains and their editorials did not vary much from paper to paper in these days. If you read one Scripps-Howard editorial page on a given day, you pretty much had read them all. The same applied to Hearst publications.

Both Daniels and Lisio noted that initial reaction to the rout in most newspapers was positive, but argued that the lack of evidence that communists were responsible and Glassford's "damaging" statements in *Collier's* and the Hearst press later turned public opinion around. An examination of newspaper and magazine coverage in October shows scant attention to the Glassford articles, except in Hearst and Scripps-Howard newspapers. The story lost much interest by October and Lisio's arguments particularly assume that people believed Glassford's honesty, though his story was published in the highly sensational Hearst publications. Lisio also cites the animosity at the American Legion national convention in September 1932 and the decision by the Legion to reverse its stand and support the bonus as evidence of the flow of public opinion against Hoover. These accounts of the convention did not draw the kind of published attention that the march had commanded. This is not to dismiss the adverse publicity Hoover sustained during the election campaign, but one must also take into account the scant attention these charges commanded. Besides, these same veterans had been labeling the marchers "communists" just months before the rout, and these men may not have been reflective of overall American opinion.

Lisio spent eight years researching the Bonus March—tracking down rumors, reports, incorrect conclusions, and sorting out a tangle of evidence to provide an accurate account of the incidents.[124] He essentially used Washington and New York newspapers and a few liberal magazines as his printed sources for both information and opinion. Daniels, though he actually cites other New York and Washington newspapers in his footnotes, lists six newspapers as main sources: *BEF News*, *Daily Worker*, *The New York Times*, *Portland Oregonian*, *Oregon Journal*, and *Washington Star*. Both authors provided a great service to historians in their use of other evidence. At the same time they seem to have left unchallenged the assumptions about the impact of the march, while employing sources too scant to draw conclusions about published opinion, let alone public opinion.

Later biographies and historical accounts seem to have relied heavily upon Lisio's and Daniel's studies. Many later authors accepted Lisio's interpretation of both the impact on Hoover and the impressions left by the media. Tebbel and Watts conclude that "the bald facts in news columns diminished Hoover's reputation."[125] Fausold subscribes to Lisio's contention that, though Hoover was praised by newspapers and magazines at first, in later weeks, months, and years, this opinion changed as Hoover's claims about communists were discredited.[126] Burner cites mostly from liberal periodicals critical of Hoover such as the *Nation*. Burner asserts incorrectly that "much newsprint" was devoted to the death of an eleven-week-old child who died of pneumonia but but was thought at first to have died of the effects of the tear gas. (Except for Hearst publications, the story was buried among coverage of the rout and its aftermath in most newspapers.)[127] Smith, like Lisio and Daniels, argues that MacArthur was the real villain but that Hoover was the victim of the debacle. However, Smith offers no evidence for his conclusion except to quote Roosevelt as saying the rout would hand him victory in November.[128]

Though scholars have finally begun to set aside the rhetoric that followed the Bonus Riot for decades, they have not clearly come to grips with the impact of the incidents in Washington in the summer of 1932. The marchers, not Hoover, were victims of poor press relations. Americans saw them in the pages of newspapers and magazines as trouble-makers, though not necessarily communists, who threatened public safety and who refused to abide by the will of Congress. That Hoover made mistakes in handling public information and that the handling of the rout reflected poor judgment cannot be disputed. It remains, however, much more of an open question than most Hoover scholars have conceded as to whether the Bonus March dealt a major blow to the Hoover Administration. The march, though, was a small symbolic event to Americans of the time, and the episode really made little impact upon readers and voters already ravaged by depression.

NOTES

1. Roger Daniels, *The Bonus March* (Westport, Conn.: Greenwood, 1971), pp. 37–39; Donald J. Lisio, *The President and Protest: Hoover, Conspiracy, and the Bonus Riot* (Columbia: University of Missouri Press, 1974), pp. 8–9.

2. Lisio, *President and Protest*, p. 8; Daniels, *Bonus March*, pp. 38–40.

3. Lisio, *President and Protest*, pp 45–46.

4. Ibid., pp. 62–64.

5. Ibid., pp. 74–75.

6. W. W. Waters, *B.E.F.: The Whole Story of the Bonus Army*, 2d ed. (New York: Arno Press and The New York Times, 1969), pp. 1–10.

7. Ibid., p. 7.

8. Daniels, *Bonus March*, p. 76.

9. Ibid., p. 76.

10. See especially coverage in the *Chicago Tribune, St. Louis Post-Dispatch, The New York Times, New York Herald Tribune, Washington Post, Cleveland Plain Dealer*, and *Portland Oregonian*. The *Oregonian* paid the *Chicago Tribune* for special coverage from its correspondents.

11. "Troops Balk 'Bonus Army,'" *Chicago Tribune*, May 24, 1932, p. 1; "If This Is a Lark, What's a Riot?" *Chicago Tribune* editorial, May 25, 1932, p. 12.

12. "Railroad Again Fools Bonus Band, Unhooks Engine," *St. Louis Post-Dispatch*, May 23, 1932, p. 1.

13. "National Guard Ordered to East St. Louis Where 'Bonus Marchers' Seized a Train," *The New York Times*, May 24, 1932, p. 1. For other examples of stories or editorials, see "Veterans Resume March on Capitol," *Portland Oregonian*, May 25, 1932, p. 1; "Problems of the Bonus Hike," *Chicago Daily News* editorial, May 28, 1932, p. 10; "Veterans Give Up Freight Cars As Guard Called Out," *New Orleans Times-Picayune*, May 24, 1932, p. 2; "Veteran Bonus Army Fails in Threat to Seize Train," *Washington Post*, May 22, 1932, p. 1; "Bonus Veterans Due in Capital Next Week," *Post*, May 25, 1932, p. 1.

14. See "Washington Police Trail War Veterans" and "Militia Rushed As 300 Vets Capture Train," *San Francisco Examiner*, May 24, 1932, pp. 1, 2.

15. Waters, *B.E.F.*, pp. 70–72; Daniels, *Bonus March*, pp. 87–122; Lisio, *President and Protest*, pp. 53–62.

16. Theodore Joslin diary, May 26, 1932, entry, Joslin Papers, Box 10, HHPL.

17. Lisio, *President and Protest*, pp. 73–74, 81.

18. Joslin diary, June 9, 1932, entry.

19. Ibid.

20. Herbert Hoover, *The Memoirs of Herbert Hoover: The Great Depression 1929–1941*, vol. 3 (New York: Macmillan, 1952), p. 225.

21. Waters, *B.E.F.*, p. 13.

22. "A Veteran Speaks His Mind," *American*, November 1932, p. 20.

23. Daniels, *Bonus March*, pp. 50–52.

24. Walter Davenport, "But the Dead Don't Vote," *Colliers*, June 11, 1932, p. 47.

25. Lisio, *President and Protest*, p. 87.

26. Ibid., p. 141.

27. Waters, *B.E.F.*, p. 94.

28. *Washington Post* editorial, June 3, 1932.

29. "Kangaroo Court Marital Warns Red Chieftains" and "Veteran Forces Defy Request to Leave Thursday," *Washington Post*, June 5, 1932, pp. 1–2.

30. "Reds Held Leaders of Bonus Marchers," *The New York Times*, June 3, 1932, p. 2; "Says Reds Inspired Bonus Marchers," *The New York Times*, June 10, 1932, p. 12.

31. "Bonus March 'Reds' Flayed," *San Francisco Examiner*, June 8, 1932, p. 4; "Communists Invade Bonus Army Ranks," *Portland Oregonian*, June 3, 1932, p. 1.

32. "Heroes—B.E.F.," *Time*, June 13, 1932, p 14.

33. See *Literary Digest*, June 11, 1932, p. 8.

34. Walter Lippmann column, "Today and Tomorrow," *New York Herald Tribune*, June 9, 1932, p. 21. For other examples of articles and editorials describing the anticommunist sentiments of the marchers, see "Bonus Force Here Denies Red Backing," *Washington Post*, June 3, 1932, p. 1; *Post* editorial cartoon, June 7, 1932, editorial page.

35. Floyd Gibbons, "Ghosts of 1917 Heroes March in Washington," *San Francisco Examiner*; also see "The 'Ghost Parade' of the Bonus Seekers," *Literary Digest*, June 18, 1932, pp. 6–7.

36. For other examples of such human interest pieces see William Key, "Atlanta's Own Bonus 'Army' Will Start 'Big Push' Today," *Atlanta Constitution*, June 7, 1932, p. 1; "Bonus Army Menaced—Epidemic Looms in Washington," *Los Angeles Times*, June 9, 1932, p. 1; *Nation*, June 15, 1932, p. 2; "Heroes," *Time*, June 20, 1932, p. 11.

37. "Veterans Relief—What Other Nations Do," *The New York Times*, June 5, 1932, Section 9, p. 1.

38. See confidential report on "Views on Proposal to Pay Soldiers Bonus in Cash," February 2, 1931, Presidential Papers—Press Relations, Box 1192, pp. 1–14, Hoover Presidential Library, West Branch, Iowa; confidential report on "Views on House Vote on Bonus Bill," June 2l1, 1932, pp. 1–9, Box 1192, Hoover Library. The newspapers in this sample did not necessarily correspond with the newspapers sampled by the author. Many were smaller newspapers in key politically volatile areas.

39. "Approval of the Bonus Bill Defeat," *Literary Digest*, July 2, 1932, p. 9.

40. See especially *Nation*, June 22, 1932, p. 691.

41. *Nation*, July 13, 1932, p. 20.

42. *St. Louis Post-Dispatch* editorial, June 3, 1932.

43. S. L. letter to the editor, *St. Louis Post-Dispatch* editorial page, June 9, 1932.

44. *Baltimore Sun* editorial, June 19, 1932.

45. "The Bonus Army," *The Commonweal*, June 15, 1932, pp 173–74.

46. Walter Lippmann column, "Today and Tomorrow," *New York Herald Tribune*, June 9, 1932, p. 21.

47. *Pittsburgh Press* editorial, June 19, 1932, p. 8.

48. *Milwaukee Leader* editorial, July 9, 1932.

49. "Veterans March on Washington to Get Bonus," *Industrial Worker* (Chicago), June 7, 1932, p. 1.

50. *Industrial Worker* editorial, June 14, 1932.

51. *United Mine Workers Journal* (Indianapolis) editorial, Aug. 15, 1932.

52. See especially "Worried Congress Wants to Go Home As 'Bonus Escape,'" June 14, 1932, p. 1; "B.E.F. Sounds Pay Call at Capitol," July 12, 1932, p. 12; "Veterans Besieging Senate As Bonus Bill Passes House," June 21, 1932, p. 1; "Government Fails to Disband 'B.E.F.': Capitol Is Picketed," July 19, 1932, p. 3; all in *Labor* (Washington).

53. See, for example, "Oregon Veterans Take Leadership," May 31, 1932, and "Veterans Refuse to Leave Capital," June 5, 1932, *Portland Oregonian*; *Chicago Daily News* editorial, May 28, 1932; *New York Herald Tribune* editorial, June 14, 1932; *Los Angeles Times* editorial, June 1, 1932; *Chicago Tribune* editorial, June 10, 1932.

54. See President's Personal File, Letters to the President, 1932, HHPL.

55. Robert Considine oral history interview with Raymond Henle, director of the Herbert Hoover oral history project, New York, Dec. 12, 1968, pp. 7–8, in oral history files, HHPL.

56. See Joslin diary, June 1–July 1, 1932, Joslin Papers, Box 10, Herbert Hoover Presidential Library, West Branch, Iowa. See especially June 13, 14, 16, 18, 19, 28, 29, and 30 entries for discussion of both the marchers and prohibition.

57. Hoover memoirs, vol. 3, pp 225–32.

58. Edgar Rickard diary, June 1–Aug, 5, 1932 entries, Rickard Papers, Box 1, HHPL.

59. *Public Papers of the Presidents of the United States: Herbert Hoover 1932–1933*, 4 (Washington: United States Government Printing Press, 1977), pp. 182–291.

60. Lisio, *President and Protest*, pp. 166–67.

61. Walter Trohan interview with author, Sept. 25, 1989.

62. Lisio, *President and Protest*, p. 142.

63. *Washington Post* editorial, July 28, 1932.

64. Waters, *B.E.F.*, pp. 177–79.

65. Lisio, *President and Protest*, pp. 140–42.

66. Daniels, *Bonus March*, p. 129.

67. Lisio, *President and Protest*, p. 127.

68. For a complete recounting of events, see several newspapers including *The New York Times* of July 29, 1932; also see Lisio, *President and Protest*, pp. 166–89.

69. See Patrick J. Hurley, Secretary of War, order to MacArthur, July 28, 1932, Presidential Papers, World War Veterans, Bonus—Press Comment, Box 373, HHPL.

70. See Associated Press chronology, especially under the headline "Chronology of Day's Swift B.E.F. Eviction: Drive Begun before Noon Waged Far into Night" in *The New York Times*, July 30, 1932; also see Lisio, *President and Protest*, pp. 190–225; Daniels, *Bonus March*, pp. 123–81.

71. MacArthur press interview, 11 p.m. July 28, 1932, p. 1, Presidential Papers—World War Veterans, Bonus—Press Comment, Box 373, HHPL.

72. "The President's News Conference of July 29, 1932" in *Public Papers of the Presidents: Herbert Hoover, 1932–33* (Washington: U.S. Government Printing Office, 1977), pp. 348–49.

73. "Newsmen in Thick of B.E.F. Fighting," *Editor & Publisher*, Aug. 6, 1932, p. 9.

74. Joslin diary, July 26, 1932, entry.

75. Joslin diary, July 29, 1932, entry.

76. President's Personal File, letters to the president, 1932, Box 373, HHPL.

77. *Cleveland Plain Dealer* editorial, July 29, 1932.

78. *San Francisco Chronicle* editorial, July 30, 1932.

79. *Philadelphia News* editorial, July 30, 1932.

80. *St. Louis Post-Dispatch* editorial, July 30, 1932.

81. *Miami Daily News* editorial, July 30, 1932.

82. Theodore Joslin, *Hoover off the Record* (Garden City, N.Y.: Doubleday, Doran, 1934), p. 276.

83. *United Mine Workers Journal* (Indianapolis) editorial, Aug. 15, 1932.

84. *Industrial Worker* editorial, August 16, 1932.

85. "The Folly of Hatred," *Colliers*, Sept. 10, 1932, p. 50.

86. *San Francisco Examiner* front page editorial, July 30, 1932.

87. Ibid., Aug. 1, 1932.

88. Floyd Gibbons, "Rout of Harrowed Vets Sad, Sullen Picture," Aug. 1, 1932, p. 2.

89. *Baltimore Sun* editorial, July 30, 1932.

90. "Bullets for the B.E.F.: Hoover Relief, New Style," Aug. 19, 1932, *New Republic*, pp. 328–29.

91. *New York World-Telegram* editorial, July 30, 1932.

92. *Washington News* page-one editorial, July 30, 1932. All Scripps-Howard newspapers carried front-page editorials after the bonus rout. See "Newsmen in Thick of B.E.F. Fighting," *Editor & Publisher*, Aug. 6, 1932, p. 9.

93. *Chicago Tribune* editorials, July 30 and Aug. 1, 1932.

94. *Los Angeles Times* editorial, July 30, 1932.

95. *The New York Times*, editorial, Aug. 1, 1932.

96. *Buffalo News* editorial, July 30, 1932.

97. *New York Herald Tribune* editorial, July 31, 1932.

98. *Washington Post* editorial, July 30, 1932.

99. *Chicago Daily News* editorial, July 30, 1932.

100. *Portland Oregonian* editorial, July 30, 1932.

101. *Time*, "Heroes—Battle of Washington," Aug, 8, 1932, pp. 5–6.

102. See especially *The New York Times*, Aug. 1–8 coverage; *Time*, "Heroes—

B.E.F.'s End," Aug. 15, 1932, pp. 9–10; and Lisio, *President and Protest*, pp. 219–25.

103. Owen P. White, "General Glassford's Story," *Collier's*, Oct. 29, 1932, pp. 10–11, 32.

104. Lisio, *President and Protest*, pp. 196–215.

105. John Tebbel and Sarah Miles Watts, *The Press and the Presidency* (New York: Oxford, 1985), p. 431.

106. Lisio, *President and Protest*, p. 231.

107. Graham White, *FDR and the Press* (Chicago: University of Chicago Press, 1979).

108. Charles E. Coffin letter to Herbert Hoover, Aug. 1, 1932, President's Personal File, Newspapers, *Indianapolis Star*, Box 84, HHPL.

109. Hoover to Coffin letter, Aug. 4, 1932, in ibid.

110. Author interview with Walter Trohan, Sept, 25, 1989.

111. See especially Claude E. Robinson, *Straw Votes: A Study of Political Prediction* (New York: Columbia University, 1932). Robinson pointed out that *Editor & Publisher* polled newspapers on the Hoover-Smith election in 1928 as to how the editors felt readers would vote. The editors predicted Smith would do much better that he did. Robinson also notes that political leaders often relied in those days on precinct chairman to gauge voter sentiment in each of their precincts. Newspaper straw polls were often completed through mailings or by telephone. The results were skewed because many voters did not have telephones or never bothered to return the mailed questionnaires.

112. Author interview with Joseph Belden, Sept. 19, 1988. Also see George Gallup and Saul Forbes Rae, *The Pulse of Democracy: The Public-Opinion Poll and How It Works* (New York: Simon and Schuster, 1940).

113. Richard Norton Smith, *An Uncommon Man: The Triumph of Herbert Hoover* (New York: Simon and Schuster, 1984), p. 140.

114. Lisio, *President and Protest*, p. 237.

115. David Burner, *Herbert Hoover: A Public Life* (New York: Knopf, 1979), p. 312.

116. Martin L. Fausold, *The Presidency of Herbert C. Hoover* (Lawrence, Kansas: University of Kansas Press, 1985), p. 203.

117. Tebbel and Watts, *Press and Presidency*, p. 431.

118. See Mark M. Dodge, *Herbert Hoover and the Historians* (West Branch, Iowa: Herbert Hoover Presidential Library Association, 1988) for a complete listing of secondary readings on Hoover. Many works on Hoover are not pertinent to this discussion because they deal with the periods before or after Hoover was president.

119. Waters, *B.E.F.*; Jack Douglas, *Veterans on the March* (New York: Workers Library Publishers, 1934).

120. Eugene Lyons, *Our Unknown Ex-President: A Portrait of Herbert Hoover* (Garden City, N.Y.: Doubleday, 1948), pp. 288–89.

121. Dorothy Horton McGee, *Herbert Hoover: Engineer, Humanitarian, Statesman* (New York: Dodd, Mead, 1959), p. 264.

122. Carol Green Wilson, *Herbert Hoover: A Challenge for Today* (New York: Evans, 1968), p 226.

123. See William E. Leuchtenburg, *The Perils of Prosperity, 1914–1932* (Chi-

cago: University of Chicago Press, 1958), pp. 262–63. Many of the earliest works on Hoover came before or during his administration and obviously would not have dealt with the Bonus March. For other early pro-Hoover works published soon after his presidency ended, see William Starr Myers and Walter H. Newton, *The Hoover Administration: A Documented Narrative* (New York: Scribner's, 1936); Harold Wolfe, *Herbert Hoover: Public Servant and Leader of the Loyal Opposition* (New York: Exposition Press, 1956); and Ray Lyman Wilbur and Arthur Mastick Hyde, *The Hoover Policies* (New York: Scribner's, 1937).

124. This according to a July 26, 1989, interview with the author.

125. Tebbel and Watts, *Press and Presidency*, pp. 430–32.

126. Fausold, *Presidency*, pp. 202–3.

127. Burner, *Herbert Hoover*, pp. 309–12.

128. Smith, *Uncommon Man*, pp. 137–40.

8

The Dawn of the Roosevelt Era

> But never think these people are not human. Or that they do not feel
> pain. They do. And sometimes for a long, long time.
>   *Baltimore Sun* columnist Roger Simon after
>   George Bush's defeat in 1992

Had he been writing 60 years earlier, Roger Simon could have been referring to Herbert Hoover. Hoover's ignominious defeat in 1932
shrouded his public career with a legacy that he could not escape for the
rest of his life. Hard work and dedication are no match for bad luck and
bad press. The loss at the polls was more than just a rejection of the
policies of the Republican Party. It was a repudiation of Hoover.

Still, early in 1932 he was confident that he could recapture the public
esteem that had marked his 18-year public career and he anticipated another term in the White House. The complete repudiation at the polls
was wholly unexpected, though 13 million people were unemployed by
late 1932, more than a fourth of the work force.[1]

In his memoirs Hoover claimed that he knew he had little chance for
reelection, but that he had resolved to fight to the end.[2] His private conversations and correspondence offer another view. Despite the unhealthy

economy, Hoover surveyed potential Democratic candidates and decided that he matched up well with all of them. He understood that the depression had generated anger and resentment, but he also knew that most Americans had voted Republican in presidential elections for 36 years. He could not believe that the depression would cause voters to leave the party to cast votes for one of the unpopular or unproven Democrats. He knew the campaign would be difficult but, despite occasional fits of despondency,[3] Hoover thought that crafty political planning and execution might stave off disaster.

Depression encouraged many to ignore tradition, and campaigning began quite early. In January 1931, a full year before the traditional election season, three-term Maryland Governor Albert C. Ritchie, a Democrat, devoted his fourth inaugural speech to national issues, indirectly initiating his bid for the White House.[4] In June Republican Gov. Gifford Pinchot of Pennsylvania employed the national governor's conference in French Lick Springs, Indiana, as a forum for a verbal fusillade against Hoover's energy policies. His intent was unmistakable. A former secretary of the interior, Pinchot was closely identified with Theodore Roosevelt and the Progressive movement. Senator George W. Norris, a Progressive from Nebraska who later supported Franklin Roosevelt, immediately announced that he was for Pinchot "five hundred times more than . . . for President Hoover."[5]

The premature campaigns offered the public a diversion from the depression, but they had little impact on the primaries, especially in Pinchot's case. No sitting president had been ousted by his own party since Chester A. Arthur lost the nomination to Grover Cleveland in 1884, and Pinchot was an anachronism, a throwback to another, more reform-minded generation. Americans in 1931 wanted jobs, not ideals.

Hoover's real intraparty threat came from Calvin Coolidge. Always closemouthed and generally secretive about his personal ambitions, Coolidge could have tapped old-line, conservative support from those eager for a return to his laissez-faire leadership. Coolidge disappointed them. A regular contributor to the *Saturday Evening Post*, in October 1931 he reviewed in his regular column his decision to step down in 1928. It had been based upon personal considerations and the nation's best interests, and he would not retreat from that position but would support Hoover, he wrote. His endorsement turned out to be his last political decision.[6] He died 15 months later. Other GOP hopefuls included Coolidge's vice president Charles Dawes, ambassador to Great Britain under Hoover; isolationist Senator William Borah, of Idaho; Hoover's old nemesis Senator Hiram Johnson, of California; and Norris.

Still, no Republican but Hoover seemed to appeal to voters in 1932, establishing much the same party scenario as in 1928. The *Literary Digest* in January asked 70 daily newspaper editors to list potential Republican and Democratic candidates. Hoover headed everyone's list. Noncandidate Coolidge came in second with 43 votes. Borah was listed next with 31; Johnson, 28; Pinchot, 26; Dawes, 25; and Norris, 24. A dozen others shared the remaining scattered votes. Two editors even cast straw ballots for Theodore Roosevelt, though he had been dead for 13 years. Except for Hoover, all potential nominees had been unsuccessful in the past or were relatively unknown. Who among these weak contenders would have been foolish enough to challenge an incumbent for the nomination during the worst unemployment crisis in national history? From the outset, Republicans knew their presidential hopes in 1932 rested with Herbert Hoover.[7]

The Democrats had surprisingly few options, too. In 1930 Governor Franklin D. Roosevelt won reelection by a landslide, capturing the attention and support of both journalists and party leaders. One exception was the influential but obviously fallible Walter Lippmann, who wrote of Roosevelt in January 1932: "[He is] an amiable man with many philanthropic impulses, but he is not the dangerous enemy of anything. He is too eager to please."[8]

Roosevelt was well positioned for the nomination. He was a first-time presidential candidate, and since his reelection in 1930, he had avoided controversy. His famous and revered family name gave him instant voter recognition, even if his sixth cousin had been a Republican. Every editor polled by the *Digest* in January 1932 mentioned Roosevelt. All but one also listed conservative Newton D. Baker, Woodrow Wilson's secretary of war, though Baker was not interested.[9] Ritchie had 63 votes; and 1928 nominee Al Smith, 56. Thirty other Democrats polled at least one vote, including Roosevelt's eventual vice presidential nominee John Nance Garner, the Speaker of the House from Texas.[10] Garner was a leading contender until he was undercut during the primaries by a protracted congressional battle over a federal sales tax.[11]

While nothing more than a collection of impressions of editors, the straw poll did offer a rough outline of the preprimary outlook. Hoover was unchallenged, while Baker's disinterest and Ritchie's lack of national exposure clearly left a Roosevelt-Smith race. Both Democrats formally declared in early 1932. Hoover soon followed.

Most newspapers and magazines reported on the 1932 campaign with enthusiasm and usually the customary bias. This led to contradictory scrutiny of the president's public record. As early as June 1931, the *Nation* published a series that explained how the Hoover Administration had failed. In contrast, William Allen White, famed editor of the *Emporia (Kansas) Gazette*, editorialized that Hoover was a genius whose programs had staved off financial disaster. White's words were reprinted and circulated by the Republican National Committee.[12]

The debate continued into the primary season. In January 1932 political analyst Elliott Thurston wrote for *Scribner's* magazine that Hoover could not be reelected. Thurston observed:

Mr. Hoover's best friends agree that he was badly oversold at the peak of an inflationary period and that the subsequent decline in values has made the contrast between the advertising that went with him and what he has been able to deliver, conspicuous to the point of painfulness.[13]

He concluded, "Mr. Hoover's only hope is that the Democrats will make some politically ruinous mistakes."[14] *Springfield (Mass.) Union* editor Henry B. Russell responded in *Scribner's* two months later that no one had foretold the calamitous market collapse and its consequences were not of the president's doing. Hoover was still the best organized, most competent person to deal with the crisis, Russell added.[15]

Thurston and Russell capsulized the themes of the campaign. Supporters contended that Hoover was a victim of circumstance and that better times were just ahead, and detractors hammered the Administration with unemployment figures and sales charts. Republicans could only point to intangibles, while Democrats eagerly cited hard facts and statistics. Hoover was forced to put the best face on a terrible political situation, while Democrats had only to ask voters to look around. Prohibition provided an emotional sidelight with Roosevelt committing himself to repeal and Hoover stubbornly opposed, but a Prohibition debate was a luxury for better times. Still, Hoover was so angered by the suggestion of a wet plank in the party platform that he threatened privately not to accept the nomination. "The president actually drafted a message today . . . declining renomination," Joslin recorded on June 14, two days before the convention.[16] The president relented when Joslin convinced him that such a plank could not be forced upon him. For the most part, though, depression was the key issue and foremost in voters' minds.

Both Hoover and Joslin underestimated Roosevelt and misjudged the public's mood. Just as the Smith-Roosevelt primary campaign got underway, Hoover exalted that the spirited Democratic race was his "first real break." Joslin wrote in his diary:

I would prefer Roosevelt to almost any other leading Democrat for the President's opponent . . . the people would come to understand he has not the ability nor the mentality to be President. As an unfortunate fact, too, he is a paralytic, depriving him of the strength to properly handle the duties of the President.[17]

Roosevelt's legs were paralyzed after he suffered an attack of infantile paralysis in 1921, and after that he walked haltingly only with the aid of crutches.

After Roosevelt's defeat in the Massachusetts primary and a narrow victory in Pennsylvania, Hoover told Joslin he did not think that Roosevelt could get the nomination. "He [Hoover] is rather disturbed," Joslin noted, "for he would like to go against the New York governor. However, when a man [Hoover] is far out in the lead you must have some one to beat him with and that some one is not in sight today."[18] Lippmann wrote that Roosevelt's loss in the Massachusetts primary dealt the New York governor a severe blow. He had been unsuccessful despite the support of the Boston Democratic machine, and his popularity outside New York was questionable, Lippmann concluded.[19] Weeks later just before the Democratic National Convention, Joslin recorded that the White House was convinced that Democratic leaders would rally around Owen Young, president of the General Electric Corporation, for the nomination.[20]

The president hoped to exploit his opponent's weaknesses and employ the same bandwagon strategy that had worked in 1928. He called upon his journalist friends to write supportive articles and help plan his campaign strategy. But unlike 1928, words of praise gushed from only the most loyal supporters, and even their exaltations had changed. In 1928 they hailed the great Engineer who could accomplish anything. In 1932 they told readers that Hoover was basically a decent, hard-working person, but they avoided arguments about dynamic leadership or a sterling public record.[21] Hoover himself wrote a few articles for magazines to offer advice and counsel to financially pinched Americans in hopes of showing them that he really did care about their misfortunes.[22]

Opposing writers either commiserated with or vilified the president. "Pity him? Of course," wrote Oswald Garrison Villard, editor of *Nation* magazine. "Who would not pity the man who, after toiling for years to achieve the greatest office in the gift of his fellow citizens, finds himself confronted by a situation beyond his intelligence to comprehend, his ability to master, his power to lead?"[23] Some opponents, including Walter W. Liggett, wrote critical biographies of the president. The organizer of a private Soviet food relief effort in 1921, Liggett had been publicly labeled a communist and then snubbed later by Hoover, the director of the U.S. government's European relief program. Liggett's vengeful book charged that Hoover had created policies that kept Europe in turmoil for years after World War I. He also claimed that many of Hoover's close friends benefitted financially from the Belgian Relief program.[24] These charges were false, but the book was released with the same precise timing as pro-Hoover books that had been circulated in 1928. This time, many were willing to listen to the anti-Hoover distortions. Liggett's book provoked Leslie Urquhart, a long- time Hoover mining associate, to respond publicly that such criticism came only from Bolshevik propagandists.[25] The sharpest attacks on the president focused on the depression, however, the most damaging claim being that Hoover did nothing while people lost their jobs and families went hungry.

Ironically, Hoover's friends hindered his campaign almost as much as his enemies. Many in Hoover's inner circle blindly assured him that he would certainly win, while other Republicans shied away from active campaign support. The first group was particularly damaging, because the anxious president wanted to believe them. As early as February 1931 Alan Fox, a member of the New York State Republican Committee, told reporters that if business improved as expected, Hoover would easily be reelected.[26] In late March 1932 *Pathfinder* magazine released a straw poll indicating that the president would out-draw any Democratic opponent by a two-to-one margin in November. The magazine reminded readers that it was too early to make unshakable predictions, but the headline trumpeted: "It Looks Like a Hoover year—And How!" The Washington-based magazine reminded readers that *Pathfinder* was an independent journal and had taken the president to task many times in the past.[27] Hoover studied the poll for a half hour in the White House and told Joslin he was much encouraged. Joslin wrote that the Hoover White House was greatly reassured.[28] The press secretary noted in his diary a few weeks later that voters either seemed to be enthusiastic supporters or angry opponents and predicted the campaign would be filled with emotion, but his confidence did not seem to waver.[29]

On the eve of the primary campaign Mark Sullivan sent a private memo to the president relaying the gist of a conversation between book publisher W. D. Howe and Adolph S. Ochs, publisher of *The New York Times*. Ochs predicted a Hoover victory, Sullivan gleefully reported.[30] Two months later Sullivan wrote that financier Bernard Baruch sensed "a distinctly better feeling on Wall Street" than in recent months. At least twice more, Sullivan sent the president quotes from businessmen all over the country who, he said, were telling him that they sensed a positive shift in the nation's economic condition. However, he also told Hoover that millionaire Joseph Kennedy (father of Democratic president John F. Kennedy) feared for the future.[31] Advertising executive Albert Lasker badgered *Chicago Tribune* publisher Robert R. McCormick to support Hoover, and Sullivan triumphantly reported that Lasker had been successful.[32] Because Sullivan continued to breakfast with Hoover three and four times a week, presumably these memos represent only a small percentage of Sullivan's daily infusion of optimism.

Other pro-Hoover newspapermen also pumped up Hoover's hopes. Malcolm W. Bingay, editorial director of the *Detroit Free Press*, wrote in June to assure the president that he had been badly treated by the media. "The great common people are beginning to resent it and you are now winning their sympathy," he concluded.[33] Two months later, Willis J. Abbot, editor of the *Christian Science Monitor*, added: "Irrespective of the times or economic conditions, I am entirely confident of your reelection."[34] In July Edward T. Butler, editor and publisher of the *Buffalo*

Evening News, wrote that Roosevelt's nomination meant certain victory for the president.[35] The *San Francisco Chronicle* carried a front page editorial in April reporting that voters were turning away from the irrational appeal of Hoover's opponents and putting "Pollyanna platitudes behind." The writers added, "If the test of leadership is that it be followed, Herbert Hoover is now the leader, not only of the Republican but of the Democratic Party—and, for that matter, of the world."[36] Frank Knox, publisher of the *Chicago Daily News*, was another avid Hoover supporter who offered the president reassurance and support. Knox was so close to Hoover that a Republican assistant state's attorney wrote to the White House in September that Knox was looked upon by Cook Country Republicans as "the personal representative of the president." *Tribune* publisher Robert R. McCormick was particularly unhappy with Knox's privileged position, and Hoover would lose many Cook County votes to Roosevelt if the rift were not mended, the letter warned.[37] Hoover sent the letter on to Knox,[38] but Knox went ahead and organized Hoover's campaign in Illinois and the Midwest anyway.[39]

What fueled such optimism? Possibly the public's hesitancy to support either Smith or Roosevelt or maybe the uncertain political climate during such distressing times. Or blind dogmatism. Or wishful thinking.

Even bitter enemies indirectly and unintentionally provided reassurance. In a January 2 radio speech William Randolph Hearst personally urged voters to support Garner and later directed one of his editors to write a Garner campaign biography,[40] but by Easter Garner's flagging campaign had frustrated Hearst. In a front page editorial appearing in late March in all 28 of his newspapers, Hearst castigated the party for a multitude of political sins, but especially for missing a golden opportunity to place a "responsible" Democrat in the White House. "Yes, General Grant was right!" Hearst thundered. "Perhaps the Democrats WILL always do the wrong thing and, perhaps it is NOT safe to entrust the country to their hands." They had handed Hoover the election as an Easter present, Hearst concluded.[41] Whatever the reasons, Hoover listened to what he wanted to hear and was not greatly concerned as the summer approached.

The president gained the endorsement of more than half the nation's daily newspapers, 52 percent, to Roosevelt's 40.5 percent,[42] but usually published support for Hoover was unenthusiastic or qualified. Hoover had only cultivated a few publishers and writers, and the insolent mood in the White House did not reassure the nation's opinion makers. Hoover's majority support only proved that most newspapers in the 1930s were owned by wealthy individuals, who endorsed Republicans. In fact Alfred Landon in 1936 enjoyed the endorsements of 57.1 percent of dailies, Wendel Willkie 63.9 percent in 1940, and Thomas Dewey 61.1 percent in 1944, though Roosevelt easily won reelection each time.

Republican politicians avoided close identification with the president and his chancy reelection campaign. Some Progressive congressmen including Norris, Robert La Follette, Hiram Johnson, Bronson W. Cutting, Donald Richberg, and Harold Ickes even supported Roosevelt, despite Hoover's traditional Progressive record.[43] Secretary of State Henry L. Stimson announced that he had to remain neutral in the campaign and made only one nonpartisan speech on foreign affairs.[44] Theodore Roosevelt's son, Ted, was going to return from his post as governor general of the Philippines to campaign for Hoover, but he balked when his sister Alice Roosevelt Longworth wired him and told him not to bother. Hoover was going to lose, she wrote.[45] Ted Roosevelt then showed reporters a letter from Secretary of War Patrick J. Hurley informing the governor general that he was needed in the Philippines.[46] "He's a quitter," an angry Hoover told Joslin in the White House. Later, Ted Roosevelt offered to campaign anyway, but Hoover declined. "I've no use for quitters," he told his press secretary. Ted Roosevelt's last name would have helped the president, but Hoover's pride was stung and he would not relent.[47]

Even long-time Hooverite journalists balked at active campaign support. Early in 1932 the White House contacted Alfred H. Kirchhofer, managing editor of the *Buffalo Evening News.* Hoover wanted him to help direct campaign publicity as he had done in 1928. This time, though, when Kirchhofer asked permission from Butler, the publisher balked. Butler and Kirchhofer in 1931 had both advised Hoover to work more amicably with reporters and to create a more activist image, but the stubborn president had not taken their advice, so the *Buffalo Evening News,* one of most pro-Hoover newspapers in the country, shied away. Kirchhofer insisted later that Butler had refused to let him join the campaign only because the financially weakened newspaper needed him on the staff. "I think he [Hoover] was disappointed, but he understood," Kirchhofer also recalled. Hoover never held a grudge, Kirchhofer added.[48] Henry J. Allen directed campaign publicity, instead. Former press secretary George Akerson returned to direct East Coast publicity.

Kirchhofer's response perhaps typifies Hoover's problem in 1932. More than half the nation's newspapers endorsed him, but the overwhelming newspaper and magazine acclamation he received in 1928 was missing. Absent, too, was the support of important newspapers and newspaper chains. Hearst and Scripps-Howard returned to the Democrats as did the *Washington Post, The New York Times,* and many Southern newspapers. The *Times* defection was the most disappointing to the president, who considered the Ochs family personal friends. Ochs left the decision to his editorial board, however, and they opted for Roosevelt. Still, the national desk tried to cover the campaign fairly and evenly. Neil MacNeil, assistant managing editor, was in charge of the 1932 campaign coverage. He remembered: "I was determined that he [Hoover] get a fair and accurate hearing in *The New York Times*, and I did it. I covered the conventions; I saw that the texts of his speeches were used accurately."[49]

The impact of Hearst's change of heart troubled some western Republicans. Mark Requa, a long-time Hoover supporter and a GOP national committeeman from California, wrote to the president's secretary Walter R. Newton, in August. "Has anyone given any consideration to the reprinting of some of the Hearst full-page endorsements of Hoover that were printed in the '28 campaign?" Requa asked.[50] Allen wrote to Baker that Herbert Kaufmann, "a brilliant" ad man, had written those advertisements and was going to compose other advertisements for the 1932 campaign, but Allen did not favor dredging up the 1928 ads. "I am afraid it would merely emphasize the fact that Hearst was with us four years ago and isn't with us now," he wrote. Then with a touch of both annoyance and disillusionment he added: "There are a lot of people in that category."[51]

But Requa persisted. Three weeks later he wrote to the Hoover campaign committee.

I would like to know just how rough this campaign can be made so far as Hearst is concerned. He is treating Hoover about as rough as anyone can be treated. . . . It seems to me when the women of the United States know that the mistress of William Randolph Hearst is entertaining Roosevelt that the reaction will not be good for him.[52]

The campaign, however, held to the code of the times and did not delve into the private lives of either Hearst or Roosevelt. In the same note Requa worried about a Hollywood pageant sponsored by Hearst's woman friend, Marion Davies. The pageant was planning to honor Hearst and was considering Roosevelt as keynote speaker. This would provide positive publicity for both. Requa wanted to somehow stop such a public relations boost. Requa suggested that Hearst's heavy-handed political activism actually offended Californians, who would like nothing better than an anti-Hearst, anti-Roosevelt drive. Requa suggested that the campaign committee plaster billboards in California with ads headlined: "Hoover or Hearst, Take Your Choice."[53]

THE GENERAL ELECTION CAMPAIGN

The Republicans met in Chicago and nominated Hoover for reelection on June 16. The convention was noticeably subdued. Excessive hoopla during such times would have alienated voters. The entire nominating process was rather mundane and uneventful, and Hoover hardly interrupted his White House routine during the three-day convention. As was tradition, the president remained in the White House. Mr. and Mrs. Hoover sat in the Lincoln Study and listened for a few hours to the nominating speeches over the radio. With the Hoovers were Akerson, Joslin, and Marie Meloney, the friendly editor of the *New York Herald Tribune* Sunday magazine.[54] After the first-ballot nomination ended at noon, Hoover eased from his chair and announced: "Well, it wasn't exactly unexpected. Guess I will go back to the office now." After laboring for hours in the Oval Office on a speech about prohibition, Hoover left his office and passed Joslin in the hallway.

"You must be happy tonight," Joslin said.

"Yes, it came out as good as could be expected in the circumstances," Hoover answered simply.[55]

When reporters congratulated him the next day, he thanked them and said that the press "had been most kind."[56] Two days later he announced that except for a few major addresses he would not take part in the forthcoming campaign, because he wanted to concentrate on running the country. Everett Sanders would serve as Republican National Committee chairman, he said, and Sanders would be in charge.[57]

Hoover accepted the nomination on August 11, exactly four years to the day after his first acceptance speech at Stanford. This time he delivered a lengthy address in Washington's Constitution Hall before an audience of four thousand. Both the Columbia Broadcasting System and the National Broadcasting Company carried the speech live. This was Hoover's first radio broadcast in over five months and only the third of the year. He acknowledged to his audience both in the hall and around the country that the nation had endured the worst economic times since Reconstruction. He reviewed all that he had undertaken to help Americans and what he proposed to do, if reelected. He touched on foreign problems and other domestic plans including his support of prohibition, but mainly the speech was a defense of his economic policies.[58] It was a typical Hoover speech: straightforward, honest, insightful, filled with facts, boring, and delivered in a hurried monotone.

Two days later, a party rift developed over the Republican platform, which Borah heatedly opposed, especially the prohibition plank which did not specifically support the Eighteenth Amendment. Hoover feared a third party try by Borah, but could find no politician who would publicly mediate the dispute.[59] Mark Sullivan visited the recalcitrant Borah at his home in Idaho, but the senator would not budge.[60] He relented only reluctantly later in the campaign. The post-convention tiff underscored Hoover's weak political support.

Two weeks later, Roosevelt was also nominated in Chicago, but on the fourth ballot and only after a bitter struggle with Smith. Hearst personally intervened to break the stalemate. Roosevelt supporters contacted Hearst in California and he agreed to convince Garner to trade his delegates from the California and Texas delegations in exchange for the vice presidential nomination.[61] When the California delegation broke on the fourth ballot, the convention stampeded to Roosevelt. The New York governor ignored tradition and delivered his acceptance speech at the convention. The governor promised a "new deal for the American people."[62] The phrase caught on later.

Since leaving the *New York World* in 1929, Charles Michelson had directed publicity for the Democratic Party and had been closely identified with Al Smith. Just after Roosevelt's nomination, Louis Howe brought Michelson to the Congress Hotel to meet Roosevelt. Howe was a former *New York Herald Tribune* reporter and the governor's campaign coordinator. "Glad to see you aboard the ship," Roosevelt told Michelson. The former *World* reporter proved to be invaluable to Roosevelt. Michelson deftly exploited Hoover's record and capitalized on his tarnished public image.[63] Hoover and the Republicans hated Michelson and for decades blamed much of the unscrupulous Democratic campaign tactics on him. In 1944, Michelson responded in his memoirs: "When we pointed out numerous mistakes to the extent and acuteness of the financial depression, we were accused of reveling in the misfortunes of the people." Michelson argued that he only was publicizing the ugly truth, but the Michelson reputation became legendary among Hoover supporters.[64]

Radio played a role different in 1932 from that in 1928. Stations and radio receivers had multiplied, and Americans had made radio a part of their daily lives by 1932. In 1932 CBS had 90 affiliates, almost double the number in 1928, and NBC had 85, ten more than four years earlier. Improved technology made radio receivers smaller and less costly and radio microphones less cumbersome. More than 12 million people owned radios by 1932, and Chicago, the site of both conventions, had excellent radio transmission facilities.[65] *The New York Times* incorrectly speculated that radio would force politicians to shorten their speeches that year.[66]

But, at the same time, listeners could barely afford to fix the radio if it broke, and political activists did not have much money to pay for election advertising. Neither party was able to spend as much on radio speeches and advertisements as in 1928. Lasker tried to raise $25,000 in October for a Coolidge speech in support of Hoover, but struggled. "Men are feeling poor," Mark Sullivan wrote to Hoover. "One man who gave $5,000 four years ago is willing to give only $250 now."[67] More speeches and political events were broadcast live over radio in 1932 than in 1928, but less money was spent on advertising and paid political persuasion.

With Roosevelt crisscrossing the nation and speaking to cheering crowds, Hoover in September was forced to abandon his plan to stay in the White House. Joslin pointed out that both Taft and Wilson had campaigned for renomination in 1912 and 1916 and so such a step was not unprecedented.[68] Plans for a series of public addresses were quickly put into place, and Hoover canvassed the country, especially the usually Republican Midwest, where he hoped to coalesce sagging support. "You don't need to tell me that Kansas, Missouri, Iowa, Minnesota and the Dakotas are lost. I know it. I have been told that twenty times," an exasperated Hoover told two newspaper editors on September 18.[69] His first broadcast campaign speech came on September 29 at the Women's Conference on Current Problems, sponsored by the *New York Herald Tribune* at the Waldorf-Astoria Hotel in New York.[70] This was an obvious ploy by Marie Meloney to entice American women to vote for Hoover. Hoover also made radio speeches in Des Moines, Cleveland, Detroit, Indianapolis, New York, St. Louis, St. Paul, and Elko, Nev. He addressed the nation by radio twice from the White House, once to deal with the unemployment question and once to appeal to women voters. One speech celebrating California Day was delivered at the Carleton Hotel in Washington just before the election and was carried only by CBS's Pacific Coast stations.[71]

Roosevelt, too, spoke frequently on radio impressing Americans with his wit and charisma and telling them in simple language that he would solve their problems, not make promises. Therein was the difference between Hoover's radio strategy and Roosevelt's. Radio's effect on the 1932 election had nothing to do with money. It had to do with change. Hoover was not a media president, and certainly not a radio president. Roosevelt definitely was. When Roosevelt spoke with his deep, rich, melodious voice, he oozed confidence and reassurance. He also kept his message simple and direct and did not try to make each speech a complex explanation of the issues of the day. "Are President Hoover's speeches too packed with facts to be assimilated by the ordinary hearer [*sic*] or reader?" asked *San Francisco Chronicle* editor Chester H. Rowell three weeks before the election. "They [politicians] observe that the President gives more facts in one sentence than the average political speech—Governor Roosevelt's, for instance—would contain in an hour." Would Americans prefer a man with facts or one with a smile, Rowell asked rhetorically.[72] Radio's influence and Roosevelt's charisma provided ready answers.

By early October both Hoover and Roosevelt were tirelessly traveling about the country, speaking to crowds of skeptical listeners, who weighed every word carefully knowing that their futures might depend on who they elected. "Aside from the value of truth, the causes and origins of this unparalleled storm [depression] are of importance only as they indicate the policies we must pursue to attain our safety," Hoover told a hushed crowd in the Des Moines Coliseum on October 4.[73] Three weeks later in Policies Stadium, Charleston, West Virginia, Hoover told the crowd of mostly miners and their families:

Our people are beginning to return to work. The signs of economic life show in every quarter. That is proof of the soundness, the ability, the character, and the willingness of the Republican Party to bring the strength and power of the Federal Government to the protection of our people in times of need.[74]

Essentially, neither the miners nor other Americans agreed. On October 22 in Detroit where unemployment had reached 50 percent, Hoover was booed lustily at the train station and his motorcade traveled past silent, hostile crowds as it made its way downtown to Olympia Arena, but the president spoke to a crowd of about 20,000 without incident.[75] Days earlier, Secret Service men were edgy about the presence of many former bonus marchers in Des Moines and had feared for Hoover's safety, but the crowd cheered enthusiastically during Hoover's address.[76] Hoover supporters were thankful for the warm reception in Des Moines and for the huge crowds that met his train the next day during a 16-city whistle stop trip beginning in Chicago and ending in Johnstown, Pennsylvania, the same city where the bonus marchers had sought refuge after the July rout. Joslin wrote after their stop in Johnstown that the crowds seemed to be greeting a conquering hero. "Yet I know that every state we passed through is likely to go Democratic. I cannot reconcile the two opposites," he added.[77]

Roosevelt, meanwhile, criticized the Smoot-Hawley Tariff and Hoover's economic programs while promising to balance the budget. His "New Deal," he said, would provide unemployment insurance, federal relief, and public works projects, but he was not specific on how and how much.[78] Smith, at first, remained aloof from the early Roosevelt campaign, licking his wounds and brooding. Roosevelt was hard-pressed to explain to reporters why Smith skipped a Long Island luncheon with the governor in late August as the campaign was beginning.[79] Eventually Smith gave Roosevelt a lukewarm endorsement after the two men reached an accord at the New York state convention in October. Crowds cheered Roosevelt wherever he traveled and unscientific newspaper and magazine polls, including the famed *Literary Digest* poll, put the New York governor far ahead of Hoover.[80] Hoover campaign people publicly predicted victory and decried the polls or produced their own unscientific voter samplings that suggested Hoover was winning.[81] Sullivan predicted that the election would be close and that New York state's 47 electoral votes would be decisive.[82]

The candidates sharpened their attacks as the campaign progressed,[83] but there was not the same mudslinging that marked the Smith-Hoover election. Though Hoover tried to portray Roosevelt as a revolutionary who would lead the country to ruin and Roosevelt described Hoover as the purveyor of the nation's miseries, neither really debated the issues. Writing in *Current History* magazine in December 1932, E. Francis Brown observed: "The campaign of 1932, like so many in American history, presented few clear-cut issues." Unlike 1928, Prohibition and religion were not major factors. Voters did not enthusiastically follow the campaign to learn which of the candidates would keep them happy or what new horizons the future would bring. They wanted to know who could guarantee new jobs and put food on the table. The tenor was different. Roosevelt's theme song was "Happy Days Are Here Again," but beleaguered Americans only wanted decent days again. Optimistic White House supporters hoped that Hoover could squeak out a narrow victory and spend the next four years repairing the economy with his brand of budget control and cautious spending.

Newspaper and magazine campaign coverage, though biased, centered around speeches and public declarations by candidates and supporters. Despite the calls for more insightful journalism from people like Walter Lippmann and Marie Meloney in 1931, stories in 1932 rarely contained objective interpretation or unbiased analysis. Instead, readers were treated to intemperate attacks from both spectrums—the Hearst newspapers and the *Los Angeles Times*, for instance—or weighted coverage of speeches and political rallies.[84] Frank Parker Stockbridge informed *American Press* readers in August that reporters would be biased and "my candid opinion, without a count of noses, is that more of the Washington reporters dislike Mr. Hoover than like him, and that the opposite is true in the case of Governor Roosevelt."[85] If he was referring to Washington reporters, Stockbridge may have been correct, because Hoover was by autumn 1932 heartily unpopular with the press corps there. He discontinued press conferences from September until after the election.[86] Roosevelt's attitude toward Washington reporters was not generally known, but correspondents in Albany found him accessible and cooperative. It is likely that Stockbridge's assessment was true, but the political persuasion of the newspaper or magazine had more to do with the campaign coverage than attitudes of the correspondents, whether they were from Washington or the home office.

Roosevelt finished the campaign with speeches and dinners in Brooklyn, while Hoover spent the last five days campaigning his way west through Pennsylvania, Indiana, Illinois, Missouri, Wisconsin, Minnesota, Nebraska, Colorado, Wyoming, Utah, and Nevada.[87] His final speech came on election eve in Elko, Nevada, where he addressed the entire nation from his rail car through a special remote national radio hookup. "And now through the magic of broadcasting we are to take you swiftly almost to the Pacific Ocean," the announcer's anxious voice told the radio audience, "over the wheat fields of Nebraska and Kansas, high over the Rocky Mountains and following through to the State of Nevada, transporting you to a train where the President of the United States is seated in front of a microphone."

In the nasal monotone that had become familiar to millions of Americans, Hoover spoke slowly and faintly into the microphone: "My fellow citizens. . . . " The sound of Hoover adjusting his chair could be heard and the voice became much louder and clearer. "We have been through an arduous campaign. It has been a campaign almost unique in the education of the great domestic and international problems which have arisen out of the events of the last fifteen years." Hoover reviewed his three-and-a-half years in office. One million men had returned to work since the adjournment of Congress, he told his listeners. He listed other successes, told his audience he had done his best, and reminded listeners that the Republican Party had always been the party of progress for the future. Toward the end of the address, all the president's papers and notes tumbled past the microphone to the floor in a series of swishing thuds that sounded to listeners like the collapse of a dam. Hoover's voice was temporarily muffled, but he continued with only a brief hesitation: "should not be led astray by the false colors of promises." He continued uneasily for several minutes before concluding: "The president must represent the nation's ideals, and he must also represent them to the nations of the world. After four years of experience I still regard this as a supreme obligation."[88] Nothing startling. No surprises and nothing really to hold on to. The delivery was hurried and amateurish and was interrupted by the papers falling to the floor. His voice contained no animation or soothing reassurance. Probably, few Americans were swayed by the complex radio hookup that conveyed an intelligent, but uninformative and amateurish last-minute appeal.

Joslin predicted on October 31 that Hoover had cut Roosevelt's lead in half, but the press secretary changed his mind a week later, writing that "things certainly look bad for the president."[89] Rickard was so confident that he bet $200 and gave his fellow wagerers four-to-one odds, though oddsmakers were offering five-to-one against Hoover.[90] Herbert and Lou Henry Hoover traveled from Elko to Palo Alto to vote on election day and await the results.

The networks carried the results to the nation that evening and the newspapers the next morning.[91] Hoover's worst fears were realized. Roosevelt swept all but six states. The Hoover electoral votes came mostly in the conservative Northeast: Delaware, Connecticut, Maine, New Hampshire, and Vermont. Pennsylvania was the only large state in the Hoover column. The president collected 59 electoral votes to FDR's 472. Roosevelt polled 22.8 million votes, 59 percent, to Hoover's 15.8 million, 41 percent. Democrats gained huge majorities in both Houses, 60 to 35 in the Senate and 310 to 117 in the House.[92]

The White House staff including Joslin would soon be without work, just like many of their fellow Americans. "Neither Walter nor I know what the future holds," Joslin wrote the day after the election.[93] Rickard's bet cost him $800, "money I can ill afford to lose," he noted bitterly. He angrily blamed the election on Walter Lippmann's flipflopping, castigating Roosevelt at the beginning of the election season and praising him at the end.[94] Lippmann spoke over NBC radio the night of the election and said the results meant that the nation could now unify in its fight against the depression.[95] Hoover told reporters the next day that he had no plans except to return to the White House and continue his work.[96] "This is a blue day," Joslin wrote. "Messages are pouring in, all expressing sincere regret."[97] Reporters in the White House now would have only four months left to joust with Hoover and, though they did not know it then, a much longer time to spend with Roosevelt.

But the real change would be in the nation's political and philosophical agenda. Not only had Roosevelt swept into office, but the Democrats had carried decisive majorities in both Houses for the first time in the century. The election was a complete repudiation of the Republicans and a total personal rejection of Hoover. Not only had the president only carried six states, but his impressive victory in 1928 meant that the 1932 election was the biggest turnaround in U.S. history. It would be a watershed election, because in the coming years Roosevelt would form a dominant Democratic coalition that would hold for 30 years more. Hoover's image as a Great Humanitarian and as a popular public figure had disintegrated. Future Americans would not even remember how he had come to be so popular, only that he had directed the rout of miserable bonus veterans from Washington and had been in charge when Americans felt the wrath of the Great Depression. Hoover left office a beaten and discouraged man, but the final months of his term brought no respite and his drooping image would have to withstand one more barrage.

LEAVING OFFICE

Newspapers of all persuasions congratulated Roosevelt on his election and called for cooperation between the old and new administrations, because difficult times still lay ahead. The sweeping electoral mandate meant that Roosevelt was free from all political ties and could pursue an independent course, Mark Sullivan wrote.[98] The *Philadelphia Public Ledger* summed up: "The election . . . gives to the Democratic Party not only complete power, but complete responsibility—and it is a sobering responsibility."[99] The *Ledger*'s words were prophetic, but for the next four months the nation remained paralyzed by lack of cooperation between its leaders and by deteriorating economic conditions. The outdated tradition of a long lame-duck period extending from November to March that had begun when horse-and-buggy travel made such an interim necessary became crucial to Americans in the winter of 1932–33.

Hoover returned to the White House from California just a week after his election defeat, determined to work industriously until his last day in office. He held two press conferences that week and spoke freely to reporters without requiring questions in advance, apparently not caring any more whether he was misquoted.[100] While en route back to Washington, he invited Roosevelt to confer with him later in the month, and the President-elect immediately accepted.[101] The British government had asked that the president accept a delay in loan payments to the U.S. government. Hoover proposed a one-year moratorium and wanted Roosevelt's concurrence. The moratorium issue would be a test as to whether the president and president-elect could provide a smooth transition during such difficult times. Roosevelt telephoned the Oval Office nine days after the election to set up a time for the conference. Hoover did not trust Roosevelt and made certain he had a witness, Secretary of War Patrick Hurley, who listened in.[102] The meeting was set for the following Tuesday, but it did not go well. Hoover was disappointed in Roosevelt's superficial knowledge of the problem and Roosevelt would not agree specifically to a joint recommendation to Congress.[103] Roosevelt eventually rejected Hoover's position on the debt question in a private telegram he sent to the White House on December 20.[104] A second meeting on January 20 in Washington on the gold standard also proved to be inconclusive. The incoming president did not want to be tied to any commitments.

In February Hoover tried once more to communicate with Roosevelt, but this time he chose a journalistic courier. Arthur Krock, *The New York Times* bureau chief, had written quite favorably about Roosevelt. Hoover asked him to come to the White House, where Krock conceded to the president that he was "the only friend he [Roosevelt] had in an executive position at *The New York Times*."

"Well, then," Hoover said, "would you undertake a mission for the incumbent president of the United States to the President-elect?"

"Mr. Hoover," Krock answered, "as long as you put it that way, I don't see how I can say, 'no.' What is the mission?"

Hoover told Krock he was concerned about a bill guaranteeing independence to the Philippines and wanted Roosevelt to refrain from criticizing Hoover publicly after he vetoed the bill. Krock conveyed the message, but Roosevelt did not react well to the request and once again agreed to nothing. According to Krock, Louis Howe told Roosevelt that the incident proved that Krock was a Hoover agent and Krock never had a close relationship with Roosevelt again.[105]

It was obvious, then, that there would be little communication between the incoming and the outgoing presidents. The economy and the stock market had rebounded well during the summer of 1932, but conditions worsened again in the fall. By the end of October so many banks had failed in Nevada that the entire state's banking system shut down for six weeks.[106] The crisis spread to other states, causing panic by the end of

February. Roosevelt made certain that voters would never forget what the last days of Republican rule meant to them. The two met twice more to attend Calvin Coolidge's funeral in January and for a tea in the White House the day before the inauguration, but a belated discussion of issues during the tea merely ended in polite disagreement.[107] During his first few days in office, Roosevelt declared a bank holiday and ordered every financial institution in the country closed for three days, while the government supposedly investigated whether they were sound financially.

The final months in office must have seemed agonizing to Hoover. While the nation foundered in economic chaos, he was powerless to do anything but issue perfunctory proclamations and prod an ineffective, lame-duck Congress. He met with reporters six more times, but the correspondents had all turned their attention to the coming Roosevelt Administration and the polite exchanges with Hoover generated little news. At a farewell Gridiron Dinner in December, the president politely thanked the club for its hospitality and told the gathered members that they ought to continue to pursue vigorously their roles as government overseers.[108]

Hoover began to make plans for post-presidential life. Just after the election, he told Joslin that he would remain out of the public eye for several months after leaving office and then in 1934 begin to organize a campaign for the 1936 nomination.[109] Hoover told reporters on February 1 that upon leaving office in March he would observe a public silence for the remainder of the year.[110] Press speculation in February that Hoover would not be head of the Republican Party during the following four years rankled the president, and he nearly called a press conference to denounce the suggestions. He decided against a public statement, though, and instructed Joslin to "laugh it off," if reporters called for comment.[111]

Postmortems on the Hoover years were surprisingly few. The country was too preoccupied with pressing day-to-day troubles and speculation over the new regime. French Strother, Hoover's administrative aide, wrote a lengthy interpretation of the Hoover years in *The New York Times* a week before the inauguration. "Herbert Hoover is of the Woodrow Wilson and Theodore Roosevelt type—original in thought, determined in purpose, dominant in personality and surcharged with creative energy," Strother wrote.[112] The same day, Mark Sullivan told *New York Herald Tribune* readers that the great success of the Hoover Administration was that he kept the American system intact despite the terrible depression.[113] Democratic Senator J. Hamilton Lewis, of Illinois, responded to Strother with his own interpretation a week later. Strother, eloquent as he was, was just trying to lay the foundation for the false argument that Hoover had initiated what Roosevelt hoped to complete, Lewis told *The New York Times*'s readers.[114]

March 4 dawned a gray, dreary day, matching the mood of the expectant country. Hoover and Roosevelt donned tuxedos and top hats and rode silently to the inauguration platform, while waving to cheering but subdued crowds. "The only thing we have to fear is fear itself," Roosevelt proclaimed in a clear, resonant voice as he addressed the nation. The country had been shattered, and Roosevelt would spend the next eight years wedging his way clear of depression, while changing the course of American politics and public life forever. Roosevelt's problems would turn in a new direction years later, but they started within days of his inauguration when Adolf Hitler became chancellor of Germany.

Boisterous, demonstrative crowds greeted the Hoovers upon their return to Palo Alto a few days later, and the couple soon settled into a quiet routine away from the public limelight. Caught up in the excitement and breakneck changes of the New Deal, reporters rarely bothered to seek Hoover's opinion on the revolution in Washington. Private Secretary Lawrence Richey stayed with the Hoovers, but Joslin did not. In the years immediately after he left the White House, Joslin wrote two books, based upon his diary and upon Hoover's speeches. The second book displeased Hoover, who had wanted to use his speeches for his own memoirs, and Joslin and Hoover remained at odds.

Hoover traveled frequently from 1933 to 1935, so much so that he and Lou rented an apartment in New York. Akerson wrote to Hoover a few weeks after Hoover left office and advised him not to say much publicly, though *Los Angeles Times* publisher Harry Chandler counseled the ex-president to do just the opposite.[115] In accordance with his pledge before leaving office, Hoover rarely spoke publicly. However, Michelson and the Democrats made certain that voters never forgot who had been president when the stock market crashed. Hoover's name was trotted out frequently at political rallies or at Democratic conventions for decades to come, making the name "Hoover" synonymous with "depression." In 1934 as a consummate insult to the vanquished president, Secretary of the Interior Harold Ickes even renamed Hoover Dam, Boulder Dam. Congress reversed Ickes in 1947.

In 1934, the ex-president published a book, *The Challenge to Liberty*, in which he set forth principles by which he thought the nation ought to be guided. The book met with negative reviews by such news figures as Arthur Krock.[116] In March of 1935 Hoover began to criticize the Roosevelt Administration publicly, but the Republican Party had moved far to the left of Hoover to keep peace with the popularity of the New Deal, and Hoover never again gained an active role in the party. He spoke for 30 minutes at the 1936 convention, but the nomination easily went to Kansas Governor Alfred E. Landon, who tried to keep Hoover out of his campaign.[117]

During the first few years out of office, Hoover gathered friends and intellectuals at his home nightly to discuss issues and philosophical points. One visitor, who came at Hoover's invitation was 26-year-old Paul Smith, financial editor of the *San Francisco Chronicle*. Smith was infatuated with Hoover and his knowledge and in 1934 resigned from the newspaper to write speeches for the ex-president. *Chronicle* publisher George Cameron wooed Smith back by promoting him to executive editor, but Hoover and Smith remained close. They toured Europe together in 1938, during which time Hoover met privately with Hitler.[118] *Chicago Tribune* Washington bureau correspondent Walter Trohan visited in New York frequently and years later noted that Hoover's greatest pleasure was derived from visits by his sons. "He was not a demonstrative man, but you could see that it pleased him a great deal when his son would lean down to give him a hug and a kiss on the cheek. His family was important to him," Trohan recalled. "He did not like Roosevelt and did not want to say much about him."[119] In his memoirs, Hoover was sharply critical of Roosevelt's policies, calling many of them fascist inspired.[120]

For 20 years, Hoover was the only living ex-president. Unlike most presidents, his image grew more tarnished as the years passed. Many new reporters came to Washington, but those left from the old days never forgave Hoover for his high-handed attitude. Roosevelt's unparalleled success in generating news stories and stirring good will among reporters only made the contrast with Hoover more stark. Roosevelt was as smooth and as manipulative as Hoover had been awkward and uninfluential. As historians and political observers sifted through the details and policies of the Hoover Administration, especially the Bonus Rout, and compared them with the New Deal, they heaped even more scorn on the former president. This despite the fact that, for all of Roosevelt's spending policies, Roosevelt came no closer to ending the depression than did Hoover. Only the outbreak of World War II brought financial prosperity again. Roosevelt, though, made people feel that he was helping them and, at least, provided some measure of individual relief and reassurance. In contrast to Hoover's stuffy speeches, Roosevelt's radio chats were folksy and appealing. They met with unparalleled popular and public acceptance, while a largely amenable press corps helped to build FDR's image. Only Republican newspaper publishers looked back upon the Hoover years fondly, as Roosevelt grew more popular. The publishers themselves, however, grew more and more out of public favor.

Lou Henry Hoover died of a heart attack in 1944. After the funeral, the home in Palo Alto was donated to Stanford University. Hoover lived in a suite at the Waldorf Towers in New York or at a winter retreat in Florida. Never lacking for money, Hoover was comfortable but unloved by those outside his immediate circle. His three-volume memoirs were published in 1950, 1951, and 1952.

In 1945 President Harry S. Truman, an admirer of Hoover and a World

War I veteran himself, asked the former president to direct postwar food relief. In a tearful scene in Truman's office, Hoover gratefully accepted the challenge and traveled 35,000 miles throughout Europe to once again oversee the movement and distribution of food to thousands of starving Europeans.[121] The ex-president also oversaw two commissions on the reorganization of the executive branch in 1947 under Truman and again in 1954 under Dwight D. Eisenhower. Deaf and nearly blind, Hoover died of colon cancer in 1964, somewhat vindicated, but never able to recapture the popularity among reporters and citizens that had marked his early career. As Roger Simon suggested in 1992, ex-presidents, especially those unpopular with reporters, suffer for a long, long time.

NOTES

1. Arthur Schlesinger, *The Age of Roosevelt: The Crisis of the Old Order 1919–1933* (Boston: Houghton Mifflin, 1957), p. 440.

2. Herbert Hoover, *The Memoirs of Herbert Hoover: The Great Depression 1929–1941* (New York: Macmillan, 1952), p. 218 [hereafter Hoover memoirs, vol. 3].

3. Hoover, for instance, told Press Secretary Theodore Joslin in late 1931: "I don't give a damn, Ted, whether I am re-nominated or not." Joslin noted in his diary that it was good for Hoover to blow off steam in private, but that he wanted another term more than anything else. Theodore Joslin diary, Presidential Papers, Individuals, Theodore Joslin, Box 10, Nov. 30, 1931, diary entry.

4. "Ritchie Makes Bid for the Presidency," *The New York Times*, Jan. 15, 1931, p. 1.

5. Pinchot's Hat Sails into the Ring," *Literary Digest*, June 20, 1931, pp. 8–9. See also "Pinchot Attacks Utilities for 'Graft,' " *The New York Times*, June 16, 1931, p. 1; "Norris to Bolt the Hoover Standard Again; He Joins with Long in Backing Roosevelt," *The New York Times*, May 6, 1932, p. 1.

6. Calvin Coolidge, "Party Loyalty and the Presidency," *Saturday Evening Post*, 204, no. 14 (Oct. 3, 1931), pp. 3–4.

7. "Speaking of Candidates," *Literary Digest*, Jan. 16, 1932, pp. 8–9.

8. Walter Lippmann column, "Today and Tomorrow," *New York Herald Tribune*, Jan. 8, 1932.

9. See Jordan A. Schwarz, *The Interregnum of Despair: Hoover, Congress, and the Depression* (Urbana: University of Illinois Press, 1970), p. 180.

10. Ibid.

11. Ibid., pp. 185–88.

12. "Hails Genius of Hoover," circular of the Republican National Committee, 1932, Reprint File for 1932, HHPL.

13. Elliott Thurston, "Hoover Can Not Be Elected," *Scribner's*, January 1932, pp. 13–16.

14. Ibid., p. 16.

15. Henry B. Russell, "Hoover Can Be Elected," *Scribner's*, March 1932, pp. 11–15.

16. Joslin diary entry, June 14, 1932.

17. Joslin diary entry, Feb. 7, 1932.

18. Joslin diary entry, April 26, 1932.

19. Walter Lippmann column, "Today and Tomorrow," *New York Herald Tribune*, April 28, 1932.

20. Joslin diary entry, May 8, 1932.

21. See, for instance, L. C. Speers, "President Hoover's Day Is a Day of Work," *The New York Times*, March 6, 1932, features section, p. 1; "The Return of the President," *New York Herald Tribune* editorial, March 7, 1932; "At Home with the President: His Unofficial Side Revealed," *The New York Times*, April 24, 1932; Will Irwin, "These Whispers about Mr. Hoover," *Liberty*, May 21, 1932, pp. 11–12; William Hard, "How Presidents Are Made," *New York Herald Tribune* magazine, June 12, 1932, features section, pp. 1, 10; Chester T. Crowell, "The President's Eighteen-Hour Day," *Washington Star*, June 19, 1932, features section, p. 1; Mark Sullivan, "The Case for the Administration," unidentified article clipping file 1932, HHPL; Vernon Kellogg, "The President As I Know Him," *Atlantic Monthly*, 150, no. 1 (July 1932), pp. 7–12; Clinton W. Gilbert, "The Kick-the-Chair Vote," *Collier's*, July 9, 1932; William Allen White, "Leading the Way to Recovery," *New York Herald Tribune* Sunday magazine, Aug. 28, 1932, pp. 1–2; Bruce Barton, "Shall I Vote for Hoover?" *Des Moines Register*, Sept. 28, 1932, p. 6.

22. See Herbert Hoover, "From President Hoover to the Ladies' Home Journal," *Ladies Home Journal*, June 1932, p. 5; Hoover, "Ideals in the Midst of Crisis," *Review of Reviews*, September 1932, pp. 26–27.

23. Oswald Garrison Villard, "Pity Herbert Hoover," *Nation*, 134, no. 3493 (June 15, 1932), pp. 669–71. See also George Milburn, "Mr. Hoover's Stalking Horse," *American Mercury*, July 1932, p. 22.

24. "Hoover Policies to Blame for Turmoil after War, New Biographer Charges," *New York World-Telegram*, Jan.8, 1932, p. 1.

25. Leslie Urquhart, "Attacks on President Hoover," *Truth*, May 25, 1932, p. 832–33.

26. "Fox Forecasts Easy Re-Election of Mr. Hoover," *New York Herald Tribune*, Feb. 3, 1931, p. 1.

27. "Pathfinder Poll Reveals Strong Hoover Sentiment" and "It Looks Like a Hoover Year—And How!" *Pathfinder*, 1997 (April 90, 1932), pp. 1–2.

28. Joslin diary entry, March 29, 1932.

29. Joslin diary entry, April 12, 1932.

30. MS to HH memo, Jan. 2, 1932. Sullivan Papers, HHPL.

31. See MS to HH memos of Aug. 5, 1932, Sept. 12, 1932, and undated memo from October 1932, Sullivan Papers, HHPL.

32. MS to HH, Oct. 14, 1932, in ibid. The *Tribune* did endorse Hoover, but not with much enthusiasm.

33. MWB letter to HH, June 20, 1932, President's Personal File, Detroit Free Press, Box 180. See also HH to MWB reply of June 23, 1932 in ibid.

34. WJA to HH letter of Aug. 8, 1932, PPF, Christian Science Monitor, Box 180, HHPL. Also see HH to WJA response of Aug. 9, 1932, in ibid.

35. EHB letter to HH, July 14, 1932, pp. 1–2, PPF, Buffalo Evening News, Box 180, HHPL.

36. "Sober Second Thought of Public Turning to Hoover," *San Francisco Chronicle*, April 27, 1932.

37. Letter from the Cook County State's Attorney's office to Presidential Secretary Walter H. Newton, Sept. 12, 1932, pp. 1–3 (Writer's signature is indecipherable), President's Personal File, Newspapers, Chicago Daily News, Box 167, HHPL.

38. HH to FK letter of Sept. 15, 1932, in ibid.

39. See FK to HH letters of Sept. 21 and 28, 1932 in ibid.

40. Schwarz, *Interregnum of Despair*, p. 185.

41. William Randolph Hearst, "A Suitable Symbol for Insurgent Democrats," *Washington Herald* signed editorial (also appearing in all other Hearst newspapers concurrently), March 29, 1932.

42. Graham S. White, *FDR and the Press* (Chicago: University of Chicago Press, 1979), p. 70.

43. Martin L. Fausold, *The Presidency of Herbert C. Hoover* (Lawrence: University of Kansas Press, 1985), p. 212.

44. Hoover memoirs, vol. 3, p. 233.

45. Joslin diary entry, Sept. 16, 1932.

46. "Hoover Barred Trip, Says Col. Roosevelt," *The New York Times*, Sept. 1, 1932, p. 1.

47. Joslin diary entry, Sept. 15, 1932.

48. Alfred H. Kirchhofer oral history interview with Raymond Henle, director of the Herbert Hoover oral history project, Buffalo, N.Y. April 4, 1969, pp. 20–21, oral history files, HHPL.

49. Neil MacNeil oral history interview with Raymond Henle, director of the Herbert Hoover oral history project, Fort Lauderdale, Fla., Feb. 25, 1967, p. 21, oral history files, HHPL.

50. MR to NB letter of Aug. 22, 1932, Presidential Papers, Individuals, William Randolph Hearst, Box 1045, HHPL.

51. HJA to NB letter of Aug. 25, 1932, in ibid.

52. Mark Requa memo of Sept. 17, 1932, in ibid.

53. Ibid.

54. Joslin diary entry, June 16, 1932.

55. Ibid.

56. *Public Papers of the Presidents of the United States: Herbert Hoover 1932–33* (Washington: U.S. Government Printing Office, 1977), p. 262.

57. Ibid., p. 264–65.

58. Ibid., pp. 357–76.

59. Joslin diary entry, June 18, 1932.

60. Joslin diary entry, Sept. 27, 1932.

61. Gene Smith, *The Shattered Dream: Herbert Hoover and the Great Depression* (New York: William Morrow, 1970), pp. 116–20.

62. Ibid., p. 122; Schlesinger, *Age of Roosevelt*, p. 314.

63. Schlesinger, *Age of Roosevelt*, p. 312; David Burner, *Herbert Hoover* (New York: Knopf, 1979), p. 314; Hoover memoirs, vol. 3, p. 232.

64. Charles Michelson, *The Ghost Talks* (New York: G. P. Putnam's Sons, 1944), pp. 32–33.

65. "Presidential Campaign Looms Big for Broadcasters," *The New York Times*, Jan. 17, 1932, p. 14.

66. Ibid.

67. MS to HH letter of Oct. 14, 1932, Sullivan File, HHPL.

68. Joslin diary entry, Sept, 7, 1932. Also see Theodore C. Wallen, "Hoover Urged to Go on Stump for Ticket," *New York Herald Tribune*, Sept. 4, 1932.

69. Joslin diary entry, Sept, 18, 1932.

70. "Appendix F—Radio Addresses by the President" and "Radio Address to Women's Conference on Current Problems," *Public Papers of the Presidents: Herbert Hoover 1932–33*, p. 1278 and pp. 446–49.

71. Ibid.

72. Chester H. Rowell, "Voters Can Understand Facts; Hoover Gets His Dander Up; Bad Economics Cost Big Money," *San Francisco Chronicle*, Oct. 18, 1932.

73. "Address at the Coliseum in Des Moines, Iowa," Oct. 4, 1932, *Public Papers of the President: Herbert Hoover, 1932–33*, p. 461.

74. "Rear Platform and Other Informal Remarks in West Virginia, Ohio, and Michigan," Oct. 22, 1932, Laidley Stadium, Charleston, West Virginia, in ibid., p. 555.

75. Albert L. Warner oral history interview with Raymond Henle, director of the Herbert Hoover oral history project, Washington, Nov. 11, 1966, p. 9, Oral History Files, HHPL; Schlesinger, *Age of Roosevelt*, p. 432; "Address in Detroit, Michigan," Oct. 22, 1932, *Public Papers of the President: Herbert Hoover 1932–33*, pp. 568–92.

76. Joslin diary entries, Oct. 3, 4, and 5, 1932.

77. Joslin diary entry, Oct. 5, 1932.

78. Schlesinger, *Age of Roosevelt*, p. 433.

79. "Governor Explains Absence of Smith," *The New York Times*, Aug. 30, 1932, p. 1.

80. "Roosevelt Leads in Polls," *The New York Times*, Sept. 5, 1932, p. 1; "Roosevelt's Lead in Polls Analyzed," *The New York Times*, Oct. 17, 1932, p. 1; "Roosevelt Gets 41 States to 7 in 'Digest' Poll," *New York Herald Tribune*, Nov. 4, 1932, p. 3; "The Poll Has Already Smashed All Records," *Literary Digest*, Oct. 29, 1932, p. 9.

81. "Winning the West," *New York Herald Tribune* editorial, Sept. 13, 1932; "Watson Finds Party Outlook Bright in West," *New York Herald Tribune*, Sept. 8, 1932, p. 1; "Moses Predicts East Will Give Hoover Victory," *New York Herald Tribune*, Sept. 2, 1932, p. 1; "Straw Votes Err, Sanders Declares," *The New York Times*, Oct. 17. 1932, p. 1; "Hoover to Win with 338 Votes, Sanders Holds," *New York Herald Tribune*, Nov. 6, 1932, p. 1; Theodore C. Wallen, "Roosevelt Hope for Vote of N.Y. Held Receding," *New York Herald Tribune*, Sept. 3, 1932, p. 1; "Hoover Sweeps Polls Taken in Five Schools," *The New York Times*, Nov. 4, 1932, p. 1.

82. Mark Sullivan, "New York State Result Likely to Decide Election," *New York Herald Tribune*, Sept. 6, 1932, p. 1.

83. Schlesinger, *Age of Roosevelt*, pp 430–37.

84. The *Los Angeles Times* carried a series of editorials in late October attacking both Roosevelt and Hearst and advising Americans to vote for Hoover.

85. Frank Parker Stockbridge, "Presidents, Candidates and Reporters," *American Press*, 50, no. 11 (August 1932), pp. 1, 26.

86. After his Sept. 13 press conference, Hoover actually met once with reporters on Sunday, Nov. 6, in southwestern Nebraska aboard his campaign train two days before the election, but discontinued all White House press meetings until after the election. *Public Papers of the President: Herbert Hoover 1932–33*, pp. 769–72.

87. For samples of coverage of the Hoover campaign swing see Albert L. Warner, "President on Final Trip; Talks in Springfield, Ill., Today, St. Louis Tonight," *New York Herald Tribune*, Nov. 4, 1932, p. 1; "Hoover Speaks 11 Times Today in St. Paul Swing; Roosevelt in Last Rally," *Washington Star*, Nov. 4, 1932, p. 1.

88. Hoover speech of Nov. 7, 1932, Elko, Nov., aural history archives, HHPL; "Radio Address to the Nation from Elko, Nevada," Nov. 7, 1932, *Public Papers of the President 1932–33*, pp. 795–99.

89. Joslin diary entries, Oct. 31 and Nov. 7, 1932. Joslin had intended to publish his memoirs as soon as he entered the service of the White House in 1931. With this in mind, it is possible that he tinkered with his diary entries after learning the result of the election to make himself look less foolish. There is a strange up-and-down attitude in this diary, especially in the days just before the balloting.

90. Edgar Rickard diary entry, Nov, 8, 1932, Rickard Papers, HHPL; Norman Klein, "Bets on Roosevelt 5 to 1 As Voters Go to the Polls," *New York Post*, Nov. 8, 1932, p. 1.

91. For samples of election coverage, see "Roosevelt Sweeps the Nation in Landslide; Congress Democratic, Wet; Lehman Wins; O'Brien Elected; Big McKee Protest Vote," *New York Herald Tribune*, Nov. 9, 1932, p. 1; "Roosevelt Total Mounts to 443," *New York Post*, Nov. 9, 1932, p. 1; "Roosevelt Winner in Landslide! Democrats Control Wet Congress; Lehman Governor, O'Brien Mayor," *The New York Times*, Nov. 9, 1932, p. 1.

92. Burner, *Herbert Hoover*, pp. 317–18.

93. Joslin diary entry, Nov. 9, 1932.

94. Rickard diary entry, Nov. 10, 1932.

95. "Lippmann Sees United Fight on Depression," *New York Herald Tribune*, Nov. 9, 1932, p. 1.

96. "The President's News Conference of Nov. 9, 1932," *Public Papers of the President: Herbert Hoover 1932–33*, pp. 805–7.

97. Joslin diary entry, Nov. 9, 1932.

98. Mark Sullivan, "Roosevelt Free from All Ties, Can Write Own Ticket to Capital," *New York Herald Tribune*, Nov. 10, 1932.

99. "The Election," *Philadelphia Public Ledger* editorial, Nov. 9, 1932. For a selection of editorial opinion see "Press Advises Nation to Back Chosen Leader," *New York Herald Tribune*, Nov. 10, 1932; and "Nation's Press, Analyzing Election, Calls for Harmony of All Factions," *The New York Times*, Nov. 10, 1932; "Mirror of the World's Opinion," *Christian Science Monitor*, Nov. 12, 1932.

100. "The President's News Conference of Nov. 9" and "The President's News Conference of Nov. 13," *Public Papers of the President: Herbert Hoover 1932–33*, pp. 805–7, 817–20.

101. J. Russell Young, "Hoover's Bid to Roosevelt for Conference a Precedent,"

Washington Star, Nov. 14, 1932, p. 1; Albert L. Warner, "Roosevelt Delighted to Confer, He Replies to Hoover, but Calls Debt Administration Problem," *New York Herald Tribune*, Nov. 15, 1932, p. 1; "Telegram to President-Elect Franklin D. Roosevelt about Intergovernmental Debts," Nov. 12, 1932, *Public Papers of the President: Herbert Hoover 1932–33*, p. 813–16.

102. Joslin diary entry, Nov. 17, 1932.

103. "Roosevelt Declines to Join President in Debt Recommendation to Congress; Hoover to Proceed with Own Program," *New York Herald Tribune*, Nov. 23, 1932, p. 1; Joslin diary entry, Nov. 22, 1932.

104. Joslin diary entry, Dec. 20, 1932.

105. Arthur Krock oral history interview with Henle in Washington, Nov. 21, 1966, pp. 4–5, Oral History Files, HHPL.

106. Burner, *Herbert Hoover*, p. 318.

107. "Hoover, Roosevelt and Smith Praise Memory of Coolidge," *New York Herald Tribune*, Jan. 6, 1933, p. 1; Schlesinger, *Age of Roosevelt*, p. 480.

108. "Address to the Gridiron Club, Dec. 10, 1932," *Public Papers of the President: Herbert Hoover 1932–33*, pp. 891–95.

109. Joslin diary entry, Nov. 28, 1932.

110. J. Russell Young, "Hoover to Observe 9 Months of Public Silence This Year," *Washington Star*, Feb. 1, 1933, p. 1.

111. Joslin diary entry, Feb. 19, 1932.

112. French Strother, "Four Years of Hoover: An Interpretation," *The New York Times*, Feb. 26, 1932, features section, p. 1.

113. Mark Sullivan, "Hoover's Great Achievement," *New York Herald Tribune* magazine, Feb. 26, 1932, p. 3.

114. James Hamilton Lewis, "Four Years of Hoover: A Reply to Strother," *The New York Times*, March 5, 1932, p. 5.

115. Akerson to Hoover letter, March 22, 1933, as quoted in Gary Dean Best, "Herbert Hoover as Titular Leader of the GOP, 1933–35," *Mid-America: An Historical Review*, 61, no. 2 (April/July 1979), p. 82. Chandler to Hoover letter, April 6, 1933, as quoted in ibid.

116. Ibid., pp. 92–93.

117. Burner, *Herbert Hoover*, pp. 331–32.

118. Leslie Winter, Jr., "The Metamorphosis of a Newspaper: The San Francisco *Chronicle*, 1935–65," pp. 48–49, 68–69, unpublished doctoral thesis, University of Illinois, 1968.

119. Walter Trohan interview with author, Sept. 19, 1989.

120. Hoover memoirs, vol. 3, pp. 408–52.

121. Donald R. McCoy, "Truman and Hoover," Parts 1 and 2, *Whistlestop: Harry S. Truman Library Institute Newsletter*, 18, nos. 3–4 (Spring and Summer 1990), pp 1–4; Burner, *Herbert Hoover*, p. 335. For a complete history of the Truman-Hoover relationship, see Timothy Walsh and Dwight M. Miller, *Herbert Hoover and Harry S. Truman: A Documentary History* (Worland, Wyoming: High Plains Publishing, 1992).

Epilogue

One of Herbert Hoover's troubles, remembered Associated Press bureau chief Byron Price, was that he was "quite inept at politics."[1] By that, Price meant that Hoover was a political neophyte, who found it difficult to negotiate distasteful but necessary compromises and to perpetuate the usual daily deceptions endemic to public office. Hoover was a business-man and an organizer, whose true genius lay in his quiet ability to suc-ceed at arduous tasks where others failed. He developed an engineering career and a record of accomplishment in government on his own, ac-cepting challenges that others brought to him but never pursuing public power and prestige to satisfy his own ego.

But, as Price recognized, presidents in the twentieth century need to persuade just as successfully as they organize and analyze, and if Hoover gained popularity because he was not a politician, he lost favor for the same reason. For all his superior intellect, Hoover could not see that the world was changing and that he could not persuade an entire country by romancing publishers and by releasing a swarm of cooperative jour-nalists to mold public opinion according to his dictates. To get his mes-sage to the country, he needed to be a politician, to influence and to persuade. This translated, in part, to getting along with the press corps and to using radio and newsreels effectively. That FDR could do this and

Hoover could not explains much about Roosevelt's popularity and Hoover's unpopularity. "Politician," in the most positive sense, means accomplishment through persuasion and influence.

Nowhere in this study, however, is there any suggestion that Herbert Hoover could have won reelection in 1932, if he had better influenced the U.S. news media. Nothing short of a dramatic turnaround in business could have saved his presidency, but his press policies were still important. They help to explain why a man who devoted his life to humanitarian charity could be reviled as an uncaring incompetent and why animosity continued to follow the ex-president even after his death.

Herbert Hoover failed to recognize that newspapers, magazines, radio, and newsreels had begun to replace the political party as the main vehicle for influencing voters. In just one generation people had begun to turn to the news media to provide them with information by which they would independently decide for whom they would vote, instead of accepting the dictates of community sentiment or the instructions of the local ward boss. Hoover grew up believing in the concept of a party press, and he abided by that perception until he was voted from office.

As relief coordinator, food administrator, and secretary of commerce, Hoover needed neither great oratory, nor duplicitous cunning. Even during his successful 1928 campaign, his much-ballyhooed recognition of modern public relations techniques only underscored his success at arranging and promoting through institutional organizations. His successes stood on their own merits, and his public relations campaign never needed to do anything but tout what he had truthfully accomplished. He won the nomination based upon a record of efficiency and successful organization. He also found a field of candidates strangely bereft of talent and public acceptance. In truth, separating himself from the other Republicans who presented themselves to the voters and from Al Smith, who engendered much antipathy among several segments of the electorate, took very little promotion. He followed two unheralded presidents, whose very impotence fueled his popularity.

In 1928, Herbert Hoover filled a vacuum. His use of public relations techniques were somewhat unique, but hardly related to the outcome of the election. The Republicans' decision to turn the campaign into a referendum on prosperity and to market Hoover as a simple champion of small-town values left him vulnerable. During his presidency, Hoover could not adapt to the change in public expectations. His weak interpersonal relations with the press and his inability to master a role as mass media performer made him seem, to the average voter, more removed and less sympathetic. His political failures were exacerbated by his media failures, but the media were no more responsible for his tarnished public image than they were the depression.

In the final analysis, Hoover spent the rest of his life shunned by the public, because he could not radically change his ideas about government's role in relation to the private business sector and because he would not listen to those who advised him to adapt new media policies. Just as he was fortunate to have succeeded such undistinguished presidents as Coolidge and Harding, he was unfortunate in having preceded Franklin D. Roosevelt. A natural public speaker and a masterful manipulator of the White House press corps, Roosevelt used his personal talents to the fullest and learned by Hoover's unfortunate mistakes. He also enjoyed the support of a sympathetic Congress and could, for many years, blame his mistakes on Hoover and the Republicans, while erring without retribution.

No president after Herbert Hoover would ever be successful in promoting his policies or arousing the nation to his cause without first mastering techniques for controlling or influencing the media. Herbert Hoover was the first president to use modern public relations techniques, but the last of the old-line presidents, who relied upon party and partisan media support to build his career and accede to the White House. Other presidents, such as Richard Nixon and Lyndon Johnson, would later harbor deep-seated antipathies for reporters and the news media, but they would learn to mask their dislike and to incorporate successful mass media promotional techniques into their political strategies. The depression brought a new era and a new focus to the presidency. Only those who could influence reporters, look presidential, speak with authority, and appear sincere would be able to claim success in the White House. Herbert Hoover, a decent man with nineteenth-century values, was a victim of circumstance and changing times to which he could not adjust.

NOTE

1. Byron Price interview with Raymond Henle, director of the Herbert Hoover oral history project, March 21, 1969, Chesterton, N.Y., p. 5, oral history files, HHPL.

Selected Bibliography

BOOKS

Bagby, Wesley. *The Road to Normalcy: The Presidential Campaign and Election of 1920*. Baltimore: Johns Hopkins University Press, 1962.

Barnouw, Erik. *A Tower in Babel: A History of Broadcasting in the United States*, vols. 1 and 2. New York: Oxford, 1966.

Baughman, James L. *Henry R. Luce and the Rise of the American News Media*. Boston: Twayne, 1987.

Bauman, John F., and Thomas H. Goode. *In the Eye of the Great Depression: New Deal Reporters and the Agony of the American People*. DeKalb: Northern Illinois University Press, 1988.

Brinkley, David. *Voices of Protest: Huey Long, Father Coughlin and the Great Depression*. New York: Knopf, 1982.

Burner, David. *Herbert Hoover: A Public Life*. New York: Knopf, 1979.

Daniels, Roger. *The Bonus March: An Episode of the Great Depression*. Westport, Conn.: Greenwood, 1971.

Douglas, Jack. *Veterans on the March*. New York: Workers Library Publishers, 1934.

Elson, Robert. *Time Inc.: The Intimate History of a Publishing Enterprise 1923–1941*. New York: Atheneum, 1968.

Fausold, Martin L. *The Presidency of Herbert C. Hoover*. Lawrence: University of Kansas Press, 1985.

Gallup, George, and Saul Forbes Rae. *The Pulse of Democracy: The Public-Opinion Poll and How It Works*. New York: Simon and Schuster, 1940.

Hawley, Ellis W. *The Great War and the Search for Modern Order: A History of the American People and Their Institutions, 1917–1933*. New York: St. Martin's, 1979.

———, ed. *Herbert Hoover As Secretary of Commerce, 1921–1928: Studies in New Era Thought and Practice*. Iowa City: University of Iowa Press, 1981.

Hoover, Herbert. *The Memoirs of Herbert Hoover: Years of Adventure 1874–1920*. New York: Macmillan, 1951.

———. *The Memoirs of Herbert Hoover: The Cabinet and the Presidency 1920–1933*. New York: Macmillan, 1952.

———. *The Memoirs of Herbert Hoover: The Great Depression 1929–1941*. New York: Macmillan, 1952.

Huthmacher, J. Joseph, and Warren I. Sussman, eds. *Herbert Hoover and the Crisis of American Capitalism*. Cambridge, Mass.: Schenkman Publishing, 1973.

Irwin, Will. *Herbert Hoover: A Reminiscent Biography*. New York: Century, 1928.

Joslin, Theodore. *Hoover after Dinner: Addresses Delivered by Herbert Hoover before the Gridiron Club of Washington, D.C. with Other Informal Speeches*. New York: Charles Scribner's Sons, 1933.

———. *Hoover off the Record*. Garden City, N.Y.: Doubleday, Doran, 1934.

Juergens, George. *Joseph Pulitzer and the New York World*. Princeton: Princeton University Press, 1966.

Kaltenborn, H. V. *Fifty Fabulous Years 1900–1950*. New York: G. P. Putnam's Sons, 1950.

Lane, Rose Wilder. *The Making of Herbert Hoover*. New York: Century, 1920.

Leuchtenburg, William E. *The Perils of Prosperity, 1914–1932*. Chicago: University of Chicago Press, 1958.

Lichtman, Alan J. *Prejudice and the Old Politics: The Presidential Election of 1928*. Chapel Hill: University of North Carolina Press, 1979.

Liggett, Walter K. *The Rise of Herbert Hoover*. New York: H. K. Fly, 1932.

Lisio, Donald J. *The President and Protest: Hoover, Conspiracy and the Bonus Riot*. Columbia: University of Missouri Press, 1974.

Lloyd, Craig. *Aggressive Introvert: A Study of Herbert Hoover and Public Relations Management, 1912–1932*. Columbus: Ohio State University Press, 1972.

Lyons, Eugene. *Our Unknown Ex-President: A Portrait of Herbert Hoover*. Garden City, N.Y.: Doubleday, 1948.

McGee, Dorothy Horton. *Herbert Hoover: Engineer, Humanitarian, Statesman*. New York: Dodd, Mead, 1959.

Mee, Charles L., Jr. *The Ohio Gang: The World of Warren G. Harding*. New York: M. Evans, 1981.

Michelson, Charles. *The Ghost Talks*. New York: G. P. Putnam's Sons, 1944.

Myers, William Starr, and Walter H. Newton. *The Hoover Administration: A Documented Narrative*. New York: Charles Scribner's Sons, 1936.

Nash, George H. *The Life of Herbert Hoover: The Humanitarian 1914–1917*. New York: W. W. Norton, 1988.

Nash, Lee, ed. *Understanding Herbert Hoover: Ten Perspectives*. Stanford: Hoover Institution Press, 1987.

Pfaff, Daniel. *Joseph Pulitzer II and the Post-Dispatch: A Newspaperman's Life*. University Park, Pa.: Pennsylvania State University Press, 1991.

Robinson, Edgar Eugene, and Vaughn Davis Bornet. *Herbert Hoover: President of the United States*. Stanford: Hoover Institution Press, 1975.

Romasco, Albert U. *The Poverty of Abundance: Hoover, the Nation, the Depression*. New York: Oxford, 1965.

Rosen, Philip T. *The Modern Stentors: Radio Broadcasters and the Federal Government, 1920–1934*. Westport, Conn.: Greenwood, 1980.

Rosten, Leo. *The Washington Correspondents*. New York: Harcourt, Brace, 1937.

Russell, Francis. *The Shadow of Blooming Grove: Warren G. Harding in His Times*. New York: McGraw-Hill, 1968.

Schiller, Daniel. *Objectivity and the News: The Public and the Rise of Commercial Journalism*. Philadelphia: University of Pennsylvania Press, 1981.

Schlesinger, Arthur M., Jr. *The Age of Roosevelt: The Crisis of the Old Order 1919–1933*. Boston: Houghton Mifflin, 1957.

Schudson, Michael. *Discovering the News: A Social History of American Newspapers*. New York: Basic, 1978.

Schwarz, Jordan A. *The Interregnum of Despair: Hoover, Congress, and the Depression*. Urbana: University of Illinois Press, 1970.

Smith, Gene. *The Shattered Dream: Herbert Hoover and the Great Depression*. New York: William Morrow, 1970.

Smith, Richard Norton. *An Uncommon Man: The Triumph of Herbert Hoover*. New York: Simon and Schuster, 1984.

Sobel, Robert. *The Great Bull Market: Wall Street in the 1920s*. New York: W. W. Norton, 1968.

Steel, Ronald. *Walter Lippmann and the American Century*. Boston: Little, Brown, 1980.

Stein, M. L. *When Presidents Meet the Press*. New York: Julian Messner, 1969.

Swanberg, W. A. *Luce and His Empire*. New York: Charles Scribner's Sons, 1972.

Tebbel, John, and Sarah Miles Watts. *The Press and the Presidency: From George Washington to Ronald Reagan*. New York: Oxford, 1985.

Vaughn, Stephen. *Holding Fast the Inner Lines: Democracy, Nationalism, and the Committee on Public Information*. Chapel Hill: University of North Carolina Press, 1980.

Warren, Harris Gaylord. *Herbert Hoover and the Great Depression*. New York: Oxford, 1959.

Waters, W. W. *B.E.F.: The Whole Story of the Bonus Army*, 2d ed. New York: Arno Press, 1969.

White, Graham J. *FDR and the Press*. Chicago: University of Chicago Press, 1979.

Wilson, Joan Hoff. *Herbert Hoover: Forgotten Progressive*. Boston: Little, Brown, 1975.

Winfield, Betty Houchin. *FDR and the News Media*. Urbana: University of Illinois Press, 1990.

ARTICLES

Barber, James D. "Classifying and Predicting Presidential Styles: Two 'Weak' Presidents." *Journal of Social Issues* 24, no. 3 (1968).

Best, Gary Dean. "Herbert Hoover as Titular Leader of the GOP, 1933–1935," *Mid-America* 61, no. 2 (April–July 1979).

Corkran, Charles W. "Hoover." *Iowa Illustrated Magazine*, special edition, 1965.

Cuff, Robert D. "Herbert Hoover: The Ideology of Voluntarism and War Organization during the Great War." *Journal of American History* 64, no. 2 (September 1977).

Davis, Joseph S. "Herbert Hoover, 1874–1964: Another Appraisal." *South American Quarterly* 68, no. 3 (Summer 1969).

Hamilton, David E. "Herbert Hoover and the Great Drought of 1930." *Journal of American History* 68:4 (March 1982).

Hawley, Ellis W. "Herbert Hoover, the Commerce Secretariat, and the Vision of an 'Associate State,' 1921–1928." *Journal of American History* 61, no. 1 (June 1974).

Koerselman, Gary H. "Secretary Hoover and National Farm Policy: Problems of Leadership." *Agricultural History* 51, no. 2 (April 1977).

Lohof, Bruce A. "Herbert Hoover, Spokesman of Humane Efficiency: The Mississippi Flood of 1927." *American Quarterly* 22, no. 3 (Autumn 1970).

Lyons, Louis M. "Calvin Coolidge and the Press." *Nieman Reports* 18, no. 3 (September 1964).

Rinn, Faneuil. "President Hoover's Bad Press." *San Jose Studies Quarterly* 1, no. 4 (Feb. 1, 1975).

Walcott, Charles, and Karen M. Hult. "Management Science and the Great Engineer: Governing the White House during the Hoover Administration." *Presidential Studies Quarterly* 20, no. 3 (Summer 1990).

Wilson, Joan Hoff. "Hoover's Agricultural Policies 1921–1928." *Agricultural History* 51, no. 2 (April 1977).

Index

About the Author

LOUIS W. LIEBOVICH is an Associate Professor of Journalism and Media Studies at the University of Illinois and was a reporter with three newspapers in the Midwest in the 1970s, the last being the *Milwaukee Sentinel*. Liebovich teaches about media history, the press and the presidency, newspaper economic history, and 20th-century journalism. His other books include *The Press and the Origins of the Cold War, 1944–1947* (Praeger, 1988), and *The Last Jew from Wegrow* (Praeger, 1991), which he edited.